Skills for Managing Rapidly Changing IT Projects

Fabrizio Fioravanti
Exitech, Italy

IRM Press

Publisher of innovative scholarly and professional information technology titles in the cyberage

Hershey • London • Melbourne • Singapore

Acquisitions Editor:	Michelle Potter
Development Editor:	Kristin Roth
Senior Managing Editor:	Amanda Appicello
Managing Editor:	Jennifer Neidig
Copy Editor:	Sue VanderHook
Typesetter:	Amanda Kirlin
Cover Design:	Lisa Tosheff
Printed at:	Yurchak Printing Inc.

Published in the United States of America by
IRM Press (an imprint of Idea Group Inc.)
701 E. Chocolate Avenue, Suite 200
Hershey PA 17033-1240
Tel: 717-533-8845
Fax: 717-533-8661
E-mail: cust@idea-group.com
Web site: http://www.irm-press.com

and in the United Kingdom by
IRM Press (an imprint of Idea Group Inc.)
3 Henrietta Street
Covent Garden
London WC2E 8LU
Tel: 44 20 7240 0856
Fax: 44 20 7379 3313
Web site: http://www.eurospan.co.uk

Library of Congress Cataloging-in-Publication Data

Fioravanti, Fabrizio.
Skills for managing rapidly changing IT / Fabrizio Fioravanti.
p. cm.
Summary: "This book covers many aspects related to IT project management, such as human relationships, team management, software methodologies, and tools and techniques for project management"--Provided by publisher.
Includes bibliographical references and index.
ISBN 1-59140-757-5 (hardcover) -- ISBN 1-59140-758-3 (softcovere) -- ISBN 1-59140-759-1 (ebook)
1. Information technology--Management. 2. Project management. I. Title.
HD30.2.F565 2006
004'.068--dc22

2005020636

British Cataloguing in Publication Data
A Cataloguing in Publication record for this book is available from the British Library.

Skills for Managing Rapidly Changing IT Projects

Table of Contents

Preface .... **x**

Acknowledgments .... **xii**

SECTION I

Chapter I
Team Working **1**
Values 2
Communication 2
Simplicity 3
Feedback 3
Creating the Group 4
Common Practices for Team Working 6

Chapter II
Time Management **10**
Values 10
Simplicity 10
Courage 11
Daily Activities 12
Weekly Planning 14
Monthly Strategy 14
Tools for Time Management 15
Conclusion 17
References 18

Chapter III
Presentation 20
Values 21
Communication 21
Phase 1: Prepare the Presentation 21
Online Presentations 21
Presentations with Slides 23
Paper Presentations 27
Phase 2: Prepare the Speech 28
Online Presentations 29
Presentations with Slides 30
Paper Presentations 32
Phase 3: The Speech 33
The Voice 33
The Body 34
The Appearance 34
The Look 34

Chapter IV
Training 36
Values 37
Communication 37
Simplicity 37
Feedback 38
Training in Practice 38
Train Your Team 39
Train the Customer 41
Train the Partner 42

Chapter V
People Management 44
Values 45
Communication 45
Feedback 46
People Management in Practice 47
Team Motivation 48
Dealing with Problems 48
Tools for People Management 50
People in the Project: How Many? 51
References 54

Chapter VI
Delegation 56
Values 56
Simplicity 56
Feedback 57
Courage 57
Delegation at Work 58
Target of Delegation Activity 58
What Can You Delegate? 59
How Can You Delegate? 59
References 61

SECTION II

Chapter VII
The Target Business Environment 64
Project Lifetime 66
Project Effort 67
Project Type 67
Project Technology 68
People Factor 69
References 69

Chapter VIII
Classical Methodologies, Techniques, and Tools for Project Management 72
Waterfall Life Cycle 73
Feasibility Study 73
Analysis 74
Project Specification 75
Development 75
Integration and Test 76
Deployment 76
Maintenance 77
Prototyping Life Cycle 77
Requirements 78
Fast Projects 79
Prototyping 79
Requirement Review 80
Engineered Product 80

Spiral Life Cycle 81
Objectives and Bounds 82
Evaluate Alternatives 83
Develop and Verify 84
Planning 84
Risk Management 84
Target and Benefit of Risk Analysis 86
Risk Indicators 86
Risk Evaluation 87
Risk Control 91
References 93

Chapter IX
Agile Development 95
Individuals and Interactions Over Process and Tools 96
Actions 97
Benefits 97
Side Effects 97
Overdose 98
Working Software Over Comprehensive Documentation 98
Actions 99
Benefits 99
Side Effects 100
Overdose 101
Customer Collaboration Over Contract Negotiation 101
Actions 101
Benefits 102
Side Effects 102
Overdose 102
Responding to Change Over Following a Plan 103
Actions 103
Benefits 103
Side Effects 104
Overdose 104
The Agile Team 104
References 106

Chapter X
eXtreme Programming 108
XP Values 109

Communication 109
Simplicity 110
Feedback 110
Courage 111
XP Rules 112
Metaphor 112
Planning Game 114
Small Releases 116
Tests 118
Simple Design 119
Refactoring 120
Pair Programming 121
Continuous Integration 122
Collective Ownership 123
On-Site Customer 124
Forty-Hour Weeks 125
Coding Standards 125
Conclusion 126
Life Cycle of an XP Project 130
References 132

Chapter XI
Agile and Defined Project Development 134
ADPD Life Cycle 135
Walking Skeleton Phase 138
Release Phase 140
ADPD Practices 140
Analysis and Design Practices 140
Development Practices 143
Test Practices 147
Deployment and Release Practices 150
General and Management Practices 151
References 156

Chapter XII
ADPD and SW-CMM 158
KPA 2.1 Requirement Management 160
KPA 2.2 Software Project Planning 161
KPA 2.3 Software Project Tracking and Oversight 162
KPA 2.4 Software Subcontract Management 163

KPA 2.5 Software Quality Assurance 163
KPA 2.6 Software Configuration Management 165
KPA 3.1 Organization Process Focus 165
KPA 3.2 Organization Process Definition 167
KPA 3.3 Training Program 168
KPA 3.4 Integrated Software Management 169
KPA 3.5 Software Product Engineering 170
KPA 3.6 Intergroup Coordination 171
KPA 3.7 Peer Reviews 171
Conclusion 172
References 174

Chapter XIII
ADPD and UML Adoption 176
UML in Short 177
UML and ADPD Life Cycle 179
Walking Skeleton Phase 179
Release Phase 186
References 189

Chapter XIV
Software Measurement 191
Metric Taxonomy 192
Functional Metrics 194
Line of Code 194
Cyclomatic Complexity 196
The COCOMO Model 198
Toward Object-Oriented Metrics 201
Object-Oriented Metrics Overview 202
Chidamber and Kemerer Suite 203
Li and Henry Metrics 204
Thomas and Jacobson Class Complexity 205
Henderson-Sellers Class Complexity 206
TAC++ Framework 206
Quality in Use Metrics 215
Fault Proneness Metrics 215
Project Metrics 216
Cognitive Metrics 218
Duplication Analysis Metrics 219
References 220

Chapter XV
Project Maintenance 224
Maintenance Models 224
Corrective Maintenance 225
Adaptive Maintenance 225
Preventive Maintenance 226
Maintenance in Classical Methodology 227
Maintenance in Agile Methodologies 228
Metric and Models for Estimation of Maintenance Effort 229
CC-Based Metrics for Maintenance 233
NAM-Based Metric for Maintenance 233
Other Metrics for Maintenance 234
Metrics and Model for Fault Detection 234
Model I 235
Model II 236
Model III 237
Model IV 238
Conclusion 239
References 239

About the Author 242
Index 243

Preface

The subject of this book is the skills that are needed for managing software projects in the Internet era, when projects evolve rapidly, requirements change often, and new methodologies, techniques, and tools for management emerge.

In this book, I have tried to transfer all my experience and the lessons learned about the different topics that are discussed — how to deal with people; how to manage a group; and how to develop, manage, and maintain a software project (Section I of the book).

While reading the book, consider that the experiences described and the methodologies and techniques discussed are based mainly on a particular target business environment that is described in Section II of the book and that is more and more common in the Internet era — small companies or small teams in large companies that deal with small to medium projects that adopt leading edge technologies and therefore are subject to vast changes during their lifetime.

I have focused on describing the Agile methodologies for software development and management, since I think that they are the most suitable approach when one is faced with a rapidly changing IT project. Obviously, I also have introduced classical methodologies, since one must know enough of all the methodologies in order to select the most suitable one.

Last, but not least, I also have presented the Agile methodology that I have developed (ADPD), which also can be employed suitably in all environments that classically are against the Agile approach, since it can be stated that ADPD is compliant to CMM-SW Level 3 and, during its adoption, software measurement and UML can be adopted profitably without abandoning the Agile approach.

I hope that you enjoy the reading of this book.

Book Organization

This book is organized into two main sections: the first is related to project management and to the skills that a team manager or a project manager must have; the second is related more directly to software production process and assessment. While the first part of the book is less technically oriented, the second part contains an overview of methodologies, software life cycles, and techniques for software development focusing on Agile programming and also giving the reader an overview of techniques for UML and software measurements adoption.

Section I is divided in six chapters: Team Working, Time Management, Presentation, Training, People Management, and Delegation.

Section II is divided in nine chapters: The Target Business Environment, Classical Methodologies, Techniques, and Tools for Project Management, Agile Development, eXtreme Programming, Agile and Defined Project Development, ADPD and SW-CMM, ADPD and UML Adoption, Software Measurement, and Project Maintenance.

At the end of each chapter is a figure that reports the lessons learned in the topic and an optional bibliography section that is related only to the chapter topics.

Fabrizio Fioravanti
Exitech, Italy

Acknowledgments

To my family: Lara, Ester, and Miriam

Without the help of my family, who allowed me time to write, this book never would have been created.

It is also important to mention other people that deserve my thanks: Medhi Khosrow-Pour (Senior Editor of Idea Group Inc.) for his invitation; Jan Travers (Managing Director of Idea Group Inc.) for her support and suggestions; Amanda Appicello (Senior Managing Editor), Michele Rossi and Kristin Roth (Development Editors of Idea Group Inc.) for working with me on this project; and last, but not least, the copy editor Sue VanderHook who corrected all of my mistakes and gave me a lot of valuable suggestions.

Fabrizio Fioravanti
Exitech, Italy

Section I

As already stated in the preface, Section I is related to project management activities and skills. The skills that I consider very important for a project manager are the values reported in the first part of each chapter: communication, simplicity, feedback, and courage. An intelligent mix of these values correctly applied to management techniques can make the difference between a good project manager and a normal project manager.

In order to evidence the activities that are related more to the management of a project, this part is divided into six chapters, summarized as follows:

- **Chapter I. Team Working.** In this chapter, the problems and techniques of working in and managing a team of people are reported. In particular, team creation and best practices for team working are reported.
- **Chapter II. Time Management.** Time management is one of the most difficult activities to carry on. This chapter shows how, with a correct daily, weekly, and monthly set of activities, time management can be an easy activity to perform. In order to facilitate this activity, the main tools related to time management, such as Gantt and PERT diagrams, also are reported.
- **Chapter III. Presentation.** One of the tasks that a project manager often has to deal with is presentation. All of the aspects of this particular instrument for transferring knowledge are considered, and therefore, presentation preparation, speech preparation, and how to speak are detailed.

- **Chapter IV. Training.** If you consider the best case in which you have a very skilled team that does not need any form of training, a project or team manager often is involved in training activities focused on the customer or on company partners. Therefore, it is important to know the importance of the fundamental techniques for training.
- **Chapter V. People Management.** Once you have created a team and learned how to manage time and present and train people, it is time to deal with people problems. In this chapter, some guidelines for correctly approaching this difficult activity are given.
- **Chapter VI. Delegation.** The last thing that a manager must learn to do is to delegate. It is the last because, before delegating to other people, you must have learned all the lessons reported in the previous chapters, since delegation is a powerful activity that can improve the productivity of your team, but it is also risky, if it is not approached in the correct way.

Chapter I

Team Working

This chapter is based mainly on my experiences as a development member of industrial and research projects in which I have participated in the first years of my career. Team working is very different from acting as a single developer or consultant who has the entire responsibility and control of the assigned work. The main difference is that in individual work, you have to develop a single part of a project that matches your skills and knowledge, while in team working, the collective effort of different individuals with different knowledge and backgrounds can be mixed together in order to increase the mean value of the cultural level of the components. The knowledge and understanding of a team is greater than the mean calculated on all the individuals of the team, since each member benefits from the cultural level, skills, and suggestions of the other members.

Often, the chances for the success of a project are based on how well the development team and project group are created. Other times, the success of the company in developing projects is due mainly to the capacity of top management to create well-mixed teams with good team managers. The first part of this book is not focused on how to manage a company (that is obviously beyond this topic) but only on how it is possible to create a team (and also manage it) that can steer the project toward a success story. Team working, as well as other activities, is supported by some values. For team working and also for each of the other activities presented and discussed in this first part of the book, the main values will be evidenced in order to collect a minimum number of values that must be present in an IT project environment.

Values

Before starting to describe how to create a team or to share roles among team members, it is necessary to examine the values that must be considered as the milestones for the creation and the survival of a team in a real working environment.

The word *value* sometimes might seem to be misused in this chapter and in the following chapter, since some of what has been reported under the "value hat" is considered as an activity or an action several times. I prefer also to call value an activity such as communication, since it can give real added value to the project if exploited correctly.

Communication

Communication is the main value to be considered within a working group. The communication channel always must be kept open in order to react promptly to problems due both to people and to technology. Communication among team members can be developed and increased in several ways: frequent meetings, shared documentation, pair programming (discussed in detail in Chapter X, related to eXtreme Programming), collective ownership of the code, and so forth.

The experience I had in the past is that verbal communication increases communication, and since the main communication channel humans have is the spoken language, it is better to have frequent meetings in which we can discuss technical questions and sometime personal matters. A meeting is not a way to lose an hour by talking about projects, but it is, for example, half an hour spent to discuss a problem or to share a knowledge or idea that can save several hours of development or unsuccessful tentative problem solving. Communication then can be supported by other media, such as documentation, code, or programming practices such as pair programming (i.e., two developers in front of the same computer). The concept of meeting contributes to aggregate the group and the concept of standing-meeting (all people participating in the meeting do not sit down but stand up in order to finish the meeting in the shortest possible time without useless discussions), thus saving time and using time to the best. Communication also is the basis for other values that have to be developed in the team.

Simplicity

Simplicity is the main aid to communication, since it is easier to communicate about a simple subject than to discuss complex strategies.

At the project level, simplicity can be approached by the means of Agile methodologies such as those addressed in this book, but for team management, simplicity means that the roles covered by each component are clear and that there is no complex set of guidelines for carrying on each task assigned to the team members.

Feedback

The other value strongly supported by communication is direct feedback, which is related to the communication of problems (regarding the project or a single team component dissatisfaction), and enforces relationships among the team manager, the developer, and the customer, who may have positive or negative comments on the status of the project, on the working environment, or on the involvement and commitment level.

The other aspect of feedback is the so-called indirect feedback, which is a measure of team productivity and team cooperation. It is simple to measure team productivity, since each project has its milestone against which the development trend has to be compared, while it is more difficult to measure team cooperation and cohesion. Communication among team members helps the manager to understand the level of cohesion and to discover problems as soon as possible, but it also is possible to track the cooperation level by periodic peer reviews of the code in order to verify if a good level in coding standards has been reached or if a strong code duplication is present. The absence or low presence of coding standards denotes that the communication has not reached the desired level, since developers have not agreed on the policies to be used for parentheses or comments, while code duplication in parts written by different developers is at least a symptom that the cooperation in problem solving is low or that the team management and task/role assignment have not been deployed well.

Creating the Group

Often, if you are not able to create the group as you want, it is due to a missing skill, the impossibility to hire the person you need, or other reasons that generally are independent of your willingness. The creation of a team with all the needed skills well distributed among the team members is the first step to obtain a successful result from your work.

Several theories on how to create a project group exist in the literature, but our focus is on teams for the development of IT projects. Hereafter, we will refer to IT development team with the general term *team*. If the target is different or the context is not IT, some of the concepts outlined in this section can be developed in a different way (especially the roles of the individuals), while the main value is still independent of the project type.

In this section, we are speaking about a team without specifying if the team is only a part of a larger group that works on a project or if the whole project is assigned to the team.

According to the literature and in several industrial contexts, there is a clear distinction between a project manager (or project leader) and a team leader. The former usually has a global view of the project and delegates to the team leaders the management and development of parts of the project having a direct contact with customers and project stakeholders; the latter usually is more technically skilled and is able to manage technical people without considering too much commercial and marketing aspects.

In Agile development, as it will be evidenced in the second part of the book, this distinction diminishes, since the team usually directly manages the project and the team itself is strongly involved with customers.

In the following, only the role of team manager will be detailed, since the focus of the book is more oriented to projects that can be managed in an Agile manner.

In the team, the following roles have to exist, and, depending on the size of the group, a single person can cover more than one role.

1. **Team manager.** The person for which this book mainly is written. The team manager must be a skilled person that has a deep knowledge of the project domain and of the competencies and tools needed to perform the work. Usually, a team manager is a full-time employee of the company.

2. **Developer.** The team worker who usually develops the code. Developers can be full-time employees or can be hired from consultants and freelancers. Generally, in order to reduce turnover risks, it is better to have at least 50% of the team composed of company employees, unless the skills required for being operative are very common and the basic understanding of the project can be reached in a short time frame.
3. **Innovator.** An innovator, together with the team manager, is one of the key persons of the team, since he or she has to contribute to the project with ideas taken from the file after the analysis of the market and the competitors' products. The innovator also can be found among developers or company consultants but is usually taken from the company Marketing Department. In that case, it is not necessary for the innovator to work on the team 100% of the time, since the innovator role can be covered by the same person for different projects. Sometimes, this role also can be covered by the customer, at least when you have an on-site customer that is a person that stably cooperates with the development team but belongs to the customer company.
4. **Glue person.** This role is not technical and is related to interpersonal relationships. It can be covered by each team member that is able to keep the group together, have ideas on how to organize the workspace in order to live better, and so forth. This role in an informal environment is covered by the team manager, while in a more formal environment, it can be discovered or naturally arise among the developers.
5. **Controller or reviewer.** A controller is the person who monitors the project results, verifies the milestones of the project, and notifies nonconformity with respect to the plan. The controller or reviewer is often external to the team, since he or she has to cover the role of peer reviewer. Therefore, this role often is covered by a customer that can be off- or onsite or by an external reviewing entity. It is unsuitable for a project or team manager to cover this role, since self-reviewing is not so objective. When external reviewing is not suitable for the company model, it is better to have a reviewing group that is composed of all the team/project managers and top management that then are able to perform the review of all projects in periodic meetings.

If you, as the manager, can choose the people to involve in the project from inside or outside the company, then you are able to build a good team that can develop well the assigned work. Often, you may not be so lucky to create an ad hoc team, and you may be compelled to choose among the people who have the best skills for covering the roles that are necessary in an IT project group. If this is the case, you can fill a table with all the team components on the rows and the needed roles on the column in order to verify who can cover the related roles. Keep this table updated, since often it is important to track how people evolve during a period of work in a development or project team. In doing so, you will be able to review roles when a more appropriate configuration appears.

The key for successfully building a team is to guide the individuals toward the concept of collective sharing of knowledge. This has to be done until the team works as a collective brain instead of an inarticulate collection of brains.

Usually, in a newly created group, the individuals are not very cooperative, since the main target is to share the minimum part of knowledge in order not to be fired, and there is no commitment in working as a group. You are successful in creating a group, only if you are able to overcome this impasse phase and guide the team on the way to cooperation. It is reached when the merit of cooperative working is recognized, when people start to discuss sharing knowledge and problems, and, in a more general sense, when people start to communicate.

Common Practices for Team Working

Once you have created and organized your team, you must deal with the problem of defining the practices that have to be adopted among the people in your group. These practices obviously are inspired by the values that have been evidenced in the initial part of this section: communication, simplicity, and feedback.

Communication in the team can be obtained by arranging short meetings as often as possible or by brainstorming, which allows an exchange of opinions among the members of the team. Communication is always related to the direct feedback that can be of two different kinds: positive and negative.

As a manger, the positive feedback must be emphasized, and all the people that perform well and resolve project or team problems have to be praised and rewarded on the basis of the obtained result. The negative feedback must be impersonal and must be focused on the problem instead of on the person that has generated the problem or the mistake. This kind of feedback must be given to the team in a general sense so that the individual is not charged with error responsibility, but this responsibility is shared among all the team members; this is true, since if an error has been made, it means that the review process or the test procedures of the team have not worked well. This generates a positive loop when the solution for the problem is found or the correction of the mistake has been performed, especially if the person who created the problem finds the solution. In that case, the person is not humiliated with negative feedback but is rewarded for the positive solution found. Direct feedback must be carefully considered, since it is difficult to create the environment for the development of a team, but it is very simple to destroy a well created team with criticisms directed to individuals. Criticisms and problem always must be considered at a team level, since this approach generates cohesion. If this is the case for pointing out critics on someone's work, it is better to do it in a one-to-one meeting between the person and the manager. In any case, the obvious suggestion is to give negative feedback as soon as the error is discovered and to solve small errors immediately instead of waiting for a solution that, if not reached, can compromise the whole project.

It has been shown how communication and, in particular, team meetings are important to allow the group to survive the project, but we also must focus our attention on how to deal with meetings and how to survive the discussions that arise during meetings.

As a general hint, it is better to discuss the topic under evaluation, since a common agreement or at least a clear decision emerges from the different points of view of the meeting participants. Sometimes, your team might agree on a line to be followed, but unfortunately, that line is not yours (as the team manager). What can you do? Often, it is better to accept the team decision and proceed in the development instead of stopping the development to push your point of view, unless your are 100% confident that the team solution introduces flaws or design mistakes in the project. Of course, if you are so confident about your point of view, you also are able to communicate to the team the reason for the desired choice you have expressed in the meeting.

As a manager, you have the duty to monitor the evolution of a choice with which you disagree in order to pay attention to the possible errors that can emerge, but if the team choice results in being the best, you have to praise your team for supporting a decision that was opposed to your point of view.

On the other hand, when the people involved in a meeting are divided in more or less two numerically identical groups with opposite views, the manager must choose the direction that he or she prefers, maintaining responsibility for the consequences of such a decision. Again, it is better to make a wrong decision that can be corrected later than fall into a deadlock that can lock your project for a period of time.

The last suggestion about team meetings is to keep in mind the value of simplicity; it is better to have a clear and simple design shared among the team members in order to avoid each decision being misunderstood by someone and the resulting code in the project not being in compliance with the specification. This is actually true, since it is very difficult for two people to understand the same concept in the identical way. Imagine how many probabilities of a concept you would have to transfer to 10 people in the same way. Simplicity and value strongly help to minimize the probability of having incompatible solutions in the project.

Lessons Learned

Target

Team working

Values

Communication
Simplicity
Feedback

Practices

Define and review team roles.
Hold frequent short meetings.
Give positive feedback in public.
Give negative feedback in private.
Success is of the person and then also of the team.
Failure is of the team and then also of the person.

Chapter II

Time Management

Time management is one of the most problematic issues to be addressed and to be understood well and transferred to the people belonging to the team.

In order to understand the meaning of time management, it is necessary to deal with the concept of time and then with the concept of the unit cost of your time for the company. During each year, you usually work (without considering extra work) between 1,600 and 1,800 hours, and then, if you divide your gross annual pay (say $50,000), you obtain an hourly cost of your time between $27 and $31. Each hour you lose during your work time costs that amount of money to your company. Usually, if you are a team manager, for each hour you lose, your team in the complex loses about five times as much, and then a larger amount of money is thrown away for your company.

In order to manage your time and the time of your team in the best way, it is necessary to approach the problem basing your efforts on some values, as suggested in the following.

Values

Simplicity

Simplicity is the main value for obtaining a correct management of your time, since simple things requires a lower amount of time to be understood, shared, communicated, and then developed and tested.

The simplicity in your projects allows you to communicate to your team in a faster way the main concepts related to the tasks to be developed. Moreover, a simple concept has a higher probability to be understood in the same way by a large number of persons, allowing your team members to share the same knowledge base. Simplicity is also the basis for the relationships among team members. Usually, the team is comprised of a small number of persons, and therefore, it is not useful to create and develop complex hierarchies, at least when the number of people involved in the same team is less than 10. If the team is larger than 10 persons, maybe some vice-management functions can be identified, and therefore, people responsible for each function can be identified in order (again) to simplify the management of the team. If this is not the case, and usually it is not, responsibilities can be assigned to the team members for an interval of time that is necessary to solve a problem, by trying also to rotate people and to choose different people for different roles. The culture and skills of each person have to be carefully considered, respecting what has been evidenced in Chapter I.

This is done in order to save time, since delegation helps to save time, but if the need of responsibility roles also emerges in the team when the number of involved people is very small, it is necessary to change your approach; otherwise, you are risking losing time taking account of an unnecessary team structure.

Courage

The other aspect that is strictly related to time management is courage, since you need courage each time you have to cut or simplify part of the project in order to respect time constraints. Courage also is needed in all the situations in which you have to stop development for a meeting that you think is necessary in order to solve a problem or to create a better environment for the development of the correct solution. Courage also is needed if the time you and your team lose with the meeting could be used profitably for developing some other code.

The need for courage is also mandatory when you have to introduce new people in the team, because the time constraints do not allow your team to develop all the scheduled features on time. Often, the introduction of people not aware of the team behavior, not skilled in the particular domain of the project under the team responsibility, or simply not used to working in a team, can hit you as a boomerang launched to save time that is coming back carrying a shipment of time loss.

Daily Activities

The best way to save time is to organize the work you have to perform during the day. If you are able to organize well the first hour of your work, you usually will be able to profitably employ the rest of the day with well planned activities.

Since you are the team manager, it is best if you can be in the office 15 to 30 minutes before your team, since it is better to perform some activities when the team members are not yet present, as will be evidenced in this section.

There are three different sources of information that must be considered when you arrive in the office at your desk: messages on the phone; notes on the desk; and last, but not least, e-mails. You should never plan your daily activities without taking care and considering the information, since often the actions you plan are automatically canceled by a note on the desk that advises you of a problem (e.g., a person that will not be at work that morning because of the flu, a problem on the code that arose five minutes after you left the office the day before, etc.); by the e-mail from your manager that asks for your presence, since you are urgently needed in a meeting 100 miles away from your office; or simply by the message on the phone left by the person that is responsible for your local deployment server who advises you of a crash on the hard disk, notifying you that in four hours the backup will be up and running. Never plan before reading and listening; the one time you forget to do it, surely you will have to start a new plan, losing time. Once you are confident that no unknown problems are facing you, then you can start your 10-minute brainstorming in front of your preferred cup of coffee. During these 10 minutes, you can plan easily the activities to be carried out that day by your team. Several managers with whom I have discussed about this "10-minutes practice" say that they cannot be sufficient to plan a work day, but I answer that it is absolutely the maximum amount of time you need to plan the current day. If you dedicate 10 minutes each day and enforce this activity by the weekly and monthly practices described in the following sections, 10 minutes will be a sufficient time.

When you have concluded your brainstorming activity, and maybe the people that make up your team have just arrived at their desk, you can start the daily meeting, which is what I call the *15-minute daily standing meeting.* I call it standing since 15 minutes are not enough if all the people are sitting down. When you are standing up, you urge conclusion, and it is the role of the manager to conclude the meeting — only when the activities for the day are understood by all the people.

The total amount of time (personal brainstorming followed by the 15-minute standing meeting that can be generally from 30 to 45 minutes) that you spend collecting information and planning and sharing your plans with the members allows each person of your team to do the same in a general sense or to better focus each team member to do a personal brainstorming related only to the activities you have scheduled for the current day. The larger your team is, the greater is the advantage in terms of saved time and then in reduced costs for the company.

The question can be: What can I do the rest of the day if I am able to plan it in a total time of 45 minutes? The activities a team manager deals with during a work day cannot be standardized, as I have proposed for the starting of the day, since they depend much on the project type, on the methodology with which the project is developed, on the documentation to be written, and on the presentation and reports that have to be prepared.

Generally speaking, the activities that all team managers perform during the day are as follows:

- Update reports, presentations, and scheduling for top management and vice presidents (VPs);
- Collect, review, and organize documentation that have to be passed to marketing and to customers;
- Peer review the project in order to discover if something is not going in the planned direction;
- Peer review some sample code produced the day before to discover bugs, missing tests, and lack of functionality (if the manager also is a skilled person from the technical point of view);
- Help team members to solve problems, both technical and organizational; and
- Write code with the team.

As you see, there is not a lot of time for a team manager to work in the code, since several other activities that are not so evident at first glance must be addressed in order to have a successful project.

Weekly Planning

You have dedicated 10 minutes of your time to a personal review of each day's assignments and schedules; however, this is not really true, since Monday is a special day. Monday is the first day of the week and then it is necessary to review the schedule for the whole week, not only for the current day. While the first 10 minutes can be dedicated to daily planning, it is necessary that after the meeting with the team you dedicate another 20 minutes to review the plan for the week in order to a have better focus on the other 10 minutes a day. The weekly planning is not a strategic planning, since a week is such a short period of time, but it can be employed usefully to select the tasks that have to be completed during that week, the tasks that should be delayed, and the tasks that must be deleted in order to fit a strategic deadline. During the weekly planning, you have to review the short-term strategies, being aware of what can be done or not in the current week. The weekly planning must be a strong aid for the activities you have to perform: meetings, presentations, and project reports to the VP. Remember that the activities that you plan at the start of the week are modifiable in each moment of the same week on the basis of the 10-minute review you perform each day, but it is also clear that an initial planning is better than no planning at all.

Monthly Strategy

As Monday is important to review the incoming week, what I call *the first day of the month* is crucial for the strategic planning of the month. I usually refer to the first day of the month not as the *first*, but as the first Monday of the month. You cannot strategically plan the month in the middle of a week, since you are distracted by the ongoing activities and by the daily problems. In this book, we suppose that each month starts on Monday (even if Monday is on the sixth day of the month). After the first 10 minutes of the day, the meeting with the team, and the 20 minutes for planning the week, you are ready for the 30-minute strategic brainstorming. During this half hour, you have to define the middle-term objectives of your project and estimate the probabilities and risks that your team will not able to complete within the scheduled deadline — the activities that marketing has sold to the customer as already done, that your manager or a VP has defined as strategic for the company, and so forth.

During these 30 minutes, you have to clarify to yourself if the deadline can be met or if a rescheduling of some activities of the project should be done. In case you see that some activities cannot be finished for the deadline, it is better to plan a meeting now with management and customers in order to advise them of that possibility and to have time to project countermeasures. It is better to know your enemy instead of combating with the ghost of impossible deadlines.

Tools for Time Management

The main tool adopted for time management and project tracking is the Gantt diagram (Coffman, 1976) in which all the tasks to be performed are placed in the time axis according to their assigned priority.

A Gantt diagram has the shape reported in Figure 1, where capital letters (A, B, C, etc.) are the tasks.

In Figure 1, two different types of activities can be identified—critical activities and activities with slack. Critical activities are the tasks that, if delayed, compel you to review the scheduling of other tasks (A is critical with respect to C, C with respect to D, E and D with respect to F), while activity with slack can be delayed without compelling to review other planned activities (B has the slack d1, while E has the slack d2). Sometimes activities with slack also can be partially critical because of resource needs or allocation, as it will be discussed in the people management section.

The critical activities can be identified better when a Gantt diagram is integrated with Program Evaluation and Review Technology (PERT) (Wiest, 1977). PERT diagrams are ordered graphs that report in the nodes the task or activities and in the arcs the precedence relationships between activities. A sample PERT diagram for the Gantt diagram in Figure 1 is reported in Figure 2.

In PERT diagrams, no information on task duration generally is reported, if it can be associated to each node while the relationships among activities are

Figure 1. A sample Gantt diagram (with tasks and slack time)

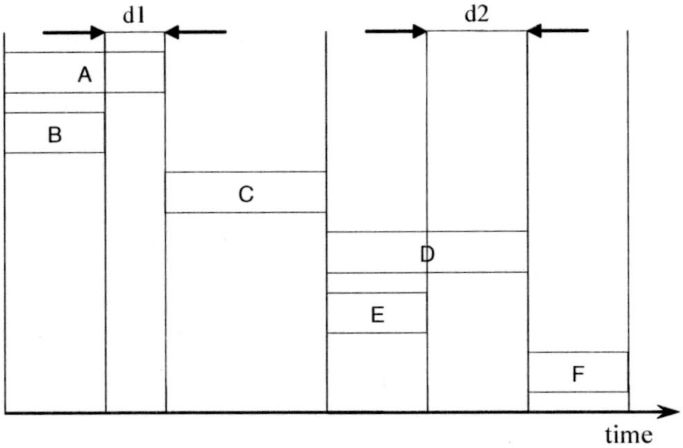

Figure 2. A possible PERT diagram for the Gantt diagram in Figure 1

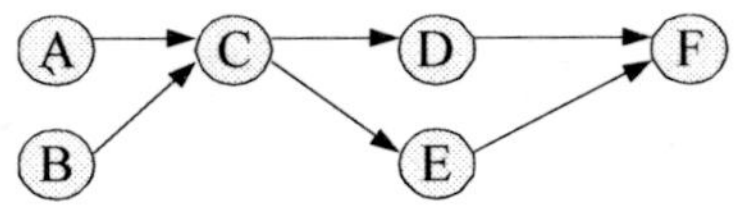

Figure 3. Integration of Gantt diagram with PERT notation in a single diagram

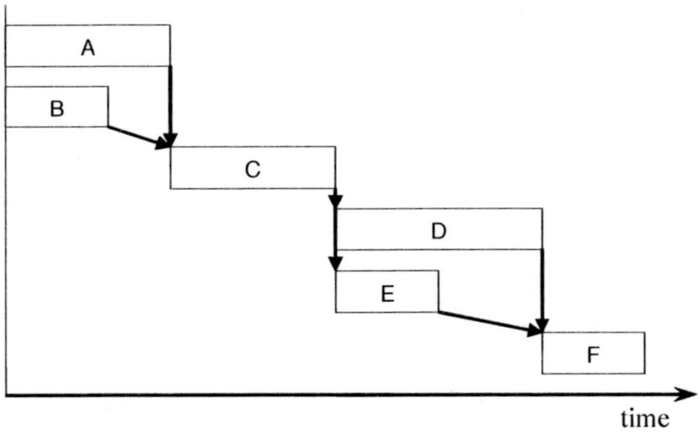

evidenced. The arcs mean that source node completion is needed before starting the end node. In the figure, task C also can start after the competition of A and B, tasks D and E only after C completion, and so forth.

We can embed information in the Gantt diagrams having a clearer picture of the meaning of critical activities. See Figure 3 for a sample integrated diagram.

Gantt and PERT diagrams are powerful instruments for scheduling activities and evidencing tasks relationships.

Conclusion

The time management strategies that have been presented have been named the *10-20-30 minutes organization*, since it requires 10 minutes a day, 20 more minutes each week, and 30 more minutes each month. All the planning you can do in these time frames must be performed, having in mind the following objectives:

- **No overtime shall be needed.** It is clear that a 40-hour work week is the best and that overtime is not the best solution for a peaceful life. Often, a wrong management of time brings overtime or a claim for more resources, which is not a good practice, as explained in the next point.
- **No claims for extra resources shall be made.** Extra resources in a project are an advantage from the perspective of long-term usage of the resources, but in the short term of an emergency, claiming extra resources is not the solution. When a new resource joins the team, you have to train him or her, explain the project, and integrate the new person into the working team. You need extra work to do that, and if an emergency arises, you have no time to dedicate to it. Correct time management and scheduling helps you avoid the need for extra resources; in the worst case, you will know that you need more resources to complete the work some time before the emergency.
- **Meet deadlines or at least control the problems.** One of the hardest tasks to control is how to meet a hard deadline. Hard deadlines generally are imposed by the management or by the customer, but remember that you, as the team manager, accept them, and therefore, you must be very careful in doing activities that your current time schedule cannot handle. An impossible deadline, once accepted, is missed, and then a great part of your work is lost with it. Before accepting such deadlines, you have to be careful to communicate to your manager that in order to meet that deadline, you have to delay some other activities or you will need more resources. You can do that only if you have a clear scheduling that can be the product of an accurate time management activity performed each day, not only at the project analysis or milestones. If you cannot plan well, at least you have to plan often.
- **Determine the short- and long-term objectives.** The daily, weekly, and monthly planning activities are the ideal time frames in which to define

short-term objectives (day and week) and long-term prospects for your project. In the last years, it has become more and more common to develop projects that have a total duration (from the start to the delivery to the customer) of no more than six months. In that sense, a monthly planning can be considered as a long-term planning activity at least for the domain of the project.

- **Reduce the stress.** This is the positive payload if the other activities are planned well. No extra work reduces stress and produces good planning and the correct visibility of the deadline to be met.

The Gantt diagrams that have been presented, if integrated with the PERT diagrams, can be very useful in keeping under control the project evolution in time by tracking current activities against what has been planned.

References

Coffman, E. G., Jr., Bruno, J. L., & Winters, P. R. (Eds.). (1976). *Computer and job-shop scheduling theory*. New York: Wesley.

Wiest, J. D., & Levy, F. K. (1977). *A management guide to PERT/CPM*. New Delhi: Prentice Hall of India Private Limited.

Lessons Learned

Target

Time management

Values

Simplicity
Courage

Practices

10-20-30 time management strategy:

- 10 minutes a day
- 20 minutes a week
- 30 minutes a month

Adopt Gantt diagrams.

Adopt PERT diagrams.

Collect information, plan, and then share the plans with your team.

Chapter III

Presentation

Presentation is a common activity for a project or team manager, since often the need arises to present the ideas, the work performed, or the work that your team has to perform, or you have to justify the work that has not been performed.

In this chapter, I will address such presentations, while presentation made for training purposes will be discussed in detail in the chapter on training (Chapter IV).

A presentation is a three-step process. In the first phase, the material presentation is produced (online presentation, slide presentation, paper presentation). Each presentation type is different and will be analyzed, since it is important to know how to prepare a presentation for each different format.

The second phase is the preparation of the speech for the presentation. Again, a different way to present the speech is needed to deal with different people attending the presentation (i.e., top management, customer, your team, etc.).

The third phase is the real speech by which you have to transfer to the audience the knowledge or messages in the presentation.

In all the phases, and especially in the third, the value of communication must be present in order to have a chance of success, as reported in the values section.

Values

Communication

Communication is the basic value around which a presentation moves. Unfortunately, communication for presenting is a skill that can be improved but not created, and therefore, if you have communication capabilities, you can use some tricks to establish a feeling with the audience, to focus the attention of the audience, and so forth, but if you have no communication skills at all, no one can teach you how to communicate.

This section is suitable for all people that want some suggestions on how to improve their communication skills, but it may not have any results for people who have no communication capabilities at all.

How many times does an interesting presentation topic become a boring event only because of the speaker? In my career, several times I have heard boring presentations, and each time, I tried to notice the errors that made the presentation — a couple years of good work — fail.

Phase 1: Prepare the Presentation

First, you have to focus your attention on the type and media of the presentation, since each media requires a different schema, different length, and different type of messages to be transmitted.

Online Presentations

Online presentations usually are made for the Web and for the stands at fairs. This presentation type must be aggressive in order to capture the attention of the reader; it must be short in order not to compel people to stay in front of the presentation monitor or Web browser for long periods of time, and it must transmit simple messages that stimulate the audience's curiosity, encouraging the reader to click on (in the case of Web) or to ask for more information (in the case of a stand at a fair).

Apart from a professional trailer that some agencies can create, with simple instruments, an online presentation can be homemade. In this section, I will consider presentations that can be made by rolling slides or simple Web animations but that can have a good impact on attending people.

In the following, we will focus on the main characteristics that such presentations must have:

- **Graphic appeal.** The background of the presentation must be aggressive so that a casual reader can consider having a look after the first glance. All the written messages and diagrams should appear with animation effects, and the transition from one slide to another must be animated.
- **Duration.** The whole duration of the presentation shall not exceed three minutes, since 180 seconds standing in front of a monitor without doing anything is a large time interval. You can try it by yourself or think about the three minutes you waited yesterday for a Web page to appear on your browser. It seems like quite an infinite amount of time.

  Consider that at a fair stand, you have less than half a minute to capture the attention of the visitor with a message that should be interesting. So you should use these three minutes to present six messages or more. The duration of each message is different and depends on the mean time to read and comprehend the slide presenting the message, which can be reduced by half in the case in which you have a professional speaker as audio background of the presentation.
- **Audio.** Audio is very important for two reasons: background music and speaking voice. If you have no way to hire a professional speaker for explaining the presented concepts, it is important to have background music that is related to the argument of the presentation. Disco music or an electronic music piece can be a good background for strong IT projects, but if you are presenting a firewall system, it is better that the music transmit tranquility and serenity in order to convince the audience that your system will give them such a feeling. Audio is as important as images and graphic appearance for capturing the interest of people. It must be considered in detail when the presentation is ready. Speaking voice is important, because it is possible to comment on graphics in a faster way with respect to written words.
- **Language.** The messages have to be expressed in a clear language with short sentences, such as advertising spots. Remember that potentially,

each message has to capture the interest of people, and therefore, people have to comprehend it independently of the already presented messages. Write each sentence considering that this might be the first time that the reader views it.

Presentations with Slides

A slide presentation is very different from an online presentation, since it is targeted to an audience that listens for it from the beginning and that is normally interested in the topic about which you are speaking.

We will analyze three different types of audiences: a large audience, such as a conference presentation or review meeting for large international projects; a meeting with management for ideas or project results presentations; and a meeting with the team you are working with.

A presentation with slides is divided in two groups: transparent slides and computer-projected slides. The first type of slide is disappearing, since portable computers are more and more diffused and have a decreasing cost, and presentation tools are available for free. In this section only the second type of presentation will be discussed, because the main concepts are the same and the only main difference is related to the graphic appearance and to animation that cannot be applied to transparent slides.

The first aspect to be analyzed is the structure of the presentation. The structure depends on the audience and on the topic you have to speak about. There are mainly four different structures that your presentation can assume: linear, sandwiched, structured, and problem-oriented.

Linear

It is maybe the simplest way of presenting something, since it involves a series of related arguments in a sequence that can bring to a conclusion but also can be a simple explanation of facts for starting the discussion at the round table in which conclusions will be drawn.

In the following, all the application fields in which a presentation can be necessary with comments related to the suitability of linear style are reported:

- **Conference.** Linear style with conclusion can be applied to conferences, but generally it is not the best presentation style, since there is no introduction to the topic, and there is no visibility on the target of the presentation. The result is that people can be bored before you reach an interesting point.
- **Management meeting.** Surely, linear style is not suitable for management meetings, since you have to capture the interest in your project and ideas in the first two slides; otherwise, the probability that the rest of the presentation will be heard and then the idea of project approved decreases exponentially as slides that are not well focused continue in the presentation.
- **Team meeting.** Linear style is appropriate for a team meeting where you have to present and comment on a set of facts or problems that can be analyzed one by one in order to start a discussion to solve the problems or to analyze the presented facts. Linear style is also appropriate for presenting technical concepts that must be understood or discussed among people that do not need introduction or background for the presentation topics. Your team is the ideal context.

Sandwiched

Sandwiched presentations are those that have in the middle the major part of the discussion, usually preceded by an introduction and followed by a conclusion.

The real sandwiched presentation, in my humble opinion, also can exist when you have the following sequence: a short introduction of the topic to catch the attention of the audience; the presentation context; and last, but not least, a detailed conclusion. The conclusion is the bread, and the real presentation is the meat. As for linear style, a comment on the applicability in a different identified context must be done.

- **Conference.** Sandwiched style is usually well suited for short presentations that are not generally usable in long conference speaking. When the conference speech is articulated in several topics (i.e., structured presentation), information on each topic can be sandwiched between an introduction and a conclusion.
- **Management meeting.** A real sandwiched presentation with an introduction at the beginning and a conclusion after the discussion topic is the

best manner to capture the attention of top management, since as the first slide appears, it is clear what target and ideas you will expose during the meeting. If you think that your idea probably will be approved, this is the best way to enforce it. In a management meeting, people will be captured by your first slide that directly announces the target; after that, you can explain the context, the advantages, and the disadvantages of your solution, and then draw extended conclusions with pros and cons.

- **Team meeting.** Sandwiched structure is generally not suited for team meetings, since you have no need to capture the attention of the audience (you are the team leader), and usually, team members would like to be included in the decision process or at least guided toward certain choices. Therefore, it is not the best solution to present a conclusion as the first slide. In this situation, it is the best way to lose the people's attention.

Structured

Structured presentation is the most frequently adopted style, since there is a sort of agenda of the topics to be discussed at the beginning and after each topic is discussed in more detail. This style is very suitable for each formal presentation in which you announce in the first slide the table of contents that will be covered during the presentation. This table of contents usually is reported when each new topic starts in order to remind the audience of the previously discussed points and how much you will tire them with other arguments!

- **Conference.** Structured presentations are adopted widely in academic presentations and, therefore, in conferences. It is perhaps the most suitable way for presenting research results, since it allows the presentation of the results in an organized manner following a clear scheduled plan that can transfer to the audience confidence about the presentation value and contents from the first slides. On the other hand, conferences need a formal way of presenting the discussion topics. In addition, if you do not present research results, the structured presentation is certainly the best choice in all formal environments.
- **Management meeting.** Structured presentations can be employed suitably in management meetings, since they give to the audience (your managers) a clear view of what you will discuss during the presentation. This is particularly true in the case in which you have to present results of

your work. On the other hand, if you have to present a new project, a structured presentation can be too formal to capture interest in your project, and maybe a more direct way of presenting can have better results.

- **Team meeting.** Formal presentations usually are not suitable for discussing technical items with your team. I strongly suggest that you do not use this format during the presentation made for your team.

Problem-Oriented Format

A problem-oriented format, also known as question-oriented, is a nice format to guide the audience toward a predefined conclusion, to express pros and cons about a certain topic, or to request the okay for a plan approval. In this format, after a short presentation and introduction of the problem to be discussed and of the background necessary to comprehend the problem, several solutions are presented, discussing for each proposed solution its advantages and disadvantages. The presentation usually ends with a summary table of pros and cons of the several solutions and usually with the evidence of the solution that the speaker would like to have approved. This format is not formal and usually is adopted for intergroup presentations.

- **Conference.** A problem-oriented format, for its lack of formality, is not suitable for a conference environment in which you usually present an on-progress or an already-concluded research, or in which you discuss a product that is sold by your company or that will be sold in a short time. In a conference, it is not expected that people have to approve your solution or agree with the path you would like to follow, and therefore, it is better to opt for another presentation format.
- **Management meeting.** During a management meeting, this format can be a success, since you can guide your managers toward the path you want and like in order to obtain the approval of a project. Remember to specify well the problem and the reason you are speaking about it in the very first slides of the presentation in order to be sure to have the focused attention of the people attending the meeting.
- **Team meeting.** This format is probably the best for guiding your team toward a decision you have already taken. It is also a good way to start discussing a problem that you have analyzed and with which you would

like to share with your team the final decision after a discussion on the several proposed solutions. In that case, often it is better to draw the table of pros and cons on a blackboard and to fill it in together with your team instead of having an already predefined table on the slide.

Color Usage in Slides

Independent of the presentation type and format, it is important to use color carefully in the slide you are presenting to the audience. Colors are very important for enhancing parts of the presentation, and at the same time, they can be the main reason for confusion in people that are listening to you, if they are not well organized or if they are misused.

Each color you use in graphics or text must be related to the related meaning, and you have to repeat the same color when you want to express concepts related to same meaning. For example, suppose you are speaking about an n-tiered application, and the first time you reference a database, you use blue; you must use the same color to refer to the database word or to the database layer in all the other slides. When the same blue appears, it must be related to the database concept. In this way, you obtain two major results: when the people in front of you see that color, they know exactly what you are speaking about, and at the same time interpretation of complex graphs are simplified by a standardized color adoption.

It is not trivial to prepare a detailed presentation with a slide. Consider that you will need between 30 minutes and one hour to have each slide in its final form. If you have a 15-minute speech, and if you think that you will use a couple of minutes for each slide, it is simple to argue that you will need about seven to eight slides and, therefore, a preparation time that is at least five to six hours, which is about 25 times the speech time you have. You can use this guideline in order to plan when you have to start to prepare a presentation.

Paper Presentations

A paper presentation is an unusual way to present, but sometimes it is necessary, especially in meeting with management, to present your proposal or results in a written form and to prepare a short speech for a discussion to be done after management has considered the proposal in detail.

For conferences, if you are a keynote speaker, it is usual to write a paper to be included in the conference proceedings, which is usually a resumé of the speech you have to present as a keynote. Keynote speakers often do not use slides to accompany their presentations, since they usually introduce an argument and do not present results of a research. Paper presentation also can be adopted with your team when you collect the documentation that each member has produced and collect it in a single document that will be discussed with all the team members.

Paper presentations are closer to the written form of a document that is not covered in this book, but some suggestions to increase the chances of success in presenting such documents are given.

- **Conference.** As discussed, the presentation of a keynote is a sort of short introductory paper to the arguments treated during the speech. It has the classical form of a paper with an introduction, a discussion on topics, and a conclusion.
- **Management meeting.** The format to be used for paper presentations is a sort of sandwiched style in which you present in the first paragraph the proposal you have in short form or the results you have obtained, and then you explain in detail the why and the pros and cons.
- **Team meeting.** Paper presentations usually are not adopted in a team meeting, unless you have to approve a document with your team (i.e., a technical manual that will be arranged by the Marketing Department to create the product manual).

Phase 2: Prepare the Speech

The second phase of a presentation deals with the problem of preparing the contents of the speech. The contents that you are preparing must be adapted to the presentation you have in your hands, but first, it must be well targeted with respect to the time you have or that has been assigned to your presentation. The first rule in a presentation speech is that overtime is not generally well received; people are interested in your speech when you do not abuse their time. After going over your allotted time, someone may stop you. You may not be able to end your speech or draw your conclusion, and therefore, the speech is a failure.

Or someone may start to get bored and not listen to you anymore. In all these cases, you have lost the opportunity to transfer the message you have prepared, and therefore, your presentation is not successful.

The preparation of the speech is different from person to person, and there is no silver bullet to use. Some guidelines can be suggested and detailed for each presentation type, but each person has to create his or her personal way to prepare the speech. Some people prefer to write the entire speech to follow during the presentation; others (me, for example) prefer to have a clear idea in mind and then create the speech on the basis of the environment, the audience, and the feeling of the moment. Each method has its advantages and disadvantages. In particular, a well prepared speech allows you to have an almost perfect presentation, but you are really in trouble if you have the wrong length of time and you have to shorten the speech on the fly. The second approach is more risky, since you can have some problems during the presentation due to the lack of the terms you would like to use, but it allows you to lengthen and shorten the speech as you want in a moment.

Apart from the path you decide to follow, it is better to try your speech in advance at least a couple of times in order to have a clear idea of time and possible problems.

Of course, speech preparation needs time. The time needed to prepare a speech depends on the type of presentation, the topic of the presentation, and the language. If the presentation has to be done in your native language, the required time will be about one-half of the time needed for another language, since the choice of terms and keywords to be used requires more time for a foreign language.

Online Presentations

Online presentations are usually commented by a professional speaker that reads something you have prepared.

To this end, the speech for an online presentation must be prepared, keeping in mind that the speaker is not you and, therefore, must be written in a detailed way, evidencing points to emphasize.

Usually, these presentations require a long time for preparation, even if the mean duration is short. This is due to the fact that the you not only have to prepare the speech, but you also have to revise it with the speaker, verify the timing, phrases, and words, and adjust all of them on the basis of the running presentation you have in front of you. After some revisions with the speaker, you are ready to follow him or her in a registration studio to verify the suitability of your effort with respect to the desired result.

It is obviously important that the speech is in sync with the running presentation and that the speech is fluent and well targeted to the audience.

Presentations with Slides

The preparation of a speech for a presentation with slides is very different from an online presentation for several reasons: the most important is that you are the speaker and the person who prepares the speech. As introduced before, it is possible to have different approaches to the preparation of the speech on the basis of your personal approach to presentations. It is unnecessary to repeat here the pros and cons of each approach. Some general guidelines about the different environments in which you can present something with slides might be useful:

- **Team presentation.** In a presentation with your team, you usually have no time boundaries, and therefore, it is better to have a clear idea of what you want to present and what you would like to obtain with your presentation. When you prepare the speech, focus the attention on the arguments to be discussed and on the results you want to obtain from your team. If you want to start an open discussion with all the members of the team, it is better that you prepare a short introductory speech to discuss quickly the slides and review the most important parts during the discussion. If your target is to convince your team that a path must be followed or that some choices are necessary for the projects or the team, you have to focus your attention on a detailed speech in which not a lot of space is left for discussion and evaluation of the proposed slides; a detailed conclusion of the speech must be addressed carefully in order to obtain the desired results. If your target is only to resume the activities performed without need for changes or discussion, it is sufficient that you prepare a summary of the arguments you want to speak about without much details.
- **Management presentation.** The presentation that you have to present to management has to be carefully prepared. The speech is very important in all situations, since if you are in a management meeting, you are in two minds: you have to convince management about the work you have

performed, or you have to convince management that the project you are proposing is a good one. In both cases, the target you want to reach must be clear, and the speech must guide the listener toward the desired target in the shortest possible time frame. This is true also because independently of the speech duration, you have no more than five minutes to capture the interest of management, and you must use this time to your best advantage. After the interest has been caught, you can relax your speech a little bit in order to explain the reasons for your choices. To this end, the first part of the speech must be very direct and clear, and the emphasis and the frequency of words should not leave space for any interruption or comments. The second part can be softer and should leave enough space for questions and comments; if you were able to interest people, you can also answer their questions, since such questions will be focused 90% on the topic. The suggestion is to detail the speech related to the first five minutes. At this point you have to prepare at least three different tracks for the second part of the speech: (1) you failed to interest people in the speech; (2) you interested people, but management is oriented to evaluate your topic in a negative way; and (3) you interested management and got a positive feedback. Certainly, the third track is the best, and you can have a relaxed second part of the speech, leaving room for management interventions. Track two is more difficult to be managed and requires special attention in presenting advantages of the proposed solution or work, allowing only pro comments at the end of the presentation in order to have all the possible weapons to use against a negative feedback. Track one is the worst, since you also have to enforce the message of the first part in the second part, but probably, it is better if the meeting is postponed to another day when you have time to revise your presentation to focus it better on capturing the interest of the audience.

- **Technical or marketing presentations for customers.** Presentations to be done for customers or partners usually do not have a strong need for a predefined duration of time, since these presentations can be one to two hours long, and therefore, 10 minutes more or less do not make a difference. The presentations to be made to customers and partners usually are repeated several times, and therefore, it is better to prepare the speech with details, having in mind how to modify the focus on the basis of the feedback of the customer and of the interest you feel with the product/service you are presenting. The effort of preparing and refining the speech is continuous, since you continuously revise the presentation; each time you repeat the presentation, you find something that can be revised, improved, or at least modified, because you discover an interesting way for meliorating the speech on the basis of the questions that the partner has asked. This process of refinement is possible only if you have prepared the speech in detail. The detailed preparation is also important, because often, some of the people that work with you have to use your presentation, and therefore, a well prepared speech allows you to have a unique message independently of the person who presents the topic. It also is an aid in time saving for other people who do not have to prepare a speech from scratch.

- **Conference presentation.** On the contrary with respect to presentations to customers, conference presentations are one-shot presentations made in front of sometimes hundreds of people. You have no time to refine the presentation, unless you are in a road-show conference, for example, but in that case, the suggestion of previous points is more appropriate, especially if time duration is shorter (between 15 and 30 minutes). You have only one opportunity to play, and therefore, you have to make the best use of this opportunity. In this situation, your practice in conference speeches must guide you toward the best approach. If you have presented a conference speech several times with successful results, you usually prepare a draft version of the speech with the main content that you only have to refine during the speech at conference time. If it is the first time, it is better to have a conservative approach and prepare the speech with more details, taking into account that the probability to be compelled to cut some parts of the speech exists, and therefore, you must be ready to change the way in which you are presenting it or the speed at which you are speaking, on the fly.

Paper Presentations

For paper presentations, the speech is usually as important as it is short. In most cases, you have no more than a couple of minutes to convince the person to whom you are giving the presentation to read the contents of the piece of paper you have in your hands.

It is important during these minutes to evidence the first part of the presentation in which you have presented the main results or conclusions. Often, since the presentation is in written form, people will read the introductory part, and as evidenced before, this is the most critical phase. The speech must stimulate the curiosity about the topic and enforce the conclusions or results. It is better to prepare well the two-minute speech with great details, since time is short and it is a one-shot speech.

Phase 3: The Speech

This section is not divided in subsections related to the target environment or audience as the others, since the suggestion on how to present and on how to speak with people are independent of the presentation type. The capability of being a speaker that has the power to interest people in the topic is a natural skill that can be improved but cannot be learned. If you are not able to present or to teach, independent of the amount of time you do such a job, you will never be able to have a strong success with your speech.

In any case, some suggestions are useful for all people and can be the difference between a terrible speech and an acceptable one, as they make the difference between an acceptable speaker and a good speaker.

There are four factors that influence the success of your speech for the most part: voice, body, appearance, and look.

The Voice

The voice and the use of the voice is the most important parameter to be considered during a speech. You have to carefully consider the use of the voice, since a wrong use of it can make your presentation fail.

The most common error is to always use the same voice tonality. This will result in an audience that falls asleep in a few minutes. It is important to vary the tonality of the voice often and to use a loud tone of voice to suggest the feeling that you can speak and be understood without a microphone.

You have to underline with the voice the most important points of your presentation without being too serious but simply by changing the voice tonality. Some exercise is needed to reach a good control of the voice, but good results are guaranteed.

The Body

The body is another important characteristic to care about. You have to consider the body as a reinforcement of the voice. The most difficult target to be obtained is the usage of hands. You never know where to put them during a speech. It is suggested not to move your hands too much, but you can simply keep them naturally down, without putting them in your pockets. You have to raise them when you want to underline a concept with the voice; in that case, the hands are useful to evidence some parts of the slide by simply pointing your finger in the right direction or using a laser pointing device to select on the screen the item you are citing with the voice.

The Appearance

The appearance also can be very important, especially for formal presentations such as conferences and management meetings. The dress is also important; if it is not necessary to have a dress code for each meeting type, it is important to have a quite simple and elegant look and feel that must capture the looks of the audience without astonishing people with strange colors put together in a random way.

Pay attention also to the shoes; it can be trivial, but they must be clean. One of the first things that people look at is the shoes, and if they are not clean, you will receive a low vote regarding your appearance.

The Look

After the voice, the look is perhaps the most important added value for obtaining a good result from your presentation.

You never look at the ground, your hands, or the room ceiling while you are speaking or listening for questions. You always have to look at people and to look for the people's look. Never look at the same person for a long time (unless you are in a very restricted meeting, and you have to present your work to the company president), but look at each person in the room, looking for mute comments and trying to identify in advance who is the person that probably will ask for more details, who is the most interested, and who is the least interested. Try also to identify how many people like your speech. If people know that you are looking at them, they will be more interested, since they will feel more involved with the passion you are demonstrating.

LESSONS LEARNED

TARGET

Presentation

VALUES

Communication

PRACTICES

Different presentation styles must be adopted for different contexts and audiences.

Three steps of giving a presentation:

- Preparing the presentation
- Preparing the speech
- Preparing how to speak

Learn how to use the voice and the body.

Chapter IV

Training

Training activities are related strictly to presentations, since each time you have to train someone, you need to present a set of topics to a group of people.

Of course, training is a very different type of presentation for several reasons: The people that are listening to you usually are not skilled in the argument and, therefore, are not inclined to destroy your presentation with negative comments; the number of persons that are listening to you usually are few in the worst case (apart from academic lessons that are out of the scope of this book); and the duration of the training session is at least half a day and also can be several days, so that you can have time to socialize with all the people.

Social aspects are very important during training, since interaction with people is not limited to the presentation time but also extends to all the coffee breaks and, in the case of a long training, to lunch or dinner, especially when you are training a partner or a customer at his or her site.

Several of the tricks reported for presentations also are valid for training, especially the suggestions related to the speech, and therefore, such suggestions will not be discussed again in this section.

For presentation, the main value that must be considered and addressed is communication, but in the training activity, some other values must be taken into account, such as simplicity and feedback. During a training session, simplicity and feedback are important as the communication capability, since simplicity usually improves and meliorates communication, and feedback aids in the dynamic revision of the presentation contents, improving simplicity and then communication.

In order to have a clearer view of their influence, a short overview of these values follows.

Values

Communication

Communication is the main skill that is needed for a good trainer. As already stated for presentations, if you have no communication skill, you can meliorate in order to obtain at least an acceptable presentation. Consider that if unfortunately you are not naturally skilled in communication, a large probability exists that you will never become a good trainer. Only a few people among those that know all the details of a topic and of a science are also capable of transferring to other people their knowledge. The number is reduced, if we also consider that the transfer should be done in a simple and direct manner and by interesting people in the topics that have to be discussed.

All the comments made in the presentation section are also valid for training activities, taking into account what already has been stated about people that are capable of teaching.

Simplicity

While communication is mandatory for performing any training activity, simplicity is the main characteristic to be considered in order to have an effective training. Unless you have information on the audience target that evidences the mean and the minimum cultural level, you must start considering that people in front of you do not have the minimum idea of the topic you will speak about.

Simplicity also means that you must prepare the documentation for the training (both paper documents and slides for presentation), always trying to find the simple way to explain the argument. Once you have built the basis, you also can introduce more complex concepts that are based on the previously discussed items. During the speech, you always have to use the simplest language that the topic allows, avoiding at least in the first part of the course a strong technical language. If you are compelled to use technical language with no skilled people, prepare some slides for giving definitions of all the terms that are related to the argument you are introducing. Another useful approach is to give the description of terms and acronyms the first time you use them. This helps to simplify the comprehension process for people that are getting the course.

Feedback

Feedback is also very important in order to understand if your training is effective enough and also if the people involved in the course are comprehending the notions you are trying to transfer to them. In order to have feedback, several methods can be used. The first method is the most direct, since you can ask people to give feedback directly to you; the main drawback is that often you do not obtain the real feedback, since people always try to mitigate negative comments and to exalt positive aspects, when the feedback is direct. The second approach is the classical one and the one that is used most-often — anonymous questionnaires by which people evaluate the contents of the course, the quality of the training, and the preparation of the teacher. This is a good way to obtain non-biased feedback.

In order to have indirect feedback, it also is important to know what people attending the course have understood and if the main concepts you have explained have been correctly transferred. The level they reach after the course is also an important parameter, especially when compared with the level before the course. Often, it is useful to prepare a test focused on the arguments of the course and to propose it before and after the course. The results usually present a success percentage of 10% to 20% before the course and a success greater than 80% after; you have to advise people that it is normal that before the course they are not able to answer most of the questions. The increment in the successfully-answered questions measures how much the course had a positive impact on the learning level of the people attending it.

Training in Practice

The preparation of a training section follows quite the same rules explained before for presentations, since when you train people, you usually present an argument regarding some topics using a presentation made with slides.

It is important to discuss the different training scenarios in which a team leader or project manager can be involved during his or her activity.

Project manager and team leaders can be involved in training in small or medium enterprises that do not have a training department. If they perform such activities, project managers are usually involved in the opening of the training, presenting general aspects of the project and major advantages of it, while usually the team manager is involved in detailing the more technical aspects.

In any case and independently of the person that trains, we will focus on some different scenarios: train your team, train the customer, and train the partner. It is out of the scope of this book to discuss training in an academic course. For some hints on seminars in academic courses, you can refer to the section related to presentations, since usually you will be involved in short seminars that are more similar to presentations than to real training sections, unless you are an academic.

Train Your Team

The training of the team can be divided in two phases. The first phase is related to the start of a new project, when you need to transfer to the development people all the concepts that are related to the target environment, to the technologies to be employed, and to the instrument that will be used during the development. The second phase of training is an atypical form of training, since it is performed day-by-day on the basis of the emerging problems and the changes in technologies.

Phase 1

During the first phase, your training will be deeply technical and focused on the topics that are specific for the project. The slides you will use have to evidence an informal approach to training and will not be detailed from the aesthetic point of view, since you are speaking to your closest colleagues, and you do not need any special effects to capture their attention. This can be true also because you are the manager, but, in particular, it must be true, because you will work together with them on the same project, having the same objectives, and needing to have success in steering the project toward a success, as they have.

It is important that during the team training, you will try to transfer the maximum number of concepts in the minimum slice of time. This does not mean that you have to be cryptic but simply that you have to point the attention only on important topics, leaving the details to the second phase of the training.

This phase of the training can be planned, and the presentation should be realized in advance in order to be sure to capture all the aspects that your team has to know before starting the project. You must give to your team all the instruments to correctly evaluate the project and the impact of technologies (new and already known) on the project. As soon as the people understand the basic concepts, you are ready to start the project and, therefore, the second phase of the training that will focus on topics that arise from the daily work or that will be related to details of already introduced technologies.

In the first phase of the training, you also have to communicate to your team the schedule of the project, its planned milestones, and its deadlines. A clear target helps people to focus their efforts better and to allow people to work, having in mind the same target and pushing the project in the same (right) direction.

It is also important to clarify and explain, if it is not already known, the methodology that will be adopted during the development of project. As soon as the methodology has been explained, it is also necessary to assign roles to the team members in order to clarify the functions and responsibility of each person, when the project type and the team size require such activity.

Phase 2

As already introduced, the second phase will be done day-by-day during the project development. This phase is a good management practice and can be considered an atypical form of training, since it cannot be planned in advance but is a sort of collection of very short training sessions focused on solving the problems that can arise during project development or to detail topics introduced in the first phase. These sessions are very similar to team meetings, if, in general, they follow a team meeting each time a problem faces the project. On the contrary, with respect to the first phase and to team meetings where all people are involved, in these training sessions, usually only a few of the team members will participate; the involved people are those that need a particular training on a specific topic.

This second phase, because of its nature, is usually not performed by using slides but is arranged on a board with chalk or felt tip pens, or in front of a piece of paper at your desk or hung on the wall. While in the first phase the interaction is limited, in this second phase, you will interact a lot with your team members, since people already know the basic concepts and need only to refine or to clarify some concept related to the details of the project.

Train the Customer

The training of customers is obviously very different with respect to team training. You can train customers having different targets in your mind. You can train a customer on a product of your company, train a customer as a service only on a product that is on the market, and train a customer on a general topic that the customer requests and that is not related to a product (this is the case for security training, quality certification training, etc.).

In all cases, the training must be very professional and formal, since you are in front of the customer.

Each one of these different types of training requires a different approach, since it is very different training people regarding a topic or regarding the use of a product or software.

The training for a product your company produces or sells always should be a *hands-on training* performed directly on the product in order to transfer to the customer a large amount of knowledge in a short time; usually, a certification of the attended course is awarded to the training participants. If background training is also necessary, it can be performed during the hands-on phase or before. From my point of view, I suggest performing all training during the same session, since it eliminates the risk of making a not useful theoretical training that is not remembered once the attendants are in front of the product.

Software and service training have to be approached in a different way, and the classical academic approach of theoretical lessons followed by a laboratory session is the best approach. A service or software can be demonstrated during a theoretical session, and then the knowledge can be tested during a lab session.

The training performed on the basis of customer request is comprised 99% percent of the time of one of two approaches already presented. Also, during a training on a general topic not related to a product, a lab session does not usually exist and is replaced by a round table discussion.

Train the Partner

A partner can be a technical or a commercial partner. In the former case, the partner in training is usually not present on the team that develops software, unless you are realizing something that is part of a larger project that has to be shared with other teams or companies. If this is the case, you have to train the partner on how your product works and on how it can be integrated with a third part application. This training is strongly technical and often it is managed in an informal way since it is a sort of "training-on-the-job". The partner training that works well, at least for software product integration, is a real on-the-job training. This training approach is based on the hypothesis that some members of the two teams or companies can work together for a small amount of time in order to transfer knowledge and experiences to each other and to share problems. It is a sort of pair programming extended to teams. In general, the training performed by only the exchange of formal documents with an optional presentation does not give valuable results.

In the latter case and, therefore, when the partnership is based on a commercial agreement, the training is closer to a customer training, since you usually have to present a product or a service that your partner can sell or install for you. Of course, the environment is usually not too formal, since you have to work together to reach the same target, but it is not informal as for a technical partner, since you have to present features of the product or service and guarantee some commercial statements instead of focusing on details of technical issues.

Lessons Learned

Target

Training

Values

Communication
Simplicity
Feedback

Practices

Train your team in two phases:

- Start of the project
- During project development

Train the customer about the product in a hands-on fashion.

Train the technical partner by pairing with the development team.

Chapter V

People Management

People management is a really complex activity that is focused mainly on problem solving and team motivation. Problem solving is a typical daily activity of each manager that has responsibility over a group of people, since people often have problems that also can impact daily work activities. Often, the solution of a problem can solve a cascaded set of problems that are related to the solved one, increasing the quality of life and the chances of success of the project.

Sometimes, problems are not real problems but are related to a person's low level of satisfaction. These problems can be solved quite easily by motivating people. In this chapter, different manners of motivating people are presented.

The success of people management is bounded also to the instrument you use to face work organization and task assignment. The last part of the chapter is dedicated to such instruments.

Values

The basic values that must be considered for successfully managing people are communication and feedback. The reason is very simple, since communication always must be used, and you must receive feedback from both your manager and from the people you are managing in order to have a clear understanding of how well you are covering your role.

People management is mainly a psychological activity (Cockburn, 1996). Obviously, I do not want to cover management aspects from that complex point of view but only to give suggestions and best practices to face management problems. The management problems are always seen from the point of view of the team manager and if they can be adopted widely, since this book is mainly dedicated to this target.

When you are a team manager and people recognize this role for you, often the developers of your team will be influenced greatly by your behavior, especially in the moments in which they are under stress. When a critical moment is facing the project or a missing deadline becomes more and more probable, and your moods shift unpredictably, your people will start to deal with their tasks in a chaotic way. If you show or at least simulate a calm behavior, specifying that we are under pressure but that you are controlling the situation, then your team will work at its best, considering that you are facing the problem or at least hoping that you see some possible solutions for the problems.

Communication

In all situations in which you have to manage people, you must learn how to communicate with them (Myers, 1999). Oftentimes, people agree with you or support your choices, if you are able to communicate your will in advance to them in the right way.

In my experience, when you have to manage several people, you use (and not lose) about 30% of your time speaking with people. Sometimes, people do not speak with you about technical problems but often for personal matters, such as holiday organization and need for vacation time. These meetings are often marginally related to the task they are doing at that moment, but they are useful for enforcing you as a leader and for having people that trust you when they have some needs. It is important for you to listen to them and to understand what they need for many reasons. The main reason is that you have to organize future work from a long-term perspective, and therefore, it is necessary to know in advance people's needs. Another important reason is bounded to the turnover of people, since unsatisfied or not considered people are usually the first that start to look for another job.

You always have to consider people's requests, since if you have to evaluate and sometimes reject their requests, it is better to lose one day of work from a person in a critical period and gain an increased productivity for a couple of weeks than to deny a vacation day and obtain a reduced productivity for the same couple of weeks.

These facts will be considered in greater detail in the section related to dealing with problems after the feedback section.

Feedback

Feedback is very important from all points of view. It is important for the payoff you give to the behavior of each team member (i.e., the management feedback), but it also is important for the feedback you receive from people (i.e., the team feedback).

We are interested mainly in covering the former aspect in this section, since the latter is better exploited in an audit process that normally is out of your control, since it is performed behind your back. When audit results come, you have to consider them in great detail from a self-criticism point of view, which helps you to focus your efforts better and strengthen your position as a leader.

Management feedback's main aim is to consolidate and improve good behaviors of team members and to try to eliminate bad behaviors. This can be obtained by giving the right feedback in terms of positive or negative payoffs. You must take care of your behavior when you give payoffs, since sometimes you risk obtaining a result that is exactly the opposite with respect to the desired result.

Let me explain that with an example. A team member often asks for your opinion regarding technical problems. If each time the team member asks for your attention you say that you are busy and do not consider him or her, you are giving a negative payoff to the behavior, resulting in this person avoiding interaction with you. On the contrary, if you answer promptly each time the team member calls, you are giving a positive payoff. Each piece of feedback can be good, if you identify that the person's behavior is good or bad. If the continuous claims are originated by a particularly difficult task that needs your attention, you have to give positive feedback. On the other hand, if this behavior is provoked by the incorrect use of the brain by the person, a negative feedback is necessary. Consider both opportunities each time you give a negative feedback or payoff to a behavior, remembering that a wrong payoff will become a problem to be solved in the future. In the previous example, it is possible that the person is not interested in the task or that the task is beyond his or her capability. In the first case, you have to motivate the person by temporarily switching him or her to a different task, while in the second case you have to train the person, since his or her knowledge is not enough for the assigned task. Bad payoff for the sake of bad payoff, without any corrective action and without being constructive to solve the problem hidden behind a bad behavior is not only negative but can be dangerous for people's motivations and, therefore, for the project success.

The behavior you must consider in terms of feedback can be summarized as follows:

- **Well done (good behavior).** Be positive with feedback and praise in public for the person and the idea that the person suggested or the solution found for a problem.
- **Badly done (bad behavior).** Be critical but constructive to improve people's capabilities; critics must be private and not public. It is important to be constructive and to create the environment that helps to reach the solution to a problem that is often masked by a badly done activity.
- **Future activities.** Always give a view of the future development of the project in order to motivate people toward the reach of a success in obtaining a completely working system. This is also useful for obtaining feedback from the team on long-term activities that you have planned.

People Management in Practice

Management activities are dedicated to problem solving 90% of the time. A great part of this time is dedicated to trying to solve people problems, especially if people do not know how to solve problems. People often ignore that they have a problem, since it is difficult to self-judge how badly one is behaving (Blair, 1995).

Team Motivation

Motivations, from a team member's point of view, are divided into two main categories:

- **Long-term motivation.** Money and advancement in the career, which usually you do not control as a team manager;
- **Short-term motivation.** Responsibility, acquirement of new skills and knowledge, broader experience, and so forth, that you can control.

The secret to motivate a team member is to offer short-term motivations, presenting them as a necessary and maybe sometimes sufficient condition to reach the desired long-term objectives.

It is not beneficial to promise advancement in career or money that you cannot control. It is better to train people with seminars and to introduce new tools for broadening the team experience, which you can control and is in your budget as a team manager. It is often true that people with broader knowledge and improved skills are the most suitable for getting a career advancement, and therefore, the path to long-term targets often must pass through short-term benefits.

Another trick to motivate people and to increase general team motivation is to have small progress with related small successes. This encourages people to work better day by day instead of having a big success after several months while people have not been motivated during the development. The flexible programming concept of small releases is very important for obtaining small progresses in a small period and, therefore, is a strong aid in increasing people's motivations from this perspective.

Dealing with Problems

When you manage people, you always have to consider the possibility of having problems. Problems are sometimes related to the project, but this is not the section in which we discuss project countermeasures when problems arise or to analyze project risks. In this section, I would like to offer some suggestion on how to face people problems or people with problems. During your daily work, you usually can identify different problems. For example, a developer

(John), when he is under pressure, starts to write very bugged code. Another developer (Kate) is always late in giving you weekly reports. Or another developer (Frank) is not capable of developing the assigned tasks. You cannot face all these problems together and at the same time, since if you act following different paths and different approaches at the same time, you cannot control which action is coupled with the related reaction. In several cases, two problems can be bound, and therefore, the solution of one of them can help to solve the other or to identify how to solve them. For example, Kate might be late because she is trying to help Frank, who is not capable of completing the assigned task. Frank needs a working code written by John in order to create his task, and he is not able to understand how to solve all the problems related to his and John's code, and so forth.

The first rule you have to always adopt is to face one problem a time. This allows you to isolate better the problem source, to understand how many, if any, other problems are bound to the one under analysis, and in general, to identify better if your efforts are bringing some good results.

Once you have identified the problem to be considered, you have to spend all your effort trying to solve it. As introduced in the value section, it is always better to know a problem rather than to ignore it, since when you know it, you can start to face it. If you ignore it, you do not know how many other problems are not being solved because you have not had the courage or the opportunity to face the unique problem you have discarded.

Now we can suppose that you have identified the problem and have decided to try to solve it. The main question is: How do I proceed in order to have a chance of success? The first matter is related to the measurement of your progresses; in order to measure something, you need something that can be measurable. In the case of John, you cannot say that he produced bugged code, but if you know that in his code, ten bugs have been found each week in the past three weeks, you have to assume that John produced code with ten bugs a week. You now have a metric to fight against. If your actions reduce this value in the following weeks, then you are winning, and you are also solving John's problem; otherwise, you are compelled to change your strategy. A problem expressed in a too general way is not simply solvable, since you are not able to verify if you are progressing toward a solution. In software, as in problem solving, a metric and the related measure is always desirable to evaluate, if you are moving toward a solution. The first brainstorm you have to get is related to how to remove generalized terms and to introduce a more formal definition of the problem.

As previously introduced, the problems are often bound to each other, and therefore, the second step is to identify if the problem is a real problem or if it is only a consequence of another problem. If the problem actually exists, you can continue in the direction of finding a solution; otherwise, it is better to stop trying to solve this problem and to switch to the root problem, with the probability of solving both problems in one shot. Remember that you have to keep track of the original problem metric in order to verify if the solution of the root problem has brought about a global solution of the related problems. The problem also can be due to transient factors, which, if eliminated or simply tolerated for a small amount of time, allow a natural solution of the problem without any intervention from you.

In any case, whenever you discover that a problem really exists and seems unrelated to transient factors, the first approach must be to speak with the person related to the problem in order to verify if he or she recognizes the problem. Often, the answer will negate the existence of the problem or to minimize the effect of it on the working environment. Now is the moment to show if you understand how to communicate with team members, since you have to explain that you are not asking about the problem because you want to punish someone but only because you want to help the person work better in a better environment without stressful conditions. If you have learned well the art of communication, the person in front of you will start to admit that maybe in your version there is something that can be possibly true. At this point, you can start to discuss with the person how you can help him or her solve the problem. If you reach this point, you will solve the problem in a short time, at least in 90% of the cases.

If you are not able to convince the person, the only mechanism that can help you find a path toward the solution is to start to give negative feedback to the person in order to compel him or her to change behavior and then solve the problem, or to start to cooperate with you to find a feasible solution together.

Tools for People Management

The Gantt diagrams presented in Chapter II also are useful for scheduling and verifying resource assignments for each task. The adoption of such diagrams allows you to verify overhead in resource assignments and resources that are not well allocated.

Figure 1. Gantt diagram with resource assignment (horizontal lines in resource assignment separate under assignment from over assignment)

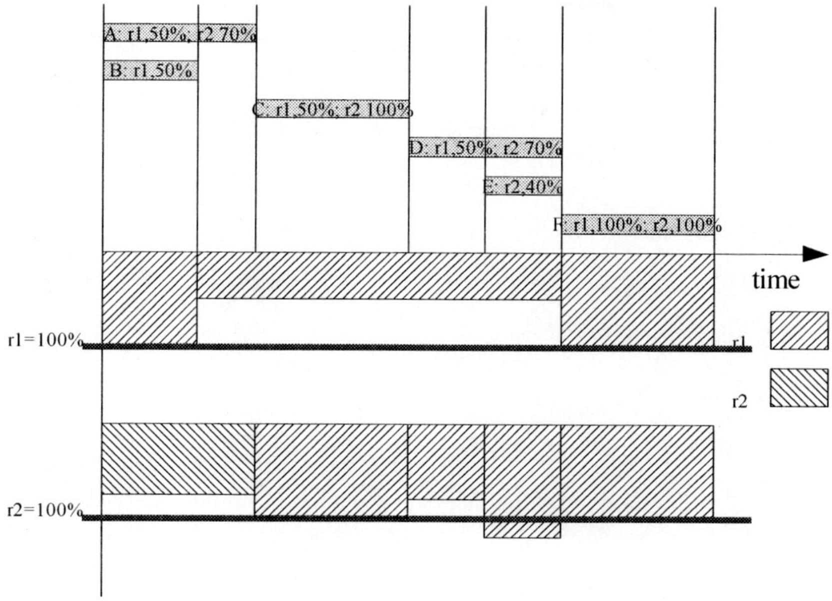

In Figure 1, together with the Gantt diagram, are the resources allocated for each task. The cumulative allocation or resources evidence that at the end of tasks D and E, there is an over assignment of r2, while r1 is only half assigned. This diagram suggests to move part of the charge and assignments on r2 to r1 during the development of task D or of task E. This operation can balance the resources and avoid scheduled overtime.

People in the Project: How Many?

In this chapter, several suggestions on how to manage people have been given, together with the correct usage of the Gantt diagram in resource allocation. The main problem is still how many resources you need for developing a project (Brooks, 1995; Miranda, 2002). This concept also can be simplified, considering only the number of developers for the project, since several other key people are present independently of the project type or size.

In Chapter XIV, related to software metrics and project measurement, a model for cost estimation named COCOMO (Boehm, 1981) is presented and discussed. Its main focus is on estimating the Effort (E) needed for the project development (i.e., the people/months necessary for the development) and the time frame (T) necessary to complete the project.

The number of people (N) involved is therefore given by the equation:

$$N = \frac{E}{T}$$

Equation 1. Number of persons (N) for a project of estimated effort (E) and estimated duration (T)

This simple equation hides an important consideration; that is, the number of people must be inferred by the estimated project duration and estimated effort. It is not possible to augment the number of people in order to reduce the time needed for completing the project, even if the equation theoretically allows it.

The real situation is very different, since a theoretical curve and the real curve bounding the development time with the number of people employed can be drawn from Figure 2.

The real curve depicted in Figure 2 suggests that after a certain number of resources, the duration of the project starts to rise again. This fact is due to the effort needed to coordinate people and to the fragmentation of the project in modules that compels a large integration time.

Equation 1 can give a rough estimate of the needed resources; its main drawback is that the number of resources is considered constant during the whole project, while in reality the number of resources needed to complete a project can vary during the project.

In order to consider this fact, Putnam used the Raleigh-Norden equation to estimate at the time (t) of the project duration (T) the number of resources (E) needed.

Boehm corrected the Putnam equation, since it was capable of correctly estimating the resources only in a limited time interval, and presented the following complex equation that can be used for t between 0 and T.

Figure 2. Time (T) needed to develop a project with N persons: Theoretical and real trend

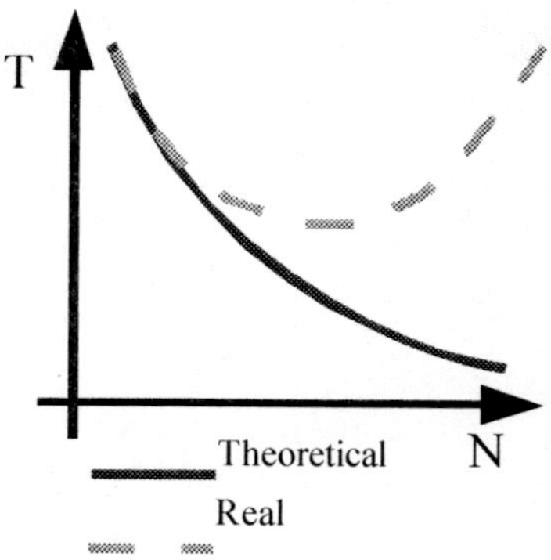

$$N = E \cdot \frac{0.15 \cdot T + 0.7 \cdot t}{0.25 \cdot T^2} e^{-\frac{(0.15T+0.7t)^2}{0.5 \cdot T^2}}$$

Equation 2. Number of resources (N) needed at time t between 0 and T on the basis of the estimated effort (E)

In order to better understand Equation 2, it can be graphically represented; a sample for $T = 36$ months and $E = 144$ people/months is shown in Figure 3.

The maximum of Equation 2 can be found simply by evaluating dN/dt, which allows you to determine that the maximum is for $t = 0{,}5*T$.

On the basis of the previous considerations, it can be estimated that the maximum number of resources needed for a project with an estimated effort of E people per an estimated duration of T months is for $t = 0{,}5*T$, having the corresponding N reported in Equation 3.

$$N_{\max} = \frac{2}{\sqrt{e}} \cdot \frac{E}{T} \approx 1.21 \cdot \frac{E}{T}$$

Equation 3. Maximum number of resources in terms of number of people needed for a project of duration T with estimated effort E

Figure 3. Graphical representation of Equation 2 for T = 36 and E = 144, where time (t) in months is on the x-axis and the number of resources in terms of people needed (N) is on the y-axis

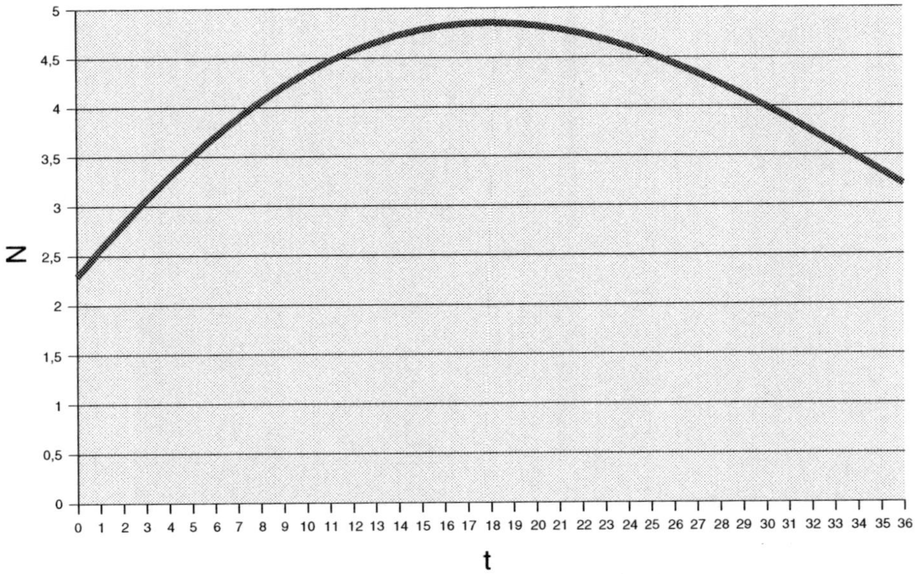

References

Blair, G. M. (1995). *Starting to manage: The essential skills*. New York: IEEE.

Boehm, B. (1981). *Software engineering economics*. Upper Saddle River, NJ: Prentice Hall.

Brooks, F. (1995). *The mythical man-month* (anniversary ed.). Reading, MA: Addison-Wesley.

Cockburn, A. (1996). The interaction of social issues and software architecture. *Communications of the ACM, 39*(10), 40-46.

Miranda, E. (2002). Planning and executing time-bound projects. *IEEE Computer, 35*(3), 73-79.

Myers, W. (1999). Early communication key to software project success projects. *IEEE Computer, 32*(5), 110-111.

Lessons Learned

Target

People management

Values

Communication
Feedback

Practices

Motivate the team with short-term benefits.
Small successes obtained often motivate the team.
Face one problem at a time.
Identify problems together with team members.
Adopt Gantt diagrams for monitoring resource assignment.
Do not add persons simply to reduce project duration.

Chapter VI

Delegation

In this chapter, delegation is introduced, and the difference between delegation and assignment is reported and evidenced.

The chapter proceeds by defining exactly what delegation means, presenting the WH (*what* and *how*) of the delegation process, since it is impossible to delegate each task, and the way in which you delegate must be carefully considered.

Values

As I have done for the other chapters on management, I will try in this section to evidence the values that are necessary for successfully applying this very particular management practice. After the values, some practical hints will be proposed that consider in great detail what delegation means (Blair, 1995; Myers, 1999).

Simplicity

Simplicity always has to be considered as strictly related to delegation. It is better to delegate tasks that are simple to people who are just starting to have new responsibilities and to delegate complex tasks to skilled people, always considering the simplest way to obtain a good result. While delegation of simple tasks is quite obvious, it may not be so easy to understand how to *simply* delegate complex tasks. In the second part of this chapter, several hints on the practical approach to delegation will be considered, but the main concept to keep in mind is always the approach to gradual delegation, giving access to information and support delegated people. This is to avoid the blind delegation in which delegated people are not aware of the tasks to be fulfilled and, therefore, can be astonished by the new responsibility without knowing how to deal with the problems they have to face.

Feedback

As evidenced in Figure 1, feedback is also part of the process of gradual delegation, since you have to give feedback to delegated people in order to control the process and to be able to suggest changes when the approach seems to be too bad. Feedback is also needed by the manager when a task is delegated to a very skilled person who also can increase the competencies of the manager by suggesting evaluation methods and solutions to problems that are different from that usually adopted by the manager.

Courage

Without any doubt, you need courage to delegate activities to someone else. If the person is able to solve the delegated problem, you have saved some work, but if you have delegated a task to a person who cannot solve it and provokes a disaster, you have on your shoulders the weight of the failure, since you are the manager and decided to delegate the task.

Figure 1. Blind delegation vs. gradual delegation

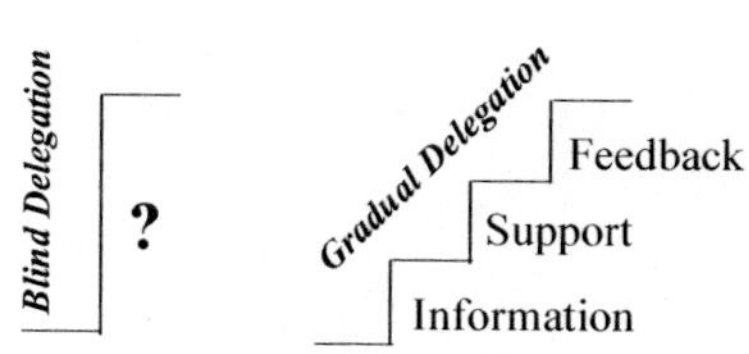

Delegation at Work

Several people I know are confused about and often wrongly interpret the delegation mechanism, confusing it with assignments. Delegating a task is an activity very different from assigning a task. The main difference is related to the fact that when you delegate an activity, you get the job done by someone (the same as assignment), but you also allow people to make decisions on your behalf. Remember that you are the manager, and if someone to whom you have delegated a job fails in the activity, then the failure is automatically yours.

You have to carefully consider what to delegate and also how to delegate a task to someone on your team.

Target of Delegation Activity

As introduced before, the target of delegation is for someone to take a task, make decisions and act on your behalf. In order to maximize the chances of success in delegating to others, it is necessary to be sure regarding the following points (Blair, 1995):

- **The delegated person knows exactly what you want.** This means that you must have a clear picture of the task in your mind in order to be able to explain it to the person. You also must be sure that the person can comprehend the task you are delegating and also has the necessary skills to understand and complete the task.
- **The delegated person has the authority to achieve the result.** This means that before you delegate a job for which a person must be responsible to other people, you have to be sure that all the other people involved know the new role of the delegated team member for the task under discussion. When you delegate something that requires access to reserved information or to reserved places, you have to be sure to delegate or obtain the needed authorization for the delegated person.
- **The delegated person must know how to do the job.** This means that the person must have the necessary skills, knowledge, and instruments to successfully complete the task.

These points show that before you delegate a job to someone, you have to prepare the chessboard and move the chess pieces to the right place in order to correctly allow delegated people to checkmate the problem.

Remember that the main aim of the delegation process is to obtain from people at least the same results that you would obtain by yourself. This implies that people have to become more skilled and can potentially reach your level. This is not a disadvantage; it is an advantage for the project manager, who now can count on skilled people to do delegated tasks.

What Can You Delegate?

Each person is inclined to delegate to others the most boring activities and all the activities that are considered less interesting or that can cause problematic time loss. This is not the correct approach to delegation. It can work sometimes for an assignment, but people probably will fail in their duties if they are facing a boring, tedious, and problematic task. One target of delegation is to enrich people, and therefore, the delegated tasks (or at least the first delegated task) have to be exciting so that people can face the problems with the right approach and possibly produce a good result.

Once you have excluded the most boring tasks, you have to choose what to delegate to people. I suggest choosing among the following:

- Delegate activities in which you are very skilled so that you are sure to communicate the target and optionally help to reach a good result.
- Delegate to each person what he or she is able to do well (possibly better than you) and ask for feedback in order to understand the decision-making process. This also can increase your abilities in tasks in which you are not very skilled.

You can delegate all interesting activities among those in the two groups mentioned previously.

How Can You Delegate?

After defining the target of delegation and what has to be delegated, it is necessary to have an overview of how to delegate tasks to people. Once you really understand the target in depth (the WH), you are ready to delegate.

You always have to remember that delegation is a challenge, since, as a result of task delegation, decisions might be made that are against yours or different from your point of view. You must not fear such challenges, since delegation not only saves the manager time but also enriches the manager, since his or her knowledge increases with different points of view and different methodologies from what he or she is used to.

Delegation does not mean loss of control, since you are compelled to verify how the delegated people work, and you must assure that the delegated tasks do not become a (big) failure. Failure in a delegated task is also your failure.

In order to accept the challenge without losing control over the results, you can apply some of the following hints to the delegation process.

- Delegate gradually in order to have people face problems step by step. These people will be able to increase their skills smoothly and to face the medium- or long-term difficult problems by themselves;
- Do not leave the delegated person alone the first time you delegate a new task. Allow a more skilled person or you to guide the delegated person in the new adventure. A real situation might be when Judy, the person that usually prepares the budget for a project, goes on vacation, and you need the weekly budget ready each Friday. You can ask to someone else, say John, to have a meeting with Judy in order to understand the processes behind her activities. Recommend also that John come back to you during the work after Judy has left the office, if he is does not understand everything completely;
- As introduced in the target of delegation, people must have the correct information in order to correctly finish their tasks. Give John access to all the files he needs for preparing the budget for Friday;
- The concept of design pattern also can be extended to decisions, creating the so-called decision pattern that can be considered the common strategy to solve a recurrent problem. Write your patterns and ask delegated people to write theirs in order to have a collection of strategies that can be useful for gradually delegating or for giving hints to people in their first delegated activity.

References

Blair, G. M. (1995). *Starting to manage: The essential skills*. New York: IEEE.

Myers, W. (1999). Early communication key to software project success projects. *IEEE Computer, 32*(5), 110-111.

Lessons Learned

Target

Delegation

Values

Simplicity

Feedback

Courage

Practices

Remember that delegation is different for each assignment.

Delegation means someone that acts and decides on behalf of you.

The failure of a delegated person is your failure.

Delegate interesting activities first.

Delegate gradually.

Control delegation results by the means of feedback.

Section II

The second part of this book is related more strictly to software project development, and methodologies and techniques for successfully steering the project toward a success story are discussed. In order to obtain such results, Section II has been divided in nine chapters.

- **Chapter VII. The Target Business Environment.** This chapter presents the business environment suitable for adopting Agile development methodologies and defines the company type, size, and commitments.
- **Chapter VIII. Classical Methodologies for Project Management.** Classical methodology must be understood well in order to evidence its strong and weak points. By comparison with Agile methodologies, strengths, and weaknesses, it is possible to identify the methodology most suitable for our environment. Several techniques, such as risk analysis, can be adopted successfully in all methodologies.
- **Chapter IX. Agile Development.** This chapter presents an overview of Agile development, evidencing the basis of this revolutionary way of interpreting software engineering and approaching software development.
- **Chapter X. eXtreme Programming.** The most well-known Agile methodology is XP. Its values and rules perhaps have contributed to the diffusion of the Agile manifesto in the programmers community. It is

impossible to write something about Agile methodologies without any reference to XP.

- **Chapter XI. Agile and Defined Project Development.** Agile and Defined Project Development (ADPD) is a methodology developed by the author and largely based on XP. Its main target is nearing the Agile methodologies with classical software quality approaches such as Software Capability Models. Apart from several rules taken as they are from XP, ADPD has modified other rules and introduced new guidelines in order to be widely accepted in the company where Agile methodologies have no chance to be introduced.
- **Chapter XII. ADPD and SW-CMM.** In this chapter, relationships between ADPD and SW-CMM are explored. In the first part of the book, a recent study on the applicability of XP in SW-CMM is performed, introducing the ADPD features that allow you to respect both Agile manifesto and SM-CMM level 3, the defined level.
- **Chapter XIII. ADPD and UML Adoption.** A lot of people think that formal languages for software representation and modeling cannot be employed suitably in Agile methodology. In this chapter, I would like to demonstrate that UML is not only useful in Agile contexts but often saves time.
- **Chapter XIV. Software Measurement.** This chapter is a summary of the metrics widely adopted in software engineering for estimating different characteristics of software engineering and software cost estimation. People can extract from this chapter interesting suggestions on the adoption of metrics for different purposes, from effort estimation to quality in use to fault prediction, selecting the most interesting metrics proposed in the literature by several authors. Some metrics extracted for the research background of the author in software measurement and assessment have been considered for inclusion.
- **Chapter XV. Project Maintenance.** Maintenance is the normal status of an Agile project. It is mandatory to address the concepts related to maintenance in a book that presents Agile methodologies and to describe how to approach rapidly changing IT projects.

Chapter VII

The Target Business Environment

During the last few years, whoever has been involved in software development and management has noticed that two different kind of projects have arisen: very large projects carried on by large companies over long periods of time (i.e., 1 to 3 years) and small to medium projects developed in a shorter period (generally less than 1 year) by small companies.

The second type of project deals mainly with recent technologies; these projects are usually Internet-related and are subject to change often and deeply in the specification (Boehm, 2000; Cusumano, 1999; Kroeker, 1999; Miranda, 2002). Moreover, since the latest technologies are on the edge and change quickly in their specifications, the technologies adopted during the project lifetime are subject to modification, and therefore, the code usually has to deal with deep modifications. The second part of this book is focused mainly on this second type of project that is often described as *rapidly changing*. In the following chapters, I will offer suggestions on how to manage and develop such projects in an environment that continuously changes and how to adapt to user modified needs and deal with technologies drift.

Several books and papers have been written with the aim of addressing the problems that arise from large projects. They teach you how to manage and develop where requirements are clear, where specification is done in advance, and where the code written today is reused without changing after 1 year. Obviously, this is still true for several large projects, especially related to banks, large industry, production companies, and similar environments where the customer knows exactly what he or she wants and is capable of becoming stable during the full life cycle of the project, the technologies, the underlying hardware, and, generally speaking, the requirements (at least with an approximation of 95% to 98% for each year).

Unfortunately, the real world of software engineers, managers, and developers is full of small companies that have customers that can draw specifications only after they have seen the first prototype, which generally does not satisfy them. In general, the IKIWISI (*I'll know it when I see it*) (Boehm, 2000) approach guides the customer, compelling deep modification of the structure, the requirements, and the code that are part of the project.

In order to avoid or at least to mitigate the effects of this refactoring on a classical management methodology such as waterfall, spiral, and so forth, Agile methods for software development and management have been created. More recently, Agile methodologies (Beck, 1999, 2000; Boehm, 2002) are trying to partially abandon their pure concepts in order to approach the world of more formal methods, such as Capability Maturity Model (Paulk, 1993, 1993a, 2001), UML (Booch, 1998; Favre, 2003; Larman, 2001; Mellor, 2002; Rumbaugh, 1999), and tools for aiding the formalization of concepts and for automating the generation of documentation.

In information technology, an amazing solution does not exist for developing and managing projects, since a single development and management methodology is not suitable for all companies, for all projects, and last, but not least, for each developer and manager.

Moreover, software engineering has no silver bullet to solve the problems related to each different type of project, and therefore, it is necessary to define the target environment for which the methodologies and techniques reported in this book are valid and can be successfully applied.

The book title refers in a generic way to rapidly changing projects. Which projects can be defined as rapidly changing? A rapidly changing project is not a rapid project, since some long projects or projects where constraints and bounds changes rapidly also can have these characteristics.

Generally speaking, if several of the assumptions that follow apply to your project, you can be quite sure that you have a rapidly changing project. You have to consider the following list as a set of rules of thumb; the reader can expand on these rules on the basis of his or her personal experience. They should not be considered a certain procedure to identify and classify projects.

1. The project lifetime (from project start to delivery of the final product) is less than 1 year;
2. The project total estimated effort does not exceed eight person/year;
3. The customer is not technical, and therefore, it is difficult for him or her to define in advance requirements the architecture and technologies;
4. The project is Web-based or oriented to e-business, where the changes in the market often require changes in some of the project requirements; and
5. The project is based on not-so-stable technologies or on technologies that are rapidly evolving toward a final specification.

As it can be simply argued, it is quite common to have such projects developed in your team, and it is also quite obvious that sometimes deadlines have been missed to the great dissatisfaction of the customer. This book aims to reduce the risks related to deadline missing and to try to establish a cooperative approach with the user in order to identify which functionality can be delayed when a deadline has to be missed, having a minimum impact on the global project.

It is important to examine in more detail each of the previous points in order to clarify better the importance of identifying the environment in which Agile projects can be developed profitably.

Project Lifetime

It is difficult to manage in an Agile manner a project whose planned duration is more than 1 year, since the usual delivery time interval of a software version in an Agile development environment is a week or a couple of weeks. Generally, it seems unsuitable to release to the customer more than 30 different versions to be evaluated, unless your customer appreciates the Agile methodologies; in that case, the customer is perhaps technical and can actively cooperate with the project development as described in Chapters X and XI, which are related to XP and ADPD.

Project Effort

The project effort is related strictly to two main factors: the number of people in an Agile team and the project lifetime or duration. Usually, an Agile team is comprised of no more than 10 people, and if the project duration is under 1 year, the maximum effort for Agile methodology is usually under eight person/year. The most common total effort for an Agile project, according to my experience, generally does not exceed three to five people/years. Sometimes, small companies (i.e., those identified for the target business environment that we are discussing) work on different projects at the same time, having the same people involved in all the projects. Accordingly, it is more suitable that an effort of one-third of the maximum effort be allocated to each project.

The second environment in which Agile methodologies can be applied is a large company that develops small projects; each project is assigned to a development team. In that case, all the people of the team are involved in the development of the same project, and therefore, the maximum project duration also can be up to eight person/year.

Project Type

It is simpler to identify projects that cannot be developed with Agile methodologies with respect to those that can apply for them, since Agile methodologies can be applied successfully when the main hypothesis of Agile programming is true. The cost of each modification is low.

This basic rule simply is not applicable in very complex project such as the following:

- **Bank and security systems.** Usually, after each modification, the system should be tested in depth. The regression testing is not always sufficient, since the possibility of interfacing with legacy systems and systems external to the bank exists, and it is not always true that these systems are available as often as an Agile developer uses regression testing. Moreover, sometimes black box testing and profiling need to be addressed for the most critical functions. In that case, the cost of a modification increases very quickly, since there is a dead interval between the end of the modification and the possibility of running the regression testing, which is necessary to validate the modification. In these situations, the code cannot be validated according to an Agile development approach.

- **Safety critical systems.** In this kind of system, it is unsuitable that all people can modify all parts of the code, since sometimes each person has to develop part of the code that is related to his or her specific knowledge. If someone else wants to modify that code, the costs of modification can be very high, since a change can require a specific training on the topic that is related to the code. Do not forget that specific responsibility assignments have to be performed in order to track who has the permission to modify part of a code that can have a negative impact on the health of one, ten, or hundreds of people.
- **Real-time systems.** Real-time systems usually are based on complex timing and strictly bound models that must be validated in advance in order to be sure that the temporal specifications for the system are satisfied. A deep modification of the system, as often happens in Agile methodologies, can compel a complete revisit of the model with the subsequent revalidation of the whole system timings and behaviors. Also, in that system type, the assumption of the low cost for the single modification is not true, and therefore, the project is not suitable for Agile development.

All the other projects can be approached with Agile methodologies. The most appropriate projects can be found in Web-related environments and among e-commerce projects, where people can see the results of the different modifications in a fast way and give fast feedback.

Project Technology

The methodology adopted for the project development and management are often influenced by the chosen technologies and by the evolution of such technologies. For example, the "project by reuse" approach is not recommended when the underlying technology can change very quickly. All projects that involve emerging technologies or technologies that are subject to change during the project lifetime are the ideal field in which Agile methodology can be applied. Standard methodology, based on component reuse, can fail when the technical basis of the components changes deeply.

People Factor

Finally, another parameter should be considered in order to verify if the methodologies described in this book or Agile methodologies in the large sense are valid for your project. It is mandatory to verify if the team that has to develop the project can work in the environment described by the methodology. The background of people involved in development can influence their approach toward Agile development, since if you have a team that has never worked in an open space, has never heard about regression testing and pair programming, and has never been permitted to change their programming styles and the way in which comments are written, then you have to spend a lot of effort introducing Agile methodologies in such a team. Sometimes it is better to move toward another methodology, unless you strategically consider the adoption of an Agile style of programming.

References

Beck, K. (1999). Embracing change with extreme programming. *IEEE Computer, 32*(10), 70-77.

Beck, K. (2000). *Extreme programming explained: Embrace change*. Los Alamitos, CA: IEEE.

Boehm, B. (2000). Requirements that handle IKIWISI, COTS and rapid change. *IEEE Computer, 33*(7), 99-102.

Boehm, B. (2002). Get ready for agile methods, with care. *IEEE Computer, 35*(1), 64-69.

Booch, G., Rumbaugh, J., & Jacobson, I. (1999). *The unified modeling language user guide*. Boston, MA: Addison-Wesley Professional.

Cusumano, M. A., & Yoffie, D. B. (1999). Software development on Internet time. *IEEE Computer, 32*(10), 60-69.

Favre, L. (2003). *UML and the unified process*. Hershey, PA: IRM Press.

Kroeker, K. L. (1999). Software [r]evolution: A roundtable. *IEEE Computer, 32*(5), 48-57.

Larman, C. (2001). *Applying UML and patterns: An introduction to object-oriented analysis and design and the unified process*. Upper Saddle River, NJ: Prentice Hall.

Mellor, S., Balcer, M., & Balcer, M. J. (2002). *Executable UML: A foundation for model driven architecture*. Indianapolis, IN: Addison-Wesley.

Miranda, E. (2002). Planning and executing time-bound projects. *IEEE Computer, 35*(3), 73-79.

Paulk, M. C. (2001). Extreme programming from a CMM perspective. *IEEE Software, 18*(6), 19-26.

Paulk, M. C. Curtis, B., Chrissis, M. B., &Weber, C. (1993, February). *Capability maturity model for software, Version 1.1* (Publication CMU/SEI-93-TR-24, DTIC No. ADA263403). Pittsburgh, PA: Software Engineering Institute.

Paulk, M. C., Weber, C. V., Garcia, S. M., Chrissis, M. B., & Bush, M. W. (1993, February). *Key practices of the capability maturity model, Version 1.1* (Publication CMU/SEI-93-TR-25, DTIC No. ADA263432). Pittsburgh, PA: Software Engineering Institute.

Rumbaugh, J., Jacobson, I., & Booch, G. (1999). *The unified modelling language reference manual*. Boston, MA: Addison-Wesley.

Lessons Learned

Target

Business environment identification

Practices

Agile projects when:

- Duration of project is less than 1 year
- Total effort is less than eight people per year
- Non-technical customer

Adoption of edge technologies

- Not Agile project when:
- Bank and security systems
- Safety critical systems
- Real-time systems

Chapter VIII

Classical Methodologies, Techniques, and Tools for Project Management

In order to better understand Agile methodologies, it is necessary to have a clear background of what software engineering has suggested in the past regarding the methodologies for approaching software development and software management (Agresti, 1986; Buxton, 1976; Ghezzi, 1990; Naur, 1969). For these reasons, in this chapter, the so-called classical methodologies for project management are considered and commented on, together with the techniques, meta-models such as the spiral life cycle, and tools such as risk management and assessment. It is important to know the background of software engineering in order to understand if Agile methodologies will fit your needs.

In this chapter, the waterfall life cycle and a couple of evolutionary life cycles (Gilb, 1988), such as prototyping and spiral life cycles (Boehm, 1988), will be analyzed.

Figure 1. Waterfall life cycle with central phases more related to development evidenced

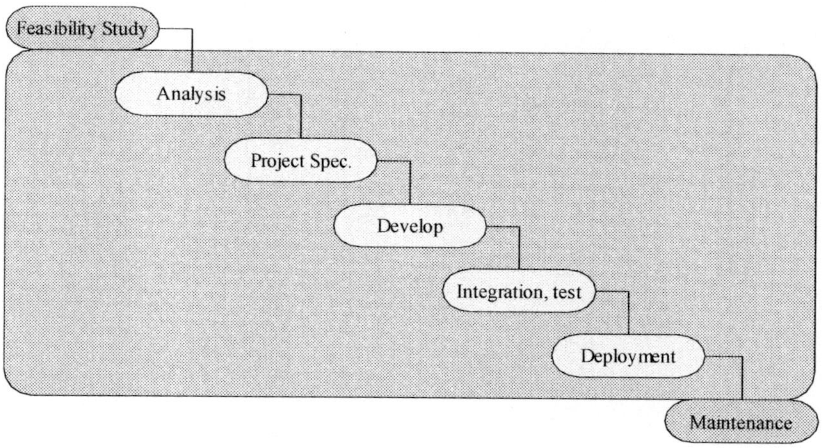

Waterfall Life Cycle

The waterfall life cycle is perhaps the first and most well-known life cycle for software development. The waterfall model divides the project development into consequent phases that have to be executed one after the other.

This model assumes that the process of software development can be divided in five phases to which two other phases (one before and one after) can be added to complete the cycle. The life cycle is summarized in Figure 1.

The central phases generally are considered the real phases of the product development and, therefore, have been evidenced, while the first and last phases can be considered respectively as necessary phases before the real starting of the project (feasibility study) and a consequence of the project development (maintenance). In the following, all these phases will be detailed more in order to give a clearer picture. All the phases are not really separated, but each phase is partially superimposed to the following apart from the feasibility study and the maintenance. This allows a partial feedback among phases, as shown in Figure 2.

Feasibility Study

The feasibility study can be defined as the make or buy phase, since it is now that the company decides if a new project has to be realized, one or more

Figure 2. Waterfall life cycle representation of phase with partial superimposing and effort represented by the area

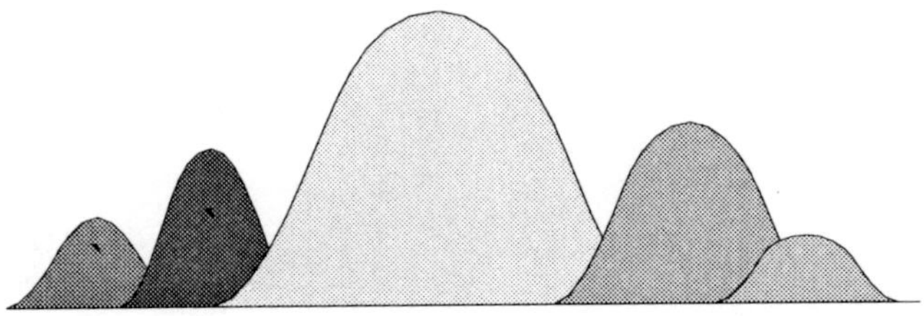

products on the market have to be integrated, or if a product should be bought.

The cost evaluation also has to be performed in this phase, since it can be the main reason that a company can discriminate between the make option or the buy option. The costs always are related to the estimation of resources needed, since if you need more resources, you have to spend more money. The output of this phase is the feasibility document (FD), in which the problem definition, the scenarios of adoption, and costs and time for the different possible choices are reported.

Analysis

If you are at this phase, the choice performed in the feasibility study has been to make the product. This is the real first phase of the project, since it is the first phase in which you really have to realize a software system. In this phase, the complete analysis of the user problems is performed, and the functional requirements are drawn in detail. The output of this phase is a couple of documents:

- **Requirement specification document (RSD)**, which contains the user requirements expressed as use cases in which the problem domain is analyzed in all its detail. This document also can assume the format of a user manual, in which the functionality is explained with the aid of some drawings of the user interface (if the system has a user interface). In practice, it is evidenced in this document *what* the application has to do.
- **System test plan (STP)**, which contains all the tests to be performed on the system in order to approve it with respect to the user requirements.

The waterfall life cycle requires that, before starting to write a single line of code and also before the choice of technologies and before the project of the system, all requirements must be established, and all tests to verify such requirements or use cases have to be defined in advance.

Project Specification

This is the phase in which the RSD objective is transformed into a software architecture to be implemented in the development phase. This is the phase in which you define *how* to do *what* has been defined in the previous section.

This phase is the core phase for the project manager, since his or her involvement is required more with respect to the other phases. In this phase, the software architecture, the technologies that have to be employed during project development, and the tools and languages to be adopted are defined.

Sometimes, it also is necessary to define how the system interacts with other systems to be realized or already present, especially in the case of legacy systems to be integrated into the architecture. The project specification phase also extends to the deployment definition, since it is necessary to establish the hardware that has to support the software architecture.

The last activity to be performed is the definition of the time line and the milestone for project verification.

The result of this phase is the project specification document (PSD), in which all the previously analyzed aspects are detailed in order to have a clear guidance during the development phase.

The PSD also contains Gantt diagrams (Coffman, 1976) and a PERT diagram (Wiest, 1977) in order to have a clear picture of the project evolution and of milestones to be met.

Development

The development phase is the main phase of the project for its duration both in time and people months, since, during this long phase, what has been analyzed and specified in the previous phases has to be realized in practice . During this phase, several other activities that are not only code writing are usually performed. The project manager has to track project evolution against deadline and milestones. Developers have to document the written code and modules (this activity is usually performed by senior developers) with special attention to knowledge sharing and transmission. The project also must be measured with software engineering metrics in order to have the possibility of verifying the quality aspects or for estimating the trend of some project figures, such as the effort spent vs. the effort that was planned to be spent, the comprehensibility and reusability of the project, and so forth. The output of this phase is the development of the code and the system, the code description document (CDD), and the actualized Gantt diagram and project measurement document (PMD) that contains the metrics measured and estimated during project evolution.

Integration and Test

The first part of this phase is dedicated to the integration of the different parts of the project in order to prepare the system for deployment in a test environment.

The integration of the parts should be easy, if all the recommendations of the analysis and project specification phases have been followed during the development phase. Unfortunately, this is not often the case, and some more development is needed in this phase. This is the way development and integration phases are partially superimposed. The second part of this phase is related to the test of the system. The system test usually is divided into two major phases: alpha test and beta test. The alpha test phase is an internal test of the system in the test deployment plan in order to verify the compliance with respect to the STP. The beta test is partially superimposed to the deployment, since the system released after the alpha test phase is installed in a deployment plant of some selected customers in order to verify the system behavior in conditions similar to the working status but not under the stress of a real working environment.

During the beta test, usually several debug engines and libraries or logs are maintained in the code in order to identify system parts to be corrected during the maintenance phase.

Deployment

In the deployment phase, the final system without all the unnecessary debug tools is installed at the customer's site. The installation of the system and the final part of the beta testing usually are started together with the maintenance phase (at least the necessary corrective maintenance), which is usually considered the conclusive phase of the project.

Maintenance

The maintenance duration can be very long and can also finish when the system becomes obsolete and no longer is used.

The maintenance phase that usually follows the project completion is the so-called corrective maintenance, during which the errors discovered during the test phase are corrected and the system's successive minor versions are released and deployed at the customer's site. Other different maintenance activities can be planned, such as adaptive maintenance and preventive maintenance.

Prototyping Life Cycle

In the literature, at least two different prototyping life cycles are reported. The first is called *throw-away prototype* and is typically adopted in a rapid application development (RAD) environment, in which the user interface has a great relevance in the project. In several RADs, it is possible to prototype an application in a short time in order to have the necessary feedback on user interface, even if the application actually implements only a few functionalities. This prototype, once the user interface and the main functionalities have been validated and approved, is simply eliminated to start the project, perhaps with another methodology. This process is not a real life cycle, since it has only one phase after which the result is used for the analysis and specification of the real project.

The second prototyping life cycle is a real life cycle and is shown in Figure 3.

The prototyping life cycle is suitable mostly for user interface-intensive applications, where the feedback that can be obtained from the user in front of a prototype can be very useful. This does not mean that this approach can be used only for complex GUI applications, since, for example, it can be applied usefully and employed in the development of Web interfaces and portals, where

Figure 3. Prototyping life cycle

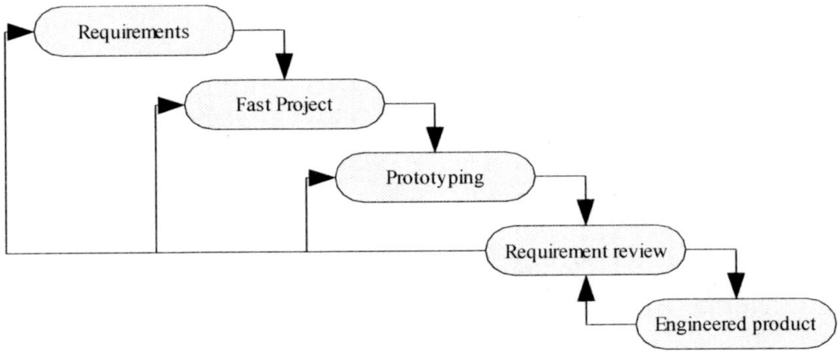

the customer sees the project gradually growing and, therefore, approaching the desired result. The prototyping life cycle is composed of two main iterative processes. The first iteration is among the requirements (fast project, prototyping, and requirement review), while the second is between requirement reviews and engineered product.

During the first phase, starting from general requirements and a fast project phase (which will be detailed in the following), the prototype of the system is prepared. In front of the working prototype, the requirements are reviewed, and an engineered product starts to exist, if requirement review is positive. Otherwise, we come back to one of the preceding phases, generating and improved working prototype and so forth. This process stops only when the engineered product is compliant with all the user requirements, and therefore, the prototype has become a product. This life cycle, among the classical life cycles, is closest to Agile development and eXtreme Programming (XP). A more detailed description of each phase with comments and suggestion on the documents to be produced is necessary to better understand this particular methodology and approach to system development.

Requirements

Requirements collection can be approached from two different points of view: the first time that requirements are collected and a new collection after a review of previously collected requirements.

In the first case, the phase is similar to the analysis phase of the waterfall life cycle, since the user requirement and use cases are collected but with the aim of producing a first prototype and not the final product. The use cases and requirements must be collected at a high level, with useful details, since they will be revised at the first iteration of review and must be focused on the main functionalities that the user wants to view in the product. During this phase, the RSD is created. This document will be improved by the different reviews of the requirements performed after the first prototype delivery.

This phase also can be reached after a review of the requirements that compel changes to the project. In that case, the requirements are collected (maybe be limiting the focus on the functionality under review) in a more detailed manner, allowing a clearer description of the user's needs in order to create an engineered product for the part of the prototype that is under analysis. The RSD must be improved each time the project passes through this phase in order to track what has been changed or what has been refined and, in the case of changes, also the motivation that procured the different use case or requirements.

Fast Projects

This phase is similar to that of project specification of the waterfall life cycle, in which it is defined how to implement the requirements specified in the previous phase. It is important also to note that this phase is not detailed in depth, since for this phase the first iteration can be distinguished by the project reviews after the first prototype. The main focus of the first time the fast project phase is approached is to define in detail the user interface in order to propose to the customer a product similar in aspect to the final engineered product, and then to implement the functionalities defined in the first requirement collection and definition phase. During the phases of review of the fast project, the functionalities specification is refined, if we reach this project review not from a review of the requirements. Other functionalities are introduced in the project, when we come from a requirement review.

Prototyping

The prototyping phase is the real coding phase. This phase also can be considered a two-step phase. It is very important to realize with particular care the user interface and projected functionalities in the first prototype, since its acceptance defines if the project will become a product or not. The acceptance of the first prototype starts the iteration process of requirement review and product engineering, which means that the initial prototype will be revised several times until a satisfactory industrial product is ready to be released on the market or deployed to the customer.

The coding approach is typically that of RAD environment and fourth generation language, where visual tools improve the development speed and also allow a pseudo-automatic generation of code.

Requirement Review

When you reach this phase, you have two main certainties: you are about to start a project that will become a product, and this is not the last time you will review the requirements.

Once the customer has viewed and approved (limited to the available functionalities), start to define in more detail the project requirements, since it is possible, adopting this particular methodology, to apply the IKIWISI approach that several customers like a lot. It is simpler for the customer to review a product specification having a prototype, even if it is in the form of a toy system, since it is possible to visually interact with the system and to identify the weaknesses or parts that are not compliant in an easier way.

During this phase, which can have as a follow up each one of the other phases, it refines the analysis of the previously approved requirement, and some new requirements are introduced. This process of embedding new knowledge into the system is aimed at obtaining something more than a prototype — an engineered or industrialized product, even if by means of continuous refinement of successive prototypes.

When all the requirements are met, the final product is released.

Engineered Product

The engineered product is the evolution of the prototype toward the final product. The main difference between a prototype and an engineered product (even if partial) is the development of stable functionality in the shell of the prototype.

Spiral Life Cycle

The spiral life cycle is one of most commonly adopted life cycles in software product development in medium and large companies. The main advantage at first glance is that it is formal enough to match quality certification needs of companies and is also agile enough to avoid compelling people to draw all the analyses and specifications in advance. The name of the methodology is clear, when we look at the shape that usually is adopted to represent such a life cycle, as shown in Figure 4.

The radius of the spiral represents the time elapsed since the start of the project or, according to some other approaches, the effort spent. According to the second approach, the spiral line is the time line, and the radius in each point of the spiral is the effort spent until that moment. I usually prefer this second approach.

The surface is divided in quarters, and the spiral is centered at the cross point of the quarters.

Figure 4. Spiral life cycle represented graphically

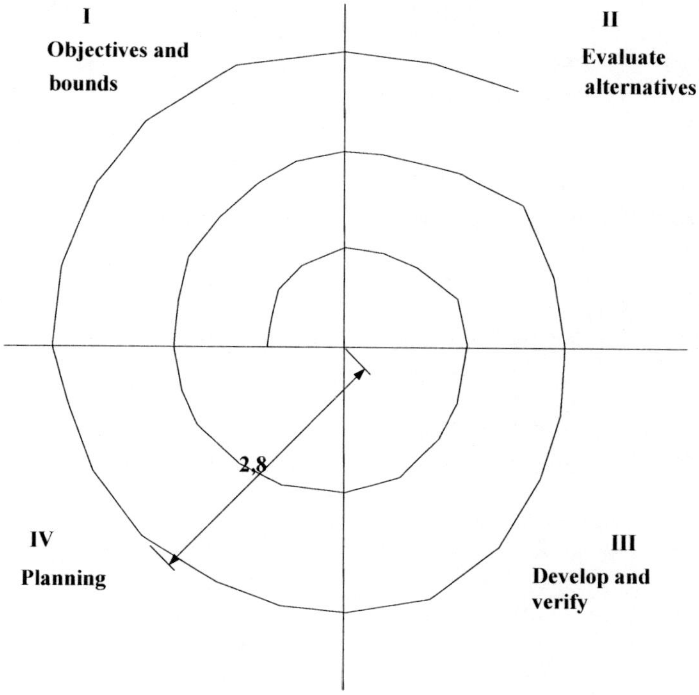

The quarters represent phases of the project:

- Objectives and bounds
- Evaluate alternatives
- Develop and verify
- Planning

A spiral-oriented life cycle is a meta-model that can apply to different development strategies. In the following, the most common will be presented.

The names of the quarters seem to be unrelated with phases discussed for waterfall of prototyping life cycle, but in the following analysis, it will be clear that the phases of the already discussed life cycle are contained in the spiral quarters. It is important to note that the spiral life cycle implements an iterative development and planning methodology that can be used in two different manners. The former is more similar to prototyping, in which a product is refined in successive iterations; in that case, after each iteration, the product gradually approximates the desired final result. The latter is a different approach, based on the fact that in each iteration, a set of functionalities is implemented and integrated into the system. After phase IV of each iteration, a milestone usually is set in order to verify if all the functionalities have been realized or if some corrective actions are needed.

In my opinion, the best approach is a mix between the first and the latter, in which requirements and specification are defined in advance for the whole project and revised at each iteration. At each iteration, a subset of the system is built, and the already-created subsystems are maintained and integrated according to developed modules and the changed requirements.

This approach is flexible enough to allow changes in the user requirements and needs, but the iteration is focused mainly on a subsystem to be implemented.

The description of the phases have to be considered, taking in account the point of view exposed in this mixed approach.

Objectives and Bounds

During the first iteration, the first quarter of the spiral is dedicated to the collection of requirements for the whole project and to the definition of the different technologies that can be suitably employed during the development. In this phase, the bounds are identified (i.e., the operating system must be the one chosen by the user and the database would have no bounds), the operating system is free among all the Unix-based systems, and the database is selected among those employed in the customer company; the development language should be Java, and so forth. The main target of this phase is to prepare the requirement specification document and the first draft of the project specification document, in which all the possible alternatives are discussed with pros and cons. The project schedule regarding time, resources, and functionalities to be implemented during each iteration and the milestone and expected results of each phase also are realized during this quarter of the first iteration.

During the other iterations, this phase is oriented to review the user requirements and project specifications detailed and partially implemented in the first iteration, to review the schedule of the project, and to verify if milestones are met and the planned results are reached. During this activity, both the RSD and PSD are updated.

Evaluate Alternatives

This phase is equal in all the iterations, since the evaluation of alternatives does not differ in the first iteration from the other iterations; the alternatives can be different, but the approach to decide is always the same. This is one of the critical phases of this life cycle, since it is strictly related to risk management, which will be discussed at the end of this chapter. This is the phase in which it is necessary to decide among the different choices that have been selected in the objectives and bounds phase.

The evaluation of alternatives allows the development team to start coding the parts of the project that have to be developed, and therefore, it is very important that each alternative is evaluated with particular care according to all the widely adopted techniques that allow the minimization of risks related to wrong choices.

During this phase, the PSD must be updated in order to have a clear track of the choices that have been selected.

This phase is also responsible for developing and maintaining the STP document, since it is impossible to define the large part of the tests, if the technical choices have not been completely performed.

Develop and Verify

This is the real productive cycle of the system under development, in which code is produced on the basis of the choices and analysis performed in the previous phases.

The development phase, usually adopted in real environments that use spiral-oriented methodologies, follows the guidelines identified for the waterfall development phase. The verify phase can be identified with the test phase of the waterfall life cycle, and therefore, the developed system is verified against the STP.

The development phase also has the duty to create and update the CDD with the full documentation of the code created in the iteration and the reviewed version of the code of the previous iterations.

Planning

Planning is the second critical phase of the process, since during the fourth quarter of the spiral, after a review of the results obtained in the development phase, the activities to be developed in the next release are planned. Planning what has to be realized in the next iteration is an activity that is performed in accordance with the customer that selects the functionalities that have the largest added value for the whole project. During this phase, the project is measured in order to track the evolution and the behavior of the main project indicators. To this end, the PMD is maintained in the planning phase.

Risk Management

Risk management (Boehm, 1989a, 1989b) is not a methodology for software development and management but is a valid support when a decision has to be made, as evidenced in the section related to the spiral-oriented life cycle, and to prevent problems that arise from a wrong management of risk factors. Risk management can be applied to the methodologies discussed in this chapter and is also a valid aid in a general sense. Risk management is a very complex activity, and discussing all of its techniques is beyond the scope of this book. In this section, an introduction to the main concepts of risk management is presented, together with some samples that can help the reader to understand the concept better and also to realize the advantages of this approach.

In Figure 5, a common decomposition of risk management is depicted. It is evidenced that risk management can be decomposed in risk evaluation and risk control. The former can be decomposed in risk identification, risk analysis, and risk classification, while the latter in planning of risk control, risk solving, and risk monitoring.

Each subpart of risk management is described briefly in the following in order to have a short introduction to each risk management aspect:

- **Risk identification.** It is related mainly to the identification of risk factors of a project and of the possible causes.
- **Risk analysis.** It evaluates the probability of a fail event with an estimation of the related loss (usually in money terms).
- **Risk classification.** To this activity is demanded the duty of classifying the various risks on the basis of their critical influence on the project.
- **Planning of risk control.** It is the identification of a control plan that allows one to face the risky situation identified in the previous sections.
- **Risk solving.** It is a set of techniques or strategies that allows one to solve risky situations, eliminating their basic causes.
- **Risk monitoring.** It is a set of techniques for evaluating how the risk level changes during the whole project.

Figure 5. Taxonomy of risk management related activities

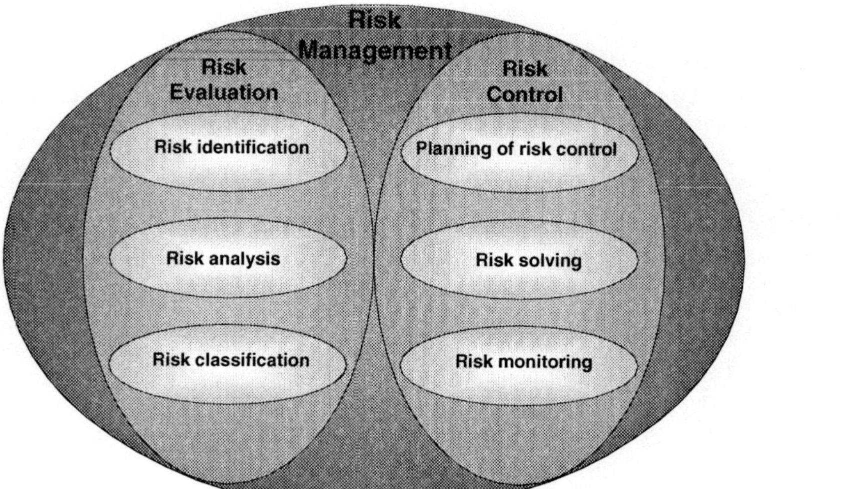

Target and Benefit of Risk Analysis

The aims and the consequent benefits of risks analysis adoption are focused on reducing the global failure probability of the project. There are other objectives that have equal importance in the global management of a software project, since they can help to save money. One of these benefits is the avoidance of code rewriting due to a wrong analysis or a wrong management of risks; another very important one is the optimization of the number of resources to use in each part of the project. It is important to put the right number of resources on the basis of the risk estimated for a certain software system. It is not useful to have the same effort of concentration in a low-risk and a high-risk module.

Risk Indicators

In order to evaluate the risks and their relevance, it is important to measure them in some way. In this section, two main factors are presented and commented on. The first is the risk exposure (RE), which is the product between the probability that a faulty event (FE) happens and the economic loss (EL) due to the faulty event, as shown in Equation 1.

$$RE = P(FE) \cdot EL$$

Equation 1. Equation of risk exposure of a faulty event

The second indicator is the Coefficient of Risk Reduction (CRR), which is evaluated in terms of ER before and after a corrective action is taken. The CRR formula is in Equation 2.

$$CRR = \frac{RE_{before} - RE_{after}}{C}$$

Equation 2. Equation of reduction risk coefficient (where C is the cost of the corrective action for reducing the risk)

CRR can be employed for evaluating the solution that gives the best benefits with respect to a certain risk reduction weighted by the cost of the solution. A larger value of CRR implies a better solution.

Suppose that you have to decide between two solutions for reducing the risk of failure of a project. Suppose also that if the project fails, you lose \$300,000, and that without any corrective action, the fault probability is 10%. You know that by applying solution S_1, which costs \$50,000, you reduce the probability to 5%, while applying solution S_2, which costs \$75,000, you reduce the fault probability to 3%. You can apply CRR evaluation to S_1 and S_2 in order to verify which solution is the best in terms of cost/benefit ratio.

$$CRR_{S_1} = \frac{0.1 \cdot 300000 - 0.05 \cdot 300000}{50000} = 0.3$$

$$CRR_{S2} = \frac{0.1 \cdot 300000 - 0.03 \cdot 300000}{75000} = 0.28$$

Equation 3. CRR for two different solutions (S_1 and S_2) aimed at reducing the risk

Equation 3 shows that CRR_{S1} is greater than CRR_{S2}, and therefore, it is better to spend a little bit less accepting a higher fault probability. If solution S_2 reduces the probability to 2%, then its CRR increases to 0.32, denoting that this 1% allows you to select the high cost solution, since its CRR is better with respect to that of solution S_1.

Risk Evaluation

In this section, the reader will find some suggestions on how to approach the risk evaluation and on techniques that can be applied suitably in the three sectors that compose risk evaluation.

Risk Identification

Risk identification is the first task to deal with when you would like to manage risks, since you can try to solve or correct only what you know. The problem is how to identify the risks factors you have in the project.

Risk management literature reports several risks for software projects organized in checklists in order to aid the user in the risk identification process. On the other hand, a checklist is not the only mechanism that can be employed. Often, the risks factors are so common that we neglect them. We can have the so-called environmental risks that are related to the environment and not to the project — external people that would like to force the project and the choice of some solutions or the selection of project management not based on skills.

Another factor that can introduce risks is the marketing that often requires so-called gold planting, which refers to the addition of functionalities that must be present because of competitor comparison, even though they are not really needed for the aim of the project or they impose a hardware or software architecture that is not optimal but gives economic or indirect advantages not related to the project.

The underestimation risk is always around the corner, since you often choose to declare a lower number of people per months or a lower number of needed resources only to have the possibility of developing the project or to gratify management. This can result in a disaster.

Other times, you can accept to develop a project because your team has a low workload in the short term, but you also have to consider the side effects that may be in the medium to long term, when you can be compelled to do extra work or to fail because you have considered only short-term bounds.

The Pareto law (80-20 law) can help you to identify modules that need particular care, since it is commonly assumed that a small part of the project can drift to the large part of the resources:

- Twenty percent of the modules will need 80% of the resources,
- Twenty percent of the modules will contain 80% of the errors, and
- Twenty percent of the modules will need 80% of the time.

The identification of a large part of those in the 20% can give you a great advantage in risks identification.

It is important to identify such 20% of classes/modules, and one of the methods can be the evaluation of fan-in and fan-out of the modules. Fan-in and fan-out, apart from a formal definition based, for example, on function points (Albrech, 1979; Dreger, 1989) can be evaluated simply by counting the number of relationships that bounds the two classes. This process can be done at run-time by the several profiling tools that are present on IDE or by specific programs that can instrument code to have a clearer picture of bounds among modules. The same process can be done (at a different level) by hand examining a UML diagram of the system or the code directly, and by identifying calls to methods and functions; specific metrics for measuring cohesion of modules also can be applied.

Finally, please always remember what Murphy's law states: "If something can go wrong, it will."

Risk Analysis

The process of risk analysis is a very complex activity that also can support the risk identification phase, selecting solutions with the lower risk or the best risk/cost factor.

One of the most useful techniques for risk analysis is the decision tree analysis, which uses a graphical representation of the decision tree in which each branch is weighted by a probability.

Suppose that your company needs a software product and that three alternatives apply:

- Develop the system internally from scratch; that is, evaluate a difficult activity at 30% with an associate cost of $200,000 and an easy task with a probability of 70% with an associate cost of $120,000.
- Modify an existing system that is suitable for 40% with a related cost of $80,000, while the remaining 60% have to be developed. The development is easy with a probability of 40% with an associate cost of $100,000 and difficult with a probability of 60% and an associate cost of $130,000.
- Buy a couple of commercial products that can fit the functionalities with a probability of 35% and an associate cost of $100,000 and of 65% for a cost of $150,000.

Figure 6. Decision tree analysis for the sample problem discussed in the text

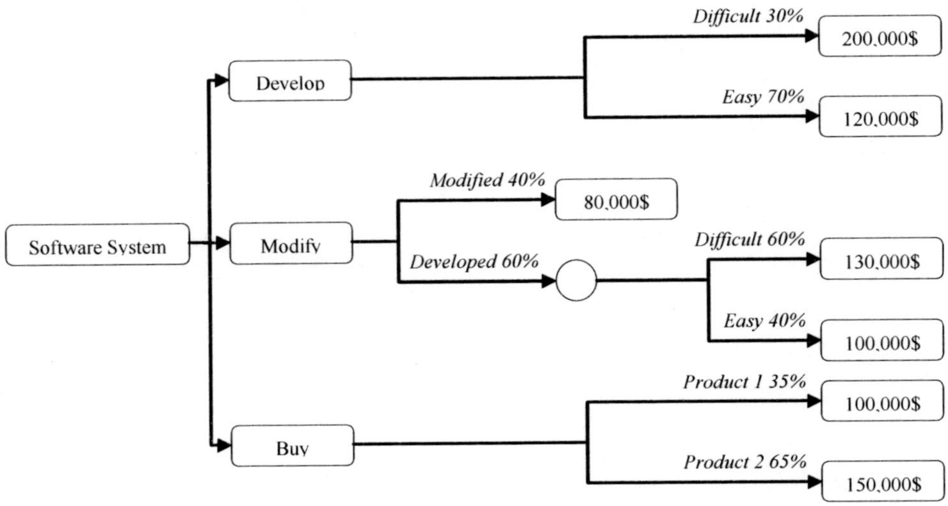

What should the company do? What is the best alternative? It is not easy to choose the right option at first glance. The decision tree represented in Figure 6 can help.

The most probable cost for each alternative is calculated according to the following formulas:

$$Develop: 0.3 \cdot 200000 + 0.7 \cdot 120000 = 144000$$
$$Modify: 0.4 \cdot 80000 + 0.6 \cdot 0.6 \cdot 130000 + 0.6 \cdot 0.4 \cdot 100000 = 102800$$
$$Buy: 0.35 \cdot 100000 + 0.65 \cdot 150000 = 132500$$

Equation 4. Cost of the different solutions

The solution that has the lowest cost is Modify, followed by Buy, while the Develop hypothesis is the last choice.

Another way to analyze the risks during the project development relies on basing timing and milestones on a probabilistic Gantt diagram instead of on a fixed length activity one. In probabilistic Gantt diagrams is an early completion date with a certain probability and a maximum completion date with another probability. The bound among activities can be influenced by these dates, and the most probable timing can be selected as a base. As soon as some activities are completed and it is, therefore, possible to fix the others, you have a picture of the activities that have a large probability of being not in time. These are the most critical activities that have to be considered in the risk analysis.

Some software estimation models, such as the COCOMO Intermediate model (discussed in Chapter XIV, related to software measurement) can give an idea of risks, since it can be tuned by several parameters that can change the estimated time for completing an activity. This is a valid aid also for creating probabilistic Gantt diagrams.

Risk Classification

Risk classification is the last activity to be performed in the risk evaluation. Once, on the basis of the previous techniques, the risks have been identified and measured, for example, by the RE factor, they can be sorted and then classified for their relevance within the project.

Risk Control

If you have completed the preceding phases, then you have identified the risks of your project. Now it is time to try to control such risks in order to avoid the appearance of solving them, as they appear.

Planning of Risk Control

The first step in trying to control the identified risks is to plan how to deal with them. This is the scope of the planning of the risk control phase. The main activity that should be performed in this phase is the creation of a plan that is synchronized with the development activities and that is focused on risk control and risk solving. In particular, a micro-plan is necessary for each risk in which the corrective action to be taken is reported, if the risk manifests. Suppose you have a risk related to the fact that one of the senior developers of your team will leave the company. You have to plan all the corrective actions. These activities can be the selection among the CV of external people or inside other teams in the same company of people having the needed skill, a plan for contacting them, and a raw contract to refine at the moment you select the person.

On the other hand, if you have identified a risk, you can limit the loss, adopting specific strategies for controlling the impact of the risk on the project and, therefore, the risk itself. For the situation previously reported, in order to avoid greater problems, you must be sure that the knowledge of each module is at least shared between two people; the documentation should be complete, accurate, and so forth. Each of these activities reduces the financial loss or the probability of the risk.

Risk Solving

When the risk you have analyzed faces the project, you are in trouble — sometimes there are little troubles, and other times big troubles. The only thing you can do is to solve the risk according to the risk plan you have created in the previous phase. Often a risk can be solved by eliminating the source or the cause of the risk. Some techniques can be helpful in risk solving and can be a support when a risk becomes a fault or to eliminate the risk's source.

Some of the techniques that can be suitably employed are:

- **Automatic or metric-driven cost estimation.** This reduces the risks of having a wrong estimation of time or to correct the estimation, if a faulty event is present.
- **Release the product according to phases and prototyping.** This reduces the risk of implementing a product far from the customer's need and helps to solve the problem of the identification of wrong functionalities in an early state.
- **Test plan.** A well created test plan or a correctly applied test methodology can be helpful in the identification of the source of several development-related problems.

Risk Monitoring

The plan for risk control must be supported by an adequate policy for risk monitoring; that is, an activity mainly focused on a continuous revision of the main risks identified for the project. The monitoring also is useful in order to verify if the application of the risk solving techniques has reduced the risk probability or not. In general, it is a good practice to have a table in which the main risks are ordered by a factor such as risk exposure, and this evaluation is repeated in a cyclic way.

References

Agresti, W.W. (Ed.). (1986). *New paradigms for software development*. Los Alamitos, CA: IEEE Computer Society Press.

Albrech, A. J. (1979). *Measuring application development productivity*. Paper presented at the IBM Applications Development Symposium, Monterey, California.

Boehm, B. (1989a). *Software risk management*. Los Alamitos, CA: IEEE Computer Society Press.

Boehm, B. (1989b). *Tutorial: Software risk management*. Los Alamitos, CA: IEEE Computer Society Press.

Boehm, B., & Papaccio, P. (1988). Understanding and controlling software costs. *IEEE Transaction on Software Engineering, 14*(10), 1462-1477.

Buxton, J. M., Naur, P., & Randell, B. (Eds.). (1976). *Software engineering: Concepts and techniques*. New York: Petrocelli/Charter.

Coffman, E. G., Jr., Bruno, J. L., & Winters, P. R. (Eds.). (1976). *Computer and job-shop scheduling theory*. New York: Wesley.

Dreger, J.B. (1989). *Function point analysis*. Englewood Cliffs, NJ: Prentice Hall.

Ghezzi, M., Jazayeri, M., & Mandrioli, D. (1990). *Fundamentals of software engineering*. Englewood Cliffs, NJ: Prentice Hall.

Gilb, T. (1988). *Principle of software engineering management*. Boston, MA: Addison-Wesley.

Naur, P., & Randell, B. (Eds.) (1969). *Software engineering: A report on a conference sponsored by the NATO Science Committee*. Presented at the NATO Software Engineering Conference, Garmisch, Germany, October 7-11 (p. 231). Brussels: NATO, Scientific Affairs Division.

Wiest, J., & Levy, F. (1977). *A management guide to PERT/CPM*. Englewood Cliffs, NJ: Prentice Hall.

Lessons Learned

Target

Classical methodologies

Practices

The waterfall life cycle is suitable only for projects with well-defined requirements.

Prototyping and the spiral life cycle can support projects with a lower stability in requirements.

Risk management can support you independent of the methodology adopted.

Measure the risk by risk indicators in order to evaluate the evolution of the risk.

Chapter IX

Agile Development

The aim of this chapter is not to compare one Agile methodology against the other but to evidence the common factors that are behind each methodology that can be defined as an Agile one in order to give to the reader a basic understanding needed to better comprehend XP (described in Chapter X) and ADPD (described in Chapter XI and exploited in Chapters XII and XIII).

Agile development and Agile methodologies have not been well considered in the past nor in the present by several people that have published papers (Briand, 2003; Rakitin, 2001) and others in different journals considering this approach too similar to hacking to be considered as a methodology for controlling and developing projects. For some project types, it is true, since safety-critical systems and real-time systems can be difficult to approach with Agile methodologies, as already stated in Chapter VII. On the other hand, several other authors and researchers have tried to consider something more —Agile development (paying particular attention to XP but considering Agile methodologies in a large sense)—and to evidence the strong points behind its approach (Beck, 1999, 2000; Boehm, 2002; Cockburn, 2001, 2001a; Paulk, 2001) and also the interaction of social issues with Agile software development (Cockburn, 1996; Highsmith, 2001).

More and more, people have adhered to an already existent Agile methodology or have developed a personal Agile methodology, and therefore, Agile development has evolved in these last years and has reached the important results of defining a manifesto with the principal guidelines that must be present in all Agile development methodologies.

To this end, the Agile Manifesto (Agile Alliance, 2001) has been published by Agile Alliance. The main assumption stated in that programmatic document is:

"Through this work we have come to value:

- *Individuals and interactions* over process and tools,
- *Working software* over comprehensive documentation,
- *Customer collaboration* over contract negotiation, and
- *Responding to change* over following a plan.

That is, while there is value in the items on the right, we value the items on the *left* more."

It is important to comment on these assumptions in order to discover the important messages that are hidden behind them, evidencing the strong points and also facing the problems of the over simplification that an incorrect understanding of these principles can bring. This analysis will be developed following a schema proposed by Cockburn, where for each statement there are possible actions, the benefits of the actions, the possible side effects, and the results of an overdose. This approach allows one to identify advantages and problems related to the argument under consideration.

Individuals and Interactions Over Process and Tools

This principle suggests that it is important to establish process and to have tools for developing and controlling the project, but it is more valuable to address social issues in a development team. As stated before, and as it will be evidenced in the following, this principle does not state that you must have an unregulated process for software development. Neither does it state that you do not have to adopt tools for measuring or planning the project. It simply means that you have to establish processes and tools that take care of individuals and interactions among individuals, since the benefits that can arise in considering social issues are very important.

Actions

Start a project by paying attention to people, and when you assign tasks to people, consider with care all people skills, assigning subsystems on the basis of that consideration, so that people can develop and contribute better to the global project.

Create an environment in which people live well, and let the team organize the workspace in the arrangement they prefer in order to have a pleasant place in which they can work. Adopt the concept of open space in order to increase communication among people and to stimulate the sharing of knowledge and exchanging of opinions. Last, but not least, write a schedule and tasks on bits of paper hung on the wall instead of keeping them secret in your computer files.

Benefits

This approach allows you to have team members that work in an environment they like, and therefore, they will regard as a remote opportunity the possibility of changing companies or teams. A person that leaves the company compels you, as the manager, to consider the introduction in the team of new and maybe unskilled resources. You can select capable people that may have little knowledge of the project domain. In any case, the increased level of communication reduces skill shortage and allows for a better distribution of knowledge among the team members.

The possibility of viewing the schedule and the schedule evolution directly in real time on the wall allows people to be more responsible for the tasks that have been assigned to them. This is because they can clearly view how delays or errors in their modules impact the work of other people and, therefore, the whole project. This is not a punitive strategy devised with the intent to terrorize employees; it is only a way to have responsible people who work together in order to produce the best results for the project. Indirectly, it is an advantage for them so they will not be compelled to do extra work and other annoying activities.

Side Effects

The main problem in an open space is related to the amount of people that can participate on the team. Ten people are usually the maximum number, unless you organize the space, closing some parts and then splitting the group, but in that case, you lose the open space concept. It is evident that you cannot have very large teams for each Agile project.

The other side effect is related to planning. Since it is very difficult to have the best scheduling at the start of the project, you must plan often and change the scheduling as often as something seems to go wrong. This continuous revision of the planned activities can expose you to critics coming from your team because of the changes in the scheduling, but it certainly helps the project to be always updated on the current status.

Overdose

The overdose of these actions can bring chaos, since people, instead of communicating, speak to each other. If the planning is not updated often to reflect the real status of the project, then people probably will fail to reach the target of the project.

Working Software Over Comprehensive Documentation

A detailed documentation can be a strong aid in a project development (Briand, 2003), if specification, requirement, and code documentation is quite stable over time; if this is not the case, you are compelled to continuously refine the documents in order to have a comprehensive documentation. This is a tremendously time-consuming activity, and if it is not performed well, it also can be a time-losing activity and a possible source of errors for the team. On the other hand, non-existent documentation can bring failure, since you lose control of what is happening or you forget some configuration tip or some particular setting.

As always, the best is in the middle between these extreme approaches. You have to write documentation, but it must be limited to the strictly necessary amount for covering the project needs. That amount must be defined in advance and cannot be pseudo-generated randomly on the basis of the wiliness of team members, as described in the action paragraph.

Actions

Start a project with a document of several pages (usually no more than 10) that describes the whole project and summarizes known specifications and known goals.

Another important step is related to the code documentation that has to be produced automatically on the basis of the comments inserted in the code (several tools for doing that exist in the market and in the open source community, such as javadoc for java, doc++ for C and C++, etc.). These tools require you to write directly on the code all the operative and descriptive comments to the functions, classes, attributes and methods that are automatically collected and formatted in a code manual.

Usually, if the knowledge is shared among several people, there is one developer who is responsible for a specific task or for part of the project. This person will produce a deliverable that helps the other people to comprehend the strategy followed and the activities performed during the development, together with the explanation of the principal choices performed.

Another important mechanism that can be automated is the adoption of change logs, which allows you to trace the reason and the subject of a modification performed on the code. These change logs also can be generated automatically by instruments such as revision control systems (RCS) or concurrent versions systems (CVS) or other more complex code versions or revision systems. All these documents must be collected and organized by the project manager in order to have one or more documents that allows you to rebuild the history of the project on the basis of this minimal set of documents.

The last trick or action can be the adoption of the so-called walking document, which is a collection of bits of paper hung on the wall that collects the project history and allows people to collect information and know details about the project simply by walking around the lab walls.

Benefits

It is not useful to write 100 pages before starting the project; in 90% of the cases, this will result in a time-losing activity, since usually only 10% of the written pages will survive after one month of the project. The solution is to write only 10 pages and save time for other activities.

The benefit of having an automatic generation of documentation (regarding code and, more generally, regarding change logs) saves a lot of time in manual code revision and documentation update and partially frees the person that collects and revises such documentation. Again, this saves time for other activities.

Another direct benefit of the adoption of an RCS is that you can revert the project to an older stable version without the need to collect and verify all the modifications to be eliminated. Advanced RCSs allow you to branch the project to test a solution that can have an unknown impact without changing anything in the current or stable version; in the case of success, these modifications can be inserted in the stable version.

The practice of the so-called walking documents is perhaps the most strange among the suggestions reported in this book. Apart from that, it can have some benefits. The main benefit of having walking documents is the possibility to transfer to people past experiences, to remind you and other people of past errors, and to have a fun set of papers on the wall that are better than an empty white wall. A professor of mine said that a clean desk is a sign of a sick mind; maybe it can be applied also to walls!

The secret for saving time in preparing a more or less comprehensive documentation is to distribute documentation assignment among people fixing the standard to be followed by each person. This automates or at least simplifies the collection process.

Side Effects

You must establish strong coding standards in order to have automatic documentation generated, and you have to stress to your team to write comments for having a self-explicative documentation for all the other people. You are also compelled to evidence to people how to write change logs and how to write deliverables in order to save time in the collection phase.

Regarding management activities, you must learn to identify what to write in the starting document of a project in order to minimize time and to maximize the ratio between effectiveness and effort spent.

The most difficult assignment among those presented consists in evidencing to developers that activities related to well-written comments and coding according to a common standard. This is an advantage and not a time-consuming activity that will not give benefits to them since, more or less, in the future, each developer will have to take a look at or modify the code written by another team component. Coding standards save time and limit errors due to misunderstanding.

Overdose

The extreme consequence of this approach consists of having no documentation or a poor documentation that is not useful for the project and for the team. This is obviously a major drawback that must be avoided. This can happen if some reference related to XP is followed strictly, since word of mouth several times is not enough, while according to Agile manifestos, the documentation has a value, and I might add that the documentation can be more valuable if written during the development of working code.

Customer Collaboration Over Contract Negotiation

Agile methodology can be applied suitably in all cases in which a fixed contract or a cost-driven project must be faced, since the adaptability and reaction time of Agile teams is usually better suited with respect to the time that can be obtained by the same team adopting standard methodologies.

On the other hand, if contract negotiation is an important activity, an on-site customer may provide more advantages, since you can revise the contract each day. This is an advantage for both the customer and the team, since sometimes the customer can request extra functionalities, but other times the customer can cut some functionality from the current version in order to meet predefined deadlines.

Actions

Ask the customer to define a simple contract and to be on the project with the team. The approach that the customer will have is collaborative in order to help you and the team in developing the project according to the customer's points of view, which is the most important, leaving to the team the technical decision and how to reach the desired results. The general suggestion is to spend as much time as possible with the customer to define and revise project objectives.

Benefits

The on-site customer can have a positive impact on the project, since changes are made on the basis of a daily agreement instead of a complex written negotiation. Moreover, the feedback of the customer that works together with the team aids during the day-by-day improvement of the product. The customer is able to control and to verify the progress and to request changes focused on product adherence to predefined goals, when necessary.

A clear distinction is made between what the customer does (e.g., requirement, specification, and functional tests) and what the team does (e.g., technical choices on the basis of requirements, unit tests, regression testing, etc.), in order to increase the capability of detecting errors and of creating a bug-free code that respects the needed functionality.

Side Effects

The side effects of this choice are minimal from a technical or team management point of view, but from a commercial point of view, a weak contract is not a widely accepted form for sales and marketing departments, and therefore, you can see the project killed because of this. The project killing can be direct if the project is cancelled or indirect if a project planned for having an on-site customer has no customer directly involved with the team in the daily activities.

The other possible side effect can be due to the customer that is not collaborative, or to the customer that would like to impose a technical decision or that does not provide a correct feedback regarding the functionalities or the functional tests.

Overdose

The overdose is a customer on-site that does not understand its role and continuously changes ideas, compelling the team to do extra work and to continuously change and adapt the code on the basis of the changed requirements.

Responding to Change Over Following a Plan

When you can establish a well-defined plan that can be followed during the entire duration of the project, you have found the silver bullet for the success of the project. Unfortunately, in doing such plans in the starting phase of an information technology project, it is usual to miscalculate the time or effort estimation about 100% of the time. In order to avoid such large errors, it is necessary to replan often, adjusting the target according to the changes that are requested. This can bring failure of the target amount of work to be done, but it allows you to better identify critical parts and to set up deadlines accordingly.

The continuous replanning of activities is related strictly to the continuous improvement of the project by responding quickly to changes.

Actions

As introduced before, it is necessary to plan, but the plan must be revised in order to address changes and to respond quickly to those changes. Each time a new customer request manifests, an adopted technology changes or improves, or a technical decision compels you to modify something, you have to revise the plans in order to address the change and to verify the influence of the change with respect to the other planned activities.

Benefits

The benefits of the active response to change is a more accurate plan. This accurate and continuously revised plan suggests whether you can meet the deadline or not. It can be a valid aid also in verifying if you are able to produce the requested functionalities, respecting at least the milestone, even if some intermediate deadlines are missed. This process allows you to track how much the past previsions were accurate, and therefore, the direct benefit is related to the experience you acquire in adjusting plans earlier in order to address the common changes that arise during the project development.

Side Effects

You have to plan activities accurately and reorganize the plan often, always keeping in mind the deadline and the milestones that should not change. The main side effect is that you can never abandon the activity that is related to planning, but you have to monitor it and revise it continuously. This must be done in order to monitor the changes and the effects related to those changes. You must consider in detail each change before approving it; otherwise, you can fall in the overdose condition.

Overdose

The principal problem with this approach is related to the possibility of having no plan at all; the result is chaos. If you plan and revise deadlines very often and perhaps move milestones, it is possible that at the end of this replanning, you have no trace of the original plan and have no real plan to follow in the future.

The Agile Team

The hypothesis that is not present in the Agile Manifesto but that must be considered carefully is related to the fact that in order to apply an Agile methodology, the cost of each change in the code must be low.

The analysis of the Agile Manifesto and the consideration made on costs of changes allows you to define the characteristics that an Agile team must have.

1. The team should be composed of no more than 10 people;
2. The technical skill on the team should be medium to high;
3. A large gap should not exist in technical skills between the least- and the best-skilled person on the team (apart from the manager, which should be outstanding), so that communication can be possible and interaction is not blocked by the total lack of knowledge of some team members;
4. Each team member must be open to communication and share his or her knowledge with the other team members; and

5. The turnover on the team should be low in order to guarantee the continuity of the knowledge.

It is important to comment on these assumptions with more detail in order to clarify how to select people that have to belong to the development team of the project.

A low number of persons on a team allows for no hierarchy. This unstructured organization improves the communication among team members and meliorates the sharing of knowledge and, therefore, the general interaction among people.

In order to have working software and people that understand the importance of writing online documentation, it is important that the people have a medium to high level of knowledge. It is difficult to transfer to unskilled people or to people that have not worked on the team the importance of doing a little extra work to save more time globally. The most important stimulus comes from people that have experienced in their life the difficult to modify undocumented code or to work on the basis of a not updated documentation. These people, when present on the team, can help the manager in a strong way in obtaining the desired results.

A skilled group of people also requires a low cost in the code modification, since novices usually have problems in doing modification in a quick and easy way because of skill shortage.

It is also important to evaluate the gap in knowledge among people on the team, since a large gap does not allow easy technical communication. People can have different skills on different topics but a large common share must exist.

The turnover is expected to be low in all environments that do not stress the team member too much. Agile methodologies have been developed, keeping in mind the target of minimizing the stress due to an uncomfortable environment. The benefit of having an environment and a group in which you work well will augment the probability that people remain on the team. Agile methodologies try to obtain such a result. If turnover is low, Agile methodologies have a great benefit, and therefore, Agile methodologies and low turnover enforce each other.

References

Agile Alliance. (2001). *Agile manifesto*. Retrieved August 10, 2004, from http://www.agilemanifesto.org

Beck, K. (1999). Embracing change with extreme programming. *IEEE Computer, 32*(10), 70-77.

Beck, K. (2000). *Extreme programming explained: Embrace change*. Boston, MA: Addison-Wesley Professional.

Boehm, B. (2002). Get ready for agile methods, with care. *IEEE Computer, 35*(1), 64-69.

Briand, L.C. (2003). *Software documentation: How much is enough?* Keynote speech presented at the Seventh European Conference on Software Maintenance and Reengineering, Benevento, Italy.

Cockburn, A. (1996). The interaction of social issues and software architecture. *Communications of the ACM, 39*(10), 40-46.

Cockburn, A. (2001a). *Writing effective use case*. New York, NY: ACM Press.

Cockburn, A., & Highsmith, J. (2001). Agile software development: The people factor. *IEEE Computer, 34*(1), 131-133.

Highsmith, J., & Cockburn, A. (2001). Agile software development: The business of innovation. *IEEE Computer, 34*(9), 120-122.

Paulk, M. C. (2001). Extreme programming from a CMM perspective. *IEEE Software, 18*(6), 19-26.

Rakitin, S. R. (2001). Manifesto elicits cynicism. *IEEE Computer, 34*(12), 4.

Lessons Learned

Target

Agile development

Practices

Agile Manifesto

Low cost for each single modification

Agile team must:

- Have less than 10 people
- Have a person whose technological skills are in the medium to high range
- Be open to communication
- Be capable of reducing turnover

Chapter X

eXtreme Programming

One of the emerging techniques that is becoming increasingly popular for managing software project is eXtreme Programming (XP) (Beck, 1999, 2000; Williams, 2000). XP surely changes the way in which we develop and manage software, as all the other methodologies related to the Agile Manifesto do (Agile Alliance, 2001; Boehm, 2002; Cockburn, 2001; Highsmith, 2001; Rakitin, 2001). XP has been the methodology that I have adopted in recent years to develop and manage software projects — before modifying it in order to create my own methodology, ADPD (Agile and Defined Project Development), which is described in Chapter XI.

In order to understand ADPD, it is necessary to acquire all the possible knowledge about XP, since ADPD is XP 80% and recognizes quite all the values of this revolutionary technique for developing and managing software projects.

The most interesting feature of XP consists in the fact that it is human oriented (Brooks, 1995). XP considers the human factor as the main component for steering a project toward a success story. On the other hand, it is important to notice that XP is guided by programming rules, even if its more interesting aspects deal with the values that are the real guides for the design, development, and management processes.

XP Values

The same values that are the basis of XP also have been discussed in the first part of the book, where the skills for management have been presented, and therefore, these values can be considered as a guide for a manager, independent of the methodology adopted in the software life cycle.

A very short general comment about each value is written, and, as a reminder for the reader, each value has been bound to the management chapters of this book that are related to it. The values on which XP is based are communication (already discussed in Chapters I, III, IV, and V), simplicity (discussed in Chapters II, IV, and VI), feedback (discussed in Chapters I, IV, V, and VI), and courage (discussed in Chapters II and VI).

Communication

Communication is the first value, since XP's main objective is to keep the communication channel always open and to maintain a correct information flow. All the programming rules I will describe later cannot work without communication among all the people involved in the project: customer, management, and developers. Communication is important not only for managing the project but also for managing people and reducing skill shortage, improving the global quality of the team. One of the roles of management is to keep communication always open (Blair, 1995); no management can exist without communication, which is true not only for software projects but for all the projects that must be completed successfully within a specified time frame having the expected results.

It has to be pointed out that there are several ways to communicate: oral communication (the main communication channel in XP), written formal documentation (not really exploited in XP) that allows one to create the project documentation before and during the project, and written informal documentation that is all the sticks attached on the wall or on the Gantt diagram of the project to evidence whose changes have been performed (this informal written communication is widely adopted in XP).

Simplicity

The first and only question that you have to answer when you face a problem is, *What is the simplest solution that can work?* As an XP team member, you are a gambler, and the bet is, *It is better to keep it simple today and to pay a little bit tomorrow for changing it, instead of creating a very complicated module today that will be never used in the future.* As introduced in Chapter VII, related to the business environment, in today's real projects with real customers, it often happens that requirements change often and deeply; it is foolish to make a complex design today that has to be rewritten completely in one month. If you keep the project design simple, then when the customer changes its mind or when the market evolution requires a change, you will be able to modify the software at a lower cost. The main hypothesis behind this assumption is that the cost of each modification is small, as introduced in Chapter IX. If a modification in a project compels you to completely start a complex analysis from scratch, as for timing constraint of a safety critical real-time system, it is obvious that it is better to plan today, but the environment in which safe critical real-time systems are developed is hardly suitable for applying Agile methodologies, as already pointed out previously in this book (Boehm, 2002).

It is necessary to evidence that simplicity does not mean that you have to realize a toy system; it means that you have to adopt the simple approach to describe and solve problems related to a complex system.

Feedback

Continuous feedback about the project status is an added value that can drastically reduce the price that you must pay when changes have to be performed. All people involved in the project must give and ask for feedback about project status and results at each stage of the project as often as possible. Feedback is communication among management, customers, and developers that is direct feedback; feedback is also tracking and measuring so that you can maintain control of the project with indirect measures on the code, on its complexity, and on the estimated time to make changes. Several parameters can be estimated during the XP planning game, as it will be discussed in this chapter, and many others can be usefully employed to track the project evolution and to reduce risks related to projects without stressing the development team too much. This is why feedback is not only communication but also deals with problems of software measurement and then with metrics. Chapter XIV of this book deals with the problems related to software measurement and then software assessment. While direct feedback is necessary in every project, indirect feedback can help in reaching the desired results. Indirect feedback is not standard, and therefore, each project can have a different need and can adopt different methodologies for indirect feedback collection. According to my experience managing and developing software products, the project that can be measured well and for which indirect feedback can be very useful in identifying weaknesses in the code are object-oriented projects. Web-oriented projects realized with non-object-oriented technologies in a non-multi-tiered environment have in general a lower need of indirect feedback, since they are based mainly on what the user sees and touches with his or hands, and therefore, direct feedback is more useful.

Courage

Courage is related to people, but it is always related to the way in which you develop your project. XP is like an optimization algorithm, such as simulated annealing or taboo search, in which you slightly modify your project in order to reach an optimal point. During this process, you also can have some time in which a modification seems to produce extra work, but often, that work will be recovered in a later part of the project. When the optimum you reach is only local, you need courage to make a strong change in order to find the global optimum. XP, with the adoption of its rules, encourages you to always refactor. You need courage not only when your project is stalled but all of the times you decide to refactor it in depth. Courage is needed when it seems impossible to respect the deadline without eliminating features, and you choose to eliminate features that can be unnecessary for that release, and therefore, that can be delayed. Courage is also needed when you, as a manager, have to delegate to someone on the team the control of some parts of the project. Delegation can bring failure if not exploited in the right way; fortunately, the other values of XP, such as feedback and communication, reduce the risks that are implicit in the delegation process.

XP Rules

On the basis of the already discussed values, the main 12 XP rules can be drawn. In the following, all these rules will be introduced and discussed in order to allow the reader to understand their impact both on programming and managing. Several of these rules also are adopted in ADPD, while others are modified, eliminated, or added on the basis of the experience and of the environment in which I have managed or developed IT projects. Apart from the changes that have been operated on these rules, it must be stated that they work well as they are, since they bring a polite and controlled environment to the manager and to the development team that is a strong aid in completing projects according to schedule. This aspect is considered both from a time and functionalities perspective.

Each project starts from ideas and needs, and therefore, it has to be summarized and specified in non-technical language that can be easily understood and corrected by a non-technical end user. This is the main reason for which XP Metaphor exists.

Metaphor

Each XP project is summarized as a metaphor or a collection of metaphors that are shared among customers, management, and developers. We must focus our attention on the possibility of starting a project having as input only a metaphor instead of a complex and complete requirement analysis. Looking at XP in the large sense, we can state that it is possible, if the other XP practices described in the next sections are implemented with metaphor. Among them, the most important are:

- **On-site customer.** The customer is with the development team, shares the metaphor, and can communicate in the metaphor terms.
- **Refactor.** Refactoring implies a continuous revision of the code and of the metaphor and allows you to start the new project cycle from a simpler initial state and from a minimal set of requirements.

Metaphor helps the customer to describe in natural language what he or she wants. If this technically raw description is refined by technical persons, it can be a good starting point for defining a more formal set of requirements. The metaphor concept is very useful to share the initial knowledge of a project in order to avoid the customer operating according to the IKIWISI (Bohem, 2000) approach, because the customer is not capable of describing in technical language what in a non-Agile life cycle can be summarized as the requirement collection phase.

Another important aspect related to the metaphor is the definition of the keywords and of the main component of a project; usually, it is helpful to express the project in terms of items that are well known to the development group. A useful example and maybe the most commonly cited one is that of the original Chrysler C3 payroll project in which XP arose. The team used the metaphor of an assembly line to discuss ways in which transactions of various kinds made their way through stages of payroll, since an assembly line was something that everyone at Chrysler understood well, while a payroll system was not understood by all so readily.

For example, the metaphor that can be assumed for an XML editor is that of a word processor (i.e., cut, copy, and paste operations plus file loading/saving and capability of writing something) that is able to write only tags with text inside. The vocabulary of the editor is the XML schema or the DTD set of tags; the spell checker is the XML well formed, and the grammatical check is the validation against the same DTD or XML schema. The proposed metaphor can be considered as an over simplification of the problem of requirement collection, but it allows you to comprehend how a general description of the project given by the customer can be a starting point for a more detailed description that can be considered as the project's initial set of requirements. The metaphor can be improved during the project life in order to have a clearer end point. Since the communication and feedback with the customer in all XP projects are very intensive, the customer will be capable of describing the needed features during project development in a language that is more similar to that of the development team.

Oftentimes, the metaphor can be taken from the real world: For building financial planning software, it can be useful to start describing the human approach to financial planning.

It is important to note that the metaphor must be monitored very well, since if it does not express what the customer really wants, it can bring the development group to build up a product that is compliant with the metaphor but not with real customer needs. One example of this emerged, for example, at the OOPSLA 2000 Educators Symposium during a planning game exercise, where a coffee maker with two carafes was sketched (one in the coffee maker and one to the side), since the customer did not specify that he wanted two carafes simultaneously. The item was compliant with the request but did not fit the customer's needs.

As soon as the metaphor has been established, the development phase can start. In order to start development, it is necessary to identify the main functionalities that arise from the general description contained in the metaphor. This process of functionality extraction from a general description of the system is the starting point for the development. The development phase in XP projects is guided by the planning game activity that is carried on during the whole life of the project.

Planning Game

During software development, commercial and marketing needs together with technical considerations have to steer the project in an equivalent way. For that reason, the planning of an XP project is decomposed in several steps. Starting from the main functionalities inferred from the general metaphor, for each functionality, a story is written. A story summarizes what the function has to do and whose results have to be obtained from it. Each story is then divided in a variable number of tasks that can be, in the case of object- oriented projects, classes or parts of them, while in Web-oriented projects, they can be Web pages or library functions.

All the stories belonging to the project or all the stories that have been selected for the release under development are sorted by relevance, where relevance is related to the benefit that the user sees in the functionality implementation and to the added value obtained by the implementation of the story for the whole project.

It is important to notice that the commitment of the user and of the team in choosing the stories to be implemented in an early phase is an added value. The added value is due to the fact that the customer always knows in advance which functionalities will be implemented first and, therefore, can define or create appropriate functional tests in order to verify their behavior and expected values. The team now has to divide each story into tasks, where a task is the smallest module that can be obtained from the story and can be implemented by a couple of programmers. Within each story, tasks are then sorted by relevance, and the more important are selected by the manager in order to choose the subfunctionality to be implemented first. This multi-level decision tree allows you to take care of customer needs (for the selection of stories), technical issues (due to the division of each story into multiple tasks), and managerial needs (choose which subfunctionality has to be implemented first). These are the ingredients for the recipe of the planning game.

In order to summarize the planning game as a set of activities to be performed by the customer and developers, we can define the following activities for the customer:

- Explain stories,
- Choose and prioritize stories,
- Define acceptance tests,
- Perform acceptance tests, and
- Decide what to do if problems are reported;

And the following for developers:

- Estimate stories,
- Implement stories,
- Track and report progress during implementation, and
- Report problems during implementation.

The previous schema is reported in the XP Game for which more details can be found at *http://www.xp.be*.

For a summary of the planning game or for each planning game iteration or product release, the following schema can be considered valid:

1. Customer writes stories and explains them to the development team;
2. Customer assigns to the story the business value in order to allow a sorting for business relevance;
3. Developer estimates the stories in terms of resources needed to implement them and of time needed to complete them;
4. Development team selects a set of stories that can be implemented in the time window of the iteration or release;

5. Customer prioritizes the stories in the order of relevance so that if some story will not be implemented, it will not be the most important; and
6. Developers implement the story, and if problems arise during development, then the customer can select the story to be eliminated.

The planning game can be implemented alone in other methodologies, but it works fine in XP, since it obtains the support from other XP rules and practices. The main practices that allow the planning game to work well are mainly the following:

- **Small releases.** Small cycle of software development and review in order to have a smooth impact of a design error in the project.
- **On-site customer.** The customer that belongs to the development team allows a faster identification of problems and a more focused (from a business perspective) choice of functionalities.

Planning has to be treated as a game in which each a person plays a role and has specific assignments to be carried out. All people as a team have the global target of obtaining the maximum value in the smallest time frame. Managers have to make decisions about priorities, production deadlines, and release dates, while developers have to decide about the estimation of the time for completing assigned tasks, choose the functionality that has to be implemented first among those selected by the customer for being implemented in the current release, and organize the work and the workspace in order to live better.

While it is evident that the presence of the customer in the development team strongly supports the planning activities, it is necessary to know what the small releases are in order to understand better their influence on the planning game.

Small Releases

The concept of the small release must be understood well, since it is one of the basic and fundamental concepts in XP and Agile methodologies, in general. A small release does not mean that in the shortest time a new release must be produced, but that as soon as a valuable set of functions has been implemented, according to what is defined in the planning game, the release must be produced and inspected by the customer and by the team. The small release concept greatly impacts the XP life cycle, since the release is the basic iteration step of the whole life cycle. The small release concept is also the basis for implementing the continuous improvement of the software product under development. Each software release should be given out as soon as possible with all the functionalities of greater value correctly working. A single release is comprised of several subreleases that implement single functionalities that are called tasks in XP. More tasks collected together to form a more complex and self-comprehending functionality determine a story that has to be implemented with other stories during the period assigned to the release. Note that in adopting this operating method, it is not possible to implement half of a functionality only to shorten the release time, since the story has to be completed within the release. The testing practice and then the unit and functional tests that are described in the next section guarantee that each release is bug-free at least from the point of view of regression testing, black box, and white box testing. Half of a functionality cannot be implemented, because each functional test will discover if the related functionality works correctly or not and then if it is fully implemented.

Small releases are the foundation for XP life cycle and programming style, and in order to be successfully implemented, it needs to have the support of the following:

- **Tests.** The implementation of a regression testing methodology during development reduces the risk of having code with errors or nonconformities with respect to the customer planned functionalities. Test methodology as implemented in XP also guarantees white and black box testing.
- **Simple design.** A simple design allows you to select in a more precise way the functionalities that have more value for the project.
- **Continuous integration.** The addition of as much working functionalities as possible is an added value for the project in general and for the implementation of small releases, since the release will match better with customer requirements and needs in an early phase.
- **Planning game.** The planning game has to select the most important features in order to have real value in the release to be produced.

Tests

Testing is perhaps the most important rule that the team must follow, since its adoption reduces the risks related to the writing of bugged code or code that brings dissatisfaction to the customer.

Tests are an added value to the project, but they are more effective in an environment where the following are also present:

- **Simple design.** It is simpler to write tests, especially functional tests, if the project is clear and simple.
- **Pair programming.** The programmer that works with you can suggest other tests to be implemented or better implementation of the test under development.

In XP, two different types of tests are identified and realized during the development of the software project: unit tests and functional tests. Unit tests allow the implementation of regression testing and white box testing methodology, while functional tests verify the system from the point of view of black box testing, allowing the discovery of partially implemented functionalities.

Programmers write unit tests in order to be confident that all the functionalities of the software product works according to the specification; in particular, for each function or for each method (in the case of object-oriented programming), a unit test should be written. It is also true that a test should be written for all the situations that can possibly not work or can become problematic, thus reducing the risks related to a missing error prevention. In any case, if it seems unnecessary to write one unit test for each method, you have to write at least a test for each part of the system that could possibly break now and in the future.

A unit test suite should be executed each time a story or a task has been completed. The code should be put in the common repository, only if all tests work correctly. This is the main basis for implementing regression testing as the basic mechanism to avoid the introduction of code that can influence a previous functionality in a negative way. Continuous improvement without a solid regression testing practice is destined to fail.

The functional part and the related tests are matters that deal with customer specification and satisfaction, and therefore, customers must participate in the writing of tests or at least in defining the tests' behaviors and expected values. To this end, the customer usually writes functional tests in order to verify high-level functionalities, testing the system as a black box that receives some input (test cases) and must respond to these inputs with predefined output results.

Regarding the functional level (it is not necessary at the unit level, since often the functions addressed by unit tests are called by a higher level part of code), remember to address the problem of monkey test, in which the system has to deal with random data in input, always giving a correct output, even if in the form of an error message.

As evidenced in this section, the test practice is not only an important task, but it is also a fundamental activity to correctly implement other XP practices, such as collective ownership, on-site customer, and continuous integration.

Simple Design

All Agile methodologies claim to keep the system as simple as possible, respecting all the operative functionalities that must be addressed in the software product.

This concept is particularly considered in XP, since each part of the system has to justify its presence by the means of its used functionalities. The question is how to identify the simplicity level at which we must stop. The answer is not easy in general, even if some guidelines can be drawn.

We can assert that the simpler project in each time instant (1) makes all the tests run, (2) implements no code or classes duplication, (3) is quite self-documenting by adopting self-explication names and commenting on all the functionalities, and (4) has the least possible number of classes and methods of functions that allow you to correctly implement the functionality.

The problem is how to measure some of these parameters. Some guidelines regarding software measurement with respect to code duplication are present in Chapter XIV, related to metrics and software evaluation, together with some metrics that can aid in identifying, at least for an object-oriented system, the correct distribution of classes and inheritance levels. The simple design practice, in order to work better, should be integrated with software metrics in order to evaluate the level of complexity of the system and should be strengthened by the following other XP rules:

- **Metaphor.** A clear, general, and shared metaphor among all the team members steers the project toward a simplification creating a common goal.
- **Refactoring.** If all developers operate according to the refactoring guidelines, the system will converge toward the simplest possible design.

Moreover, the peer review of the system, which is not addressed explicitly by XP but is implicit in its values and rules, is the best point to evidence if the system architecture has to be revised in order to simplify it. The refactoring process described in the next section also can be a good starting point for the peer review process and then for addressing the problem of system simplification.

Refactoring

Refactoring is the basic brick of the wall named continuous improvement. It is not possible to develop and meliorate a software product without implementing a refactoring process aimed to simplify the system and to reduce the effort needed for adding functionalities. Continuous refactoring as a stand-alone activity is impossible and somehow dangerous, if it is not supported by a set of other rules and practices that allow its implementation. The main factors that influence the possibility to refactor are some other XP rules that enforce this practice with some of the others:

- **Collective ownership of the code.** You can modify each part of the system that your team is developing, since you are able to understand and simplify each part. This is true, since you have participated in the development, test, and simplification of the design in all system parts for the pair programming concept.
- **Coding standards.** You are able to modify each part of the system, since you are not compelled to completely reformat the code before each modification you have to perform. Moreover, you know that comments are present and that each comment has a well-known format and meaning.
- **Test.** If you have a regression testing environment, you are sure that your changes do not impact on previously created functionalities.
- **Pair programming.** The concept of pair programming enforces the collective ownership, and then of refactoring, since pairs change on the

basis of the functionality to be written, and then each developer has worked more or less on each part of the system during the software product life.

- **Simple design.** A simple design aids in reducing the effort for refactoring, since it diminishes the effort to comprehend the system, and therefore, the impact of refactoring can be planned better.

If the previous activities are considered and if XP is fully implemented in the team, it is possible to refactor the project as often as it is necessary. In order to refactor, before adding a new functionality, it is necessary to verify if the system can be simplified in order to spend less work and time to add it. Before the test phase, programmers ask themselves if it is possible to simplify the old system in order to make it smarter. These techniques are at the basis of continuous refactoring. Keep in mind that refactoring is carried out to simplify the system and not to implement new functions that are not useful.

Pair Programming

All the code must be written by two programmers in front of the same computer (Spinellis, 2001; Williams, 2000). This can be a good way to instruct new team members and to reduce skill shortage. In any case, it can be considered a good practice to increase productivity and reduce fault probability, since one person is continuously stimulated by the other to produce quality code and to correct the errors that the other inserts into the program. Also, a not-so-skilled programmer can be a valid aid in pair programming, since he or she can ask questions of the more skilled person that can produce a better testing suite. Feedback helps the less skilled to improve his or her system knowledge, and the right question at the right moment can be a contribution for the more skilled to find a solution that can simplify the code.

In order to implement pair programming in practice, it is necessary to create an environment that is comfortable for working in pairs; sometimes, it is difficult for programmers that have not previously worked in pairs to interact with the other developer profitably, and therefore, some other XP practice reduces the psychological impact and supports the team members during the first approach to pair programming:

- **Coding standards.** All programmers write code according to a pre-defined standard related to code formatting and comments placement in order to write code that is understandable at first glance by the others.
- **Tests.** Tests must be written cooperatively in order to improve them and to improve pair commitments.
- **Simple design.** The programmer's pairs that operate with a simple and clear design in mind reduce the possibility to have different opinions on how to implement a feature.
- **Forty-hour week.** If all the team members are more relaxed, the probability of contrasts is reduced, and then pair programming can be more successfully applied.

The common misunderstanding about pair programming in real companies is related to the fact that double the resources are needed when pair programming is implemented. Recent studies (Cockburn, 2000; Williams, 2000) show that the total effort (with the same number of programmers) for producing the same project is a little bit more with pair programming, not double, as expected. But on the other hand, the quality of the code is better, and the number of errors to be corrected during the maintenance phase after the product release is reduced. These studies show that with the correct adoption of pair programming, the total cost for a project instead of doubling is reduced or at least equivalent. On the other hand, some more exhaustive and comprehensive studies have to be conducted in order to guarantee that pair programming is a technique that reduces costs. In any case, pair programming, if correctly implemented, increases the quality of the final product and reduces the probability of undiscovered errors.

Continuous Integration

During project development, the code is tested and integrated several times a week and, in some cases, a few times a day. The integration process of a functionality ends only when all the previous tests (regression testing) and the new unit and functional tests work correctly. The continuous integration reduces the probability of conflicts in the code committed to the central repository of software. It is better to commit changes and improvements as soon as all the tests are working, but not before. The addition of bugged code in the repository propagates to all the other developers, and they start to see tests that are failing and cannot understand easily that the error is not due to the code they are writing.

In order to support this rule, other XP practices are adopted:

- **Test.** It is mandatory to have an implementation of regression testing in order to be sure to have developed code that is compatible with all the previous assumptions and that respects the already accepted requirements.
- **Refactoring.** Refactoring is a strong aid in doing such activity, since the simplification of the system and the development of small components increase the probability to integrate code very often.

Collective Ownership

Whoever sees the possibility to simplify or improve a part of the code has to do it. With individual code property, only the person that has developed a module is able to modify it, and then the knowledge about the system decreases quickly. This also is a valid aid for future maintenance, since more than one person is able to modify the code. Moreover, during project development, it is a valid support for the manager. Let me consider the possibility that the unique code owner of a module accepts employment at another company; in that case, ... well, ... you are really in trouble, unless you have adopted the collective ownership of code. Collective code ownership does not only mean that the team has adopted a revision control system or a software repository (that in any case is mandatory for successfully implementing collective code ownership), but mainly that nearly all the team members are able to modify each part of the system. This practice reduces the impact on the project due to people that leave the company or the team. Another positive impact is due to the reduced need of having comprehensive documentation, since the knowledge can be shared among all the team members. The XP rules that allow or enforce collective ownership are as follows:

- **Continuous integration.** This rule is highly influential in reducing the probability of conflicts in the code.
- **Pair programming.** Knowledge is shared naturally among team members, since the programmer pairs rotate on the basis of the skills needed to

implement each functionality, thus increasing the probability that each person has worked or participated in the development of each part of the code.

- **Test.** It is mandatory to be sure that the code under modification works. Tests also can be a support for people that develop code, since in the test suite is hidden the description of all functionalities and interactions among system modules.
- **Coding standards.** Predefined coding standards increase the probability that anyone can work in any part of the system without becoming confused trying to understand how another developer uses braces.

On-Site Customer

An on-site customer can be an added value for the project globally, if he or she can support the team during the requirement definition (see metaphor and planning game value), development (see the planning game value), and test phases (see test-related section). The other main involvement of the customer is related to the feedback that he or she has to provide to the team when a release is committed. Moreover, the on-site customer is a greater advantage, if the following practices are included in the used methodology:

- **Test.** The customer writes functional tests or at least specifies how functional tests must work.
- **Planning game.** The customer has an important role in the planning game, since he or she can drive the project priorities and then the functionalities to be implemented first.

A customer has to be present in the work group and has to give feedback to developers. This is strategic, since the customer presence during the development allows all team members to have feedback directly during the early stages of product development instead of having feedback (maybe partially negative) only after the software release. As introduced before, a customer also has to write functional tests in order to verify if the system works correctly (in terms of correct output in front of correct input and continuing to work in the presence of wrong input data) and has to select the functionalities and modules that add the greater value to the system in order to select which functionalities should be present in the next release of the software.

The hypothesis behind the previous assumption is that the customer is skilled at least for performing the tasks that he or she is assigned to deal with. A non-skilled customer on-site can have a more negative effect with respect to the absence of the customer.

Forty-Hour Weeks

You cannot work 60 hours each week for a long time. You'll become tired and stressed, and your code will result in a lower quality product. In addition, your capability to interact with other people will decrease (Brooks, 1995).

According to me, all practices can enforce this concept, but it can be generally true that if you can work without much stress, all the other practices will benefit, especially pair programming, which is the activity more strictly related to human interaction. Moreover, the main rule that influences this practice is the planning game, which allows the team to implement first the main functionalities, reducing the probability of missing a deadline for a certain revision and, therefore, also reducing the risk of extra work.

Coding Standards

The adoption of a coding standard simplifies in the long term the life of the programmers in the team, since all programmers will have the same style for writing code. Coding standards have as the main positive side effect the minimization of shock due to looking at a code not formatted with your personal standards or not commented on according to specified rules. The adoption of a common formatting standard eliminates the different standards that each programmer has. The most influenced items are in parentheses and comments.

In particular, comments (especially those for automated documentation generation) have to be standardized; parentheses and indentations should be uniform among all the code in order to facilitate comprehension and collective ownership.

Without any doubt, it is difficult to convince a programmer to use a company coding standard that differs from the personal one, but you can win this battle by convincing the team that the cooperative work can save individual time, diminish stress, and increase the knowledge of the system. Certainly, coding standards are influenced mainly by the pair programming methodologies that simplify the adoption of commonly adopted standards, since programmer pairs change as often as individual skills are needed in a part of the project.

Conclusion

XP obviously has no silver bullet for solving development and management issues for software projects, and at the same time, it is not the methodology that can work with all teams, in all environments, and for each project type. XP provides you with several copper bullets that, if adopted together in a dynamic environment, can improve the way in which you develop and manage your project. If you claim that XP as a whole methodology cannot be suitable for your projects, you can agree that some of its guidelines can be applied successfully in all environments.

To conclude this chapter, a picture evidencing how the XP rules interact with each other is presented in Figure 1. A directional arc in Figure 1 means that the source rules influence destination one. Moreover, a rule that influences many others will have a lot of exiting arcs, while a rule that is influenced by many others has several entering arcs. Without any doubt, it is evident that the relationships among XP rules are several, and it is also evident that strong interconnections exist among some of them.

In order to better understand the impact of each rule on XP methodology, in Table 1, the number of rules influenced (OUT) and influenced by (IN) other rules are reported. The total number of arcs (TOTAL) also is summarized in the same table in order to show the rules that are mostly interconnected. The fourth and last column measures the DIFF parameter, which is OUT-IN, that measures the exportability of the practice in other methodologies, since it is related to the number of influenced rules minus the number of rules that support the practice. The rules that have a large number for OUT with a contemporary low number for IN are those that can be exported to other methodologies, since they have a general positive impact on several activities without needing strong coupling with other practices. The rules having a large TOTAL number of arcs are the practices that are mandatory to allow the implementation of XP in a project environment.

The number reported in Table 1 can be a valid support to develop a critical analysis of XP rules. Considering that, in a general sense, XP adoption requires all the practices defined in this section; the rules that are mandatory for XP adoption can be evidenced, and it also can be deduced which rules can be

Figure 1. Relations among different XP rules

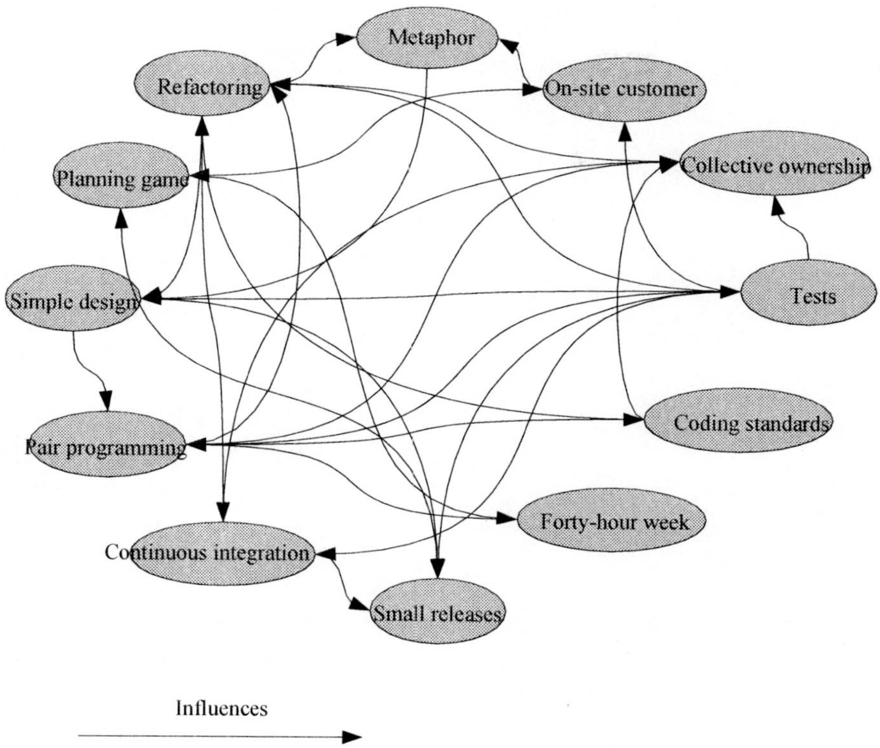

exported to other environments and methodologies, since they can be considered added value practices in all environments.

Considering that Table 1 is ordered by TOTAL, it is possible to extract the rules that are mandatory for XP adoption:

- **Pair programming.** This is the most referenced rule in the XP description performed, since it influences four rules and is influenced by four others. In order to have a correct implementation of XP, pair programming has to be adopted as the first milestone in the XP methodology adoption plan.
- **Refactoring.** Refactoring is related to the value of courage that is a strong push for XP activities. The continuous improvement by refactoring is one of the key areas for the success of an XP project.
- **Tests.** XP is based on tests. Unit tests and functional tests are the bases for all the activities that have to be developed in an XP team.
- **Simple design.** It is one of the "musts" of all Agile methodologies, and it is also a fundamental practice for an XP environment.

Table 1. Fan-in and fan-out of XP rules (table is sorted by TOTAL)

Rule	OUT	IN	TOTAL	DIFF
Pair programming	4	4	8	0
Refactoring	2	5	7	-3
Tests	5	2	7	3
Simple design	4	2	6	2
Small releases	1	4	5	-3
Collective ownership	1	4	5	-3
Planning game	3	2	5	1
Continuous integration	2	2	4	0
On-site customer	2	2	4	0
Coding standards	3	1	4	2
Metaphor	1	2	3	-1
Forty-hour week	1	1	2	0

In order to perform the analysis related to the value that can be exported into other methodologies, we have to sort the table by DIFF column. In doing so, we obtain Table 2, which can be a valid aid in performing the already cited identification of such rules.

The following list summarizes the added value practices that can be easily exported to other programming environments and that can be a basic framework for developing an Agile methodology. They differ from XP but are based on the same values and relay similar practices.

- **Tests.** A regression testing environment allows the team to identify errors introduced in the code by modification of previously working functionalities. Tests also allow you to keep the code repository clean, since it is mandatory that all tests must work before putting anything into the shared code repository. All these advantages are independent of the adopted methodology and should be implemented in all projects.
- **Coding standards.** Having a coding standard shared among all developers of the team allows you to modify code written by another programmer without the need of reformatting it completely. Certainly, it is useful when pair programming is present in the development methodology, and it is also more useful when no pairs among programmers exist, since at least theoretically a double number of formatting styles exist.

Table 2. Fain-in and fan-out of XP rules (Table is sorted by DIFF)

Rule	OUT	IN	TOTAL	DIFF
Tests	5	2	7	3
Coding standards	3	1	4	2
Simple design	4	2	6	2
Planning game	3	2	5	1
Forty-hour week	1	1	2	0
On-site customer	2	2	4	0
Continuous integration	2	2	4	0
Pair programming	4	4	8	0
Metaphor	1	2	3	-1
Collective ownership	1	4	5	-3
Small releases	1	4	5	-3
Refactoring	2	5	7	-3

- **Simple design.** As evidenced in the previous sections, each Agile project has as its main target to keep the project simple. A simple project is not a synonym of a raw project; it means that the project has to be kept simple, considering the constraints imposed by its domain. Assuming that you do not violate the constraints of the domain, it is always a best practice to have a simple design in mind in order to avoid errors due to misunderstanding, which can bring developers to implement wrong functionalities in a correct way or correct functionalities in a wrong way.
- **Planning game.** A planning game is a complex activity in XP and involves not only the development team but also the customer and management of the project. The main concepts that are behind planning game practice are simple and can be easily exported in environments different from XP teams: (1) divide the project modules into pieces that are as small as possible in order to be developed quickly by a single programming unit (one developer or two developers in the case of pair programming); (2) prioritize the modules and their subfunctionalities in order to have a clear view of what has to be implemented first; and (3) try to develop first the functionality with the greater impact and added value for the whole project.

In the next chapter, these concepts will be reconsidered when ADPD methodology is introduced.

In order to completely understand XP, it is also necessary to introduce its life cycle, which is coupled very strongly with its values and rules. XP life cycle application allows you to obtain the best from each programming practice presented in this chapter.

Life Cycle of an XP Project

The waterfall life cycle and evolutionary programming paradigms, such as spiral-based ones, make an assumption about activities to be performed during the development of a task: a clear sequence of activities have to be carried out before coding. Classically, the phases that are considered during a task development are the following: requirement, analysis, design, code and test, and integration.

In general, these activities are not considered for each functionality or task but for the global project or for large modules, so that before writing a single line of code, the whole analysis and design phase has to be completed. At the same time, the test activity is performed after the code has been written, and it is mainly related to external or functional testing (black box testing) without considering unit testing or regression testing (white box testing). If the project is split in some iteration, a large part of the analysis and design is performed before starting the first iteration of coding, and only the refinement of analysis and design is performed. The concept of refactoring is generally absent, or at least it is not as strong of a concept as it is in XP.

XP projects are not managed with a life cycle defined at the level of the whole project, but the life cycle is defined at task or story level, and it is different from the traditional life cycle previously defined.

This is mainly due to the approach to software development of XP rules. The phases among which a task development is divided are:

- **Requirements and analysis.** These actions usually are performed together, since the customer is on-site and the feedback about functionalities to be implemented is faster and more precise. This allows you to reduce the effort and the time needed with respect to a more classical approach.
- **Design.** In XP projects, we never project for tomorrow, but we only address the problems related to the task selected by the on-site customer. This allows you to reduce the time-to-market, so that the effort for this

phase can be employed profitably for other task phases. The design is limited to the features that have to be implemented in the current release with the aim of producing a simple project.

- **Refactoring.** Continuous refactoring is one of the rules of XP, and then a refactoring phase has to be performed before any modification is introduced into the system. During this phase, the system is analyzed in order to verify if the possibility of system simplification exists. This task can take much more time than the design phase, since all the subsystems related to the task under development have to be revised and eventually improved and/or simplified. Since small releases are a must in XP, the refactoring activities are very close to each other, so that a continuous refactoring process is approximated.
- **Write tests.** During this phase, the classes/modules or functions of the systems to implement the new functionalities are realized in the form of a skeleton. The written code is only present for the purpose of satisfying, even with dumb code, the unit tests that we have to write in this phase. Unit tests must cover all the aspects that have the probability of not working correctly. This phase is very important and is strongly coupled with the phases in which the functional code has to be written. In this phase, only unit tests are defined and written. It is obvious that, if during another phase the need for a test arises, developers have to write it.
- **Test integration.** In this phase, all the classes developed in the previous one are integrated into the system, and it is verified if all the unit-tests that had been developed in the past continue to work. The effectiveness of this phase deals with the opportunity to verify that the design of the new functionality will not impact other system operations that were stable in the past. This is the phase in which regression testing is carried out.
- **Code.** In this phase, the code for the new functionalities is inserted into the skeleton provided by the write-test phase. Several phases of this kind have to be carried out before the final release of the task. Each coding phase has to be followed by a test and integration step.
- **Integration and test.** During this phase, it is verified if all the previous unit tests and functional tests work correctly. If all is okay, then the code is approved and is considered stable.

Since the previous phases are present for each task of the system, a sequence of these phases is present during the development of the whole system, approximating a continuous sequence of mini-waterfall life cycles one after the other (Beck, 2000).

References

Agile Alliance. (2001). *Agile manifesto*. Retrieved August 10, 2004, from http://www.agilemanifesto.org/

Beck, K. (1999). Embracing change with extreme programming. *IEEE Computer, 32*(10), 70-77.

Beck, K. (2000). *Extreme programming explained: Embrace change*. Boston, MA: Addison-Wesley Professional.

Blair, G. M. (1995). *Starting to manage: The essential skills*. New York: IEEE.

Boehm, B. (2000). Requirements that handle IKIWISI, COTS and rapid change. *IEEE Computer, 33*(7), 99-102.

Boehm, B. (2002). Get ready for agile methods, with care. *IEEE Computer, 35*(1), 64-69.

Brooks, F. (1995). *The mythical man-month* (anniversary ed.). Reading, MA: Addison-Wesley.

Cockburn, A., & Highsmith, J. (2001). Agile software development: The people factor. *IEEE Computer, 34*(1), 131-133.

Cockburn, A., & Williams, L. (2000). *The cost and benefit of pair programming*. Paper presented in EXtreme Programming and Flexible Processes in Software Engineering—XP2000, Cagliari, Sardinia, Italy, June 21-23.

Highsmith, J., & Cockburn, A. (2001). Agile software development: The business of innovation. *IEEE Computer, 34*(9), 120-122.

Rakitin, S. R. (2001). Manifesto elicits cynicism. *IEEE Computer, 34*(12), 4.

Spinellis, D. (2001). Fear of coding, and how to reduce it. *IEEE Computer, 34*(8), 99-100.

Williams, L., Kessler, R. R., Cunningham, W., & Jeffries, R. (2000). Strengthening the case for pair programming. *IEEE Software, 17*(4), 19-25.

Lessons Learned

Target

eXtreme Programming (XP)

Practices

XP is human-oriented in that the human is central in the development methodology.

The same values reported in management chapters also are the basis for XP.

XP rules enforce each other, creating and defining a complete methodology for project development.

Some rules are fundamental for XP:

- Pair programming
- Refactoring
- Tests
- Simple design

Some rules can be exported to other methodologies:

- Tests
- Coding standards
- Simple design
- Planning game

Chapter XI

Agile and Defined Project Development

In this chapter, the ADPD methodology will be presented and discussed. The name and the consequent acronym are due to the fact that I would like to create a methodology that is agile and, therefore, compliant to the Agile Manifesto, but that at the same time can be widely accepted and then also deployed in organizations that are not inclined to accept Agile development. The ADPD's main aim is to eliminate the criticisms that often bound Agile methodologies with hacking or unstructured development. To obtain such results, the methodology must be compliant at least with the Software Capability Maturity Model, commonly known as CMM-SW (Paulk, 1993, 1993a) Level 3: the defined level. It also explains the second term of the acronym. Third and fourth terms are quite obvious and do not necessitate any further investigation.

The compliance with CMM-SW Level 3 allows me to successfully apply this methodology in an environment where a standardization in terms of software or product quality is a must, since the Defined Level of CMM-SW allows you to match the requirements of most of the companies that usually do not agree with Agile methodologies and management.

These are the main reasons for which I started to define a new methodology, mainly based on the concept of the first Agile methodology I have applied in real projects; that is, XP (Beck, 1999, 2000).

I have inserted in ADPD all the positive aspects and techniques that are part of XP and that I was able to apply successfully in daily project management. I modified all the improvable aspects, inserting some new hints to the project manager and guaranteeing at least the compliance with CMM-SW Level 3.

ADPD Life Cycle

The successful application of a methodology is mainly due to the comprehension of its life cycle and of the advantages and dues that the methodology offers or compels you to deal with.

ADPD has been created with a main target in mind: reduce the costs of maintenance. In a past publication by the same editor, I have evidenced how Agile methodology and, particularly, XP application can bring constant maintenance costs (Fioravanti, 2003) during the project life time, and I have tried to transfer this aspect to ADPD in order to limit one of the major drawbacks of classical methodologies that consists in the fact that the maintenance costs are not constant during the project life cycle. This is due to the organization of the life cycle in large monolithic blocks, where, if an error occurs at some point, it compels you to re-discuss a large part of the work already done.

We can evidence this fact considering different life cycles, such as the monolithic waterfall life cycle and the iterative spiral life cycle, compared to agile (with particular reference to ADPD). The steps that are present in each life cycle can be considered the same or at least very similar. What really differs is the instant of application of each step and the consequent organization of these steps. For each methodology, it is supposed to have the following steps: analysis, design, develop, test, and release/deploy.

The waterfall life cycle has these phases organized in a sequence: one after the other without any feedback but only with an interaction between the adjacent phases. An error in a phase compels you to review between 25% and 50% of the work already done in that phase and at least 25% of the work performed in the previous phases. For example, if you discover that you have a design error, you are compelled to review the global design of the system, reworking it in part, and you have to verify if the analysis performed before is compliant with the new reworked design, since a design flaw often impacts the requirement satisfaction. This fact suggests that for the waterfall life cycle, it is true that the impact of errors on maintenance time, in terms of effort to be spent, increases dramatically as time goes on. If you consider that, apart from design flow, the large part of errors is discovered during the test and deployment phases, you can be sure that the discovery of errors costs a lot.

Figure 1 shows the trend of effort during project development divided among the different phases of the project. This graph also shows the cumulative effort and the cost of maintenance over time.

In order to mitigate this problem, the iterative life cycles, such as the spiral, have suggested that the project be divided in some iteration in order to try to minimize the impact of maintenance effort on the project. In order to have a comparison, it has been supposed to have a project with the same cumulative effort as in the previous sample in order to have a total cost that is independent of the chosen life cycle.

Due to the division of the project in iterations, which allows you to accept subsets of the project that can be considered stable, the mean maintenance cost decreases with respect to the waterfall sample.

Figure 1. Development life cycle (upper part) with the related maintenance and development effort (lower part) for waterfall life cycle

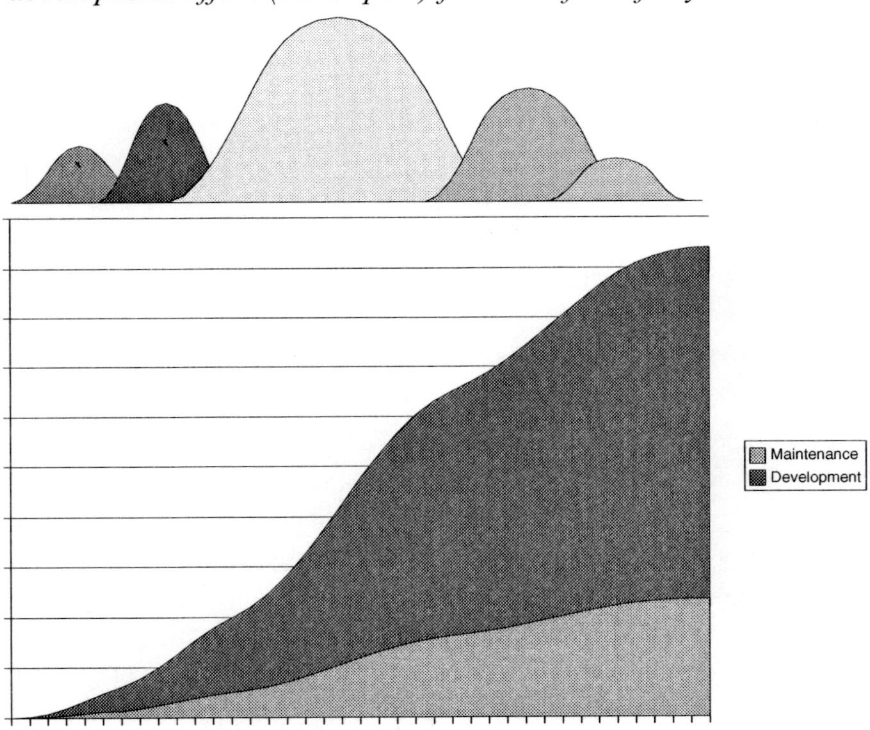

In Figure 2, the same parameters for the waterfall life cycle are adopted in order to graphically compare the results.

Repeating this process of divide et impera, shortening the iteration and repeating them often, the main maintenance costs become low and can be considered quite constant during the project life cycle, while the total cost is the same. This is the main hypothesis of Agile life cycle and also of ADPD life cycle: consider the same phases of a classical life cycle but use very short iterations to be repeated very often.

The iterations are so close to each other that the analysis and design phases can be considered as a unique phase for each iteration, while the other phases are equivalent with respect to the other life cycles.

Another important difference between classical methodology and ADPD is represented by the first iteration, which is longer with respect to the others and is focused mainly on obtaining a walking skeleton of the application. The walking skeleton phase is then followed by several release iterations of the

Figure 2. Development life cycle (upper part) with the related maintenance and development effort (lower part) for spiral life cycle

Figure 3. Development life cycle (upper part) with the related maintenance and development effort (lower part) for ADPD life cycle

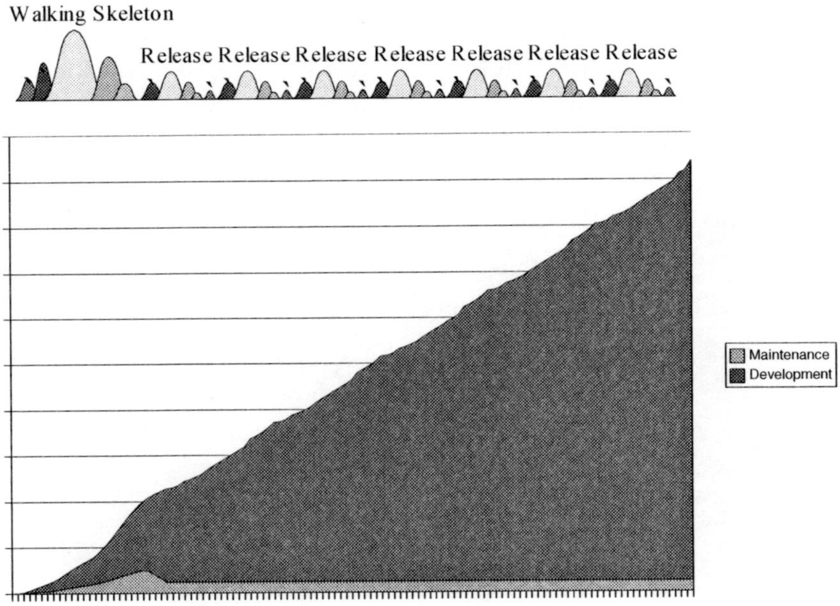

product, in which at each iteration, one or more functionalities are added. These phases will be detailed in the following, while in Figure 3 the ADPD life cycle by using the same graphical representation used previously is depicted.

Walking Skeleton Phase

Walking skeleton (WS) is the first phase of the project, and its main aim is to develop the system architecture without implementing any real functionality, or at least to implement only dummy or toy functionalities in order to verify if the global infrastructure of the project is solid enough to start release iterations.

During this phase, the distinction between analysis and design is kept, since this iteration is normally longer with respect to the others, and particular care is needed in the general architectural realization.

The analysis phase during the WS development is implemented, designing a high-level use case that will guide the general requirement selection to be carried with the customer. The use case adopted in this phase is mainly a business use case without any reference to the architectural or technical details.

During the design phase, the architecture for such business use case is decided, and the single use cases are detailed. The design phase has the responsibility for the definition of the main structure of the classes that can be suitably described by CRC (Classes, Responsibilities, and Collaborators) cards.

In order to better understand how important the WS phase is and also to explain how to implement it during the development, we simulate the WS phase of a classical three-tier Web application.

Suppose that you want to create an e-commerce site in which you have some Web pages where you place an order, confirm the basket, and pay the total amount due, a middle-tier application that receives such data and connects to a database or to external services. In the WS phase, you will create a Web page with only a couple of articles that can be ordered by the user, without any graphic appeal. The only data present for the articles to be put in the basket is the database ID that identifies each article. Once you have selected the articles and quantities to be put in the basket, you have to pass to another very simple Web page in which you confirm the order and select the payment method. This page is realized, eliminating all unnecessary frills and without considering real details, but only passing a flag describing the payment method. The middle-tier application receives these data and updates a dummy table on the database that contains only the IDs of the order and the flag of payment. A confirmation page with data extracted from DB is sent to the user.

If all is working well, you can fix some important points, since you are sure that:

1. The connection between the middle-tier application and the database is correct and that the database is working.
2. The connection between the Web page and the middle-tier application is working, and therefore, the application server is up and running.
3. The Web page works correctly, and therefore, the Web server is working well and is well integrated with the application server.
4. The customer can view an on-the-field simulation of the transactions after only a few days of work, giving the feeling that you are working hard for that project.

The consequence is that the architecture to implement the system is ready and running, and therefore, you can start to plan with the customer the functionalities to be implemented first and start to release the first version of the application, since at least the infrastructure is approved.

The development phase of the WS is followed by a test and release phase, in which different rules and practices, described in the following, have to be applied.

Release Phase

The release phase is the classical phase of all Agile methodologies with analysis and design of the functionality selected for that phase in the first part, the development and test following that phase, and the deploying and release of the planned product functionalities at the end. During all these phases, it is necessary to apply ADPD practices in order to successfully release the product in each phase.

ADPD Practices

All ADPD practices are commented on in the following. These practices are divided between general and management practices, and rules to be followed in different phases of the release life cycle. It is important to evidence that each practice enforces the others, and therefore, it is fundamental to adopt all of them in order to have the benefits promised by the methodology.

Analysis and Design Practices

During analysis and design, the same activities that are commonly performed in the classical methodologies are carried out also in ADPD. The main difference consists in the target of the phase, which is no more a long-term planning but is bounded to the short duration of the next release. The importance of having small releases very close to each other reduces the time needed for these phases, even if some formal and important activities have to be performed.

Small Releases

The importance of having small releases already has been evidenced from the point of view of maintenance costs that are reduced and can be considered constant during the full evolution of the project. The other very important aspect that has to be considered is related to the fact that it is simpler to define for the customer a short-term target with well-defined activities than long-term activities that perhaps the customer will need to change considerably in the future.

The small-releases concept is focused on selecting the most important activities to be completed in the short term. The advantage of this approach is that usually, the most important activities in the short term are the functionalities that the customer can define with a minimum risk of errors, since they have been discussed thoroughly and focused.

The concept that also is used in ADPD is the following assumption: if you cannot plan well, you at least have to plan often. You are aided in this process by the adoption of small releases.

This practice is mandatory for a successful ADPD adoption.

On-Site Customer

The presence of the customer during the development of the project is an important added value for the project, since customer presence allows for immediate feedback on the evolution of the project. It also helps to have very small releases, since the on-site customer can provide suggestions on the functionalities to be implemented and also approve the already developed features in a short time.

Unfortunately, in a practical project and especially in small projects, it is not possible to have the customer on site, unless you transfer your development team to the customer's site. When you cannot have the customer on site, you must build a test deployment plant at the customer's site in order to obtain at least the fast approval of developed features. Moreover, several other mechanisms can be used to have a virtual customer at your site: instant messaging, video conferences, extranet by means of virtual private networks, and other useful technologies.

It also should be noted that the formal documents and tasks to be produced diminish if the customer is present, since often a collection of pieces of paper with CRC and task cards is enough to establish and maintain a correct communication with the customer.

This practice is strongly suggested, although not mandatory (if replaced by a virtual customer) for ADPD adoption.

Planning Game

The following steps can be followed to obtain a good result from the planning game adoption. It is evident that apart from minor changes, the ADPD planning game is very similar to the namesake XP rule.

- For each release-phase, a minimum and maximum duration is set in order to respect the concept of small releases and to have predefined deadlines for the selected functionalities.
- Define with the customer the functions (stories) that have to be realized in the next release. Assign to the stories a priority between one and 100 in accordance with customer needs, and also evaluate the value and impact that the realization of the story has on the whole project.
- Divide each identified story into parts with the following characteristics: (1) each part is a well-defined function; (2) each part is a stand-alone function or need that is already a realized function; and (3) each part can be developed and tested in no more than two to three days by a programmer or a couple of programmers, in the case of pair programming. Each part, as for XP, is called *task*.
- Developers and the team manager assign to each task a priority that is a number between one and 100 and that is in the range of plus or minus 10 with respect to the story to which it belongs. This allows you to implement the tasks of a story in a limited period of time with each task close to the other, but with the possibility of postponing am unimportant task of a story after a more important task of another story.
- Developers select the tasks in order of priority and, on the basis of their knowledge, assign to each task the estimated effort in person/days and the estimated duration in time.
- Once the priorities have been assigned and the time to complete each task has been estimated, it is possible to schedule the revision to be realized.

- When the scheduling of the activities has been completed, the first action to be taken is to approve the scheduling with the customer, taking particular care to the story priorities and assignments made by the team on the basis of the main priority assigned by the customer. You have two options: the scheduling fits the release time or not. In case it does not fit, you have to discuss with the customer whose stories have to be postponed in the next release (which will be ready in no more than two to four weeks). Once the stories are identified and the scheduling is updated, the development starts accordingly. If it fits in the assigned release time, you can choose to try to end the phase earlier or to add some other functionalities. In general, it is better to try to finish earlier, since a review of the functionalities to be added can be a loss of time, since the customer once again has to plan the priorities of the new functionalities compared with the existing ones.

Management of Requirements

In the case of the adoption of an Agile methodology, you have to manage requirements, since requirements are the main components of the planning game. You also have to monitor the requirements in order to track the changes and the choices performed by the customer. This process can be done without a lot of overhead, since it can be performed simply by filling out a card for each task. The collection and modification of these cards allows requirement tracking and also the evaluation of the fulfillment of estimated time for stories and tasks.

The typical task card is reported in Figure 4. This is only a sample of how a task card can be realized on paper, but, of course, it also can be in electronic form or, better yet, in Web form, which allows an automated scheduling of activities according to the priorities and a visual verification of estimated vs. real effort spent. In that case, you have to spend some time developing the automation system, but you can reuse it in all future projects. A system for the collection of time cards is a valid aid for the creation of models for costs estimation, since it is an important source of information related to the effort spent on each task.

Development Practices

The activities that already have been discussed are not related to the main scope of the project development—programming. In this section and in the next, the

Figure 4. Story and task card for ADPD management of requirements

Story and Task Card					
Project ____________			Customer ____________		
Date ____________	Activity Type	New___	Bug Fix___	Change___	Test___
Story/Task ID ________	Priority	Story ________		Task ______	
Developer(s) ____________			Manager ____________		
Estimated Effort (hours/days)____________				Date: ________	
Real Effort (hours/days)____________				Date: ________	
Task Description					
Notes					
Tracking					

Date	Release	Comment

ADPD practices related to programming and testing will be presented and commented on. These sections will emphasize the development practices, while in the last section you will find the management practices that are strongly related to development.

Pair Programming

Pair programming is one of the fundamental activities in each XP project. It is not so strongly emphasized in ADPD, although its adoption can be recommended. Pair programming is an added value when it is possible to implement it, but it cannot be a requirement; otherwise, you prevent the use of an Agile methodology such as ADPD in several environments that are not ready or simply are too small to allow the application of pair programming.

ADPD encourages the use of pair programming without saying that it is a mandatory practice. In any case, let me analyze the advantages of this development practice. One of the advantages of pair programming is the training-on-the-job function of sharing knowledge and reducing skill shortage for developers that are new to the project or to a technology adopted in the project.

In any case, when it is impossible to apply pair programming, ADPD suggests an alternative method for sharing knowledge: the 15-minute daily meeting that is detailed in the management section.

Coding Standards

During development, the adoption of coding standards is a mandatory practice in order to avoid losing time trying to interpret how another developer put braces in the code. Save this time, and use it to improve colleague code, when possible.

Coding standard is not only for parentheses and indentation but also can be applied to comments and variable names.

Comments must be written in order to generate automatic documentation and must be placed in a standard place (i.e., always before the code to which the comment is related) or written with a standard notation, as in the following sample:

```
void myfunc()
{
// Start - developer name - date
... here there is the code to be commented
// End - developer name - date
}
```

A variable and constant name must follow a uniform notation throughout the code. Constants always can be written in capital letters and variables in Camel Notation (e.g., thisIsMyVariableName), with the first letter capitalized (e.g.,

Thisismyvariablename), or without capitalized letters but with underscores (e.g., this_is_my_variable_name). Variable names should not be too generic (i.e., foo or foobar), but they must express what they contain. For not typed languages, such as PHP, and also for typed ones, it is possible to prefix the variable with a short version of the type, so that you can distinguish the type at first glance (e.g., intMyVariable, strMyVariable, where the former is an integer, and the latter is a string).

You can lose some seconds typing, but you will gain a lot of time reading the code of another developer or reading the code you wrote three months ago.

Adoption of Concurrent Version System

The adoption of a CVS repository is a mandatory practice for ADPD, since it guarantees several advantages during software development. Some of these advantages are listed and discussed as follows:

- **Concurrent changes are allowed.** This means that the commit of a file performed by more than one user is managed and allows the last user who performed the commit to decide which modification has to be kept. This prevents unauthorized overwriting of files without any prompt, when more than one person is working on the same piece of code. It is usually unsuitable for different people to work on the same code during the release phase, but it can happen, especially during the walking skeleton phase, since there is not much code to work on.
- **Traceability.** Another advantage of a generic revision control system is the traceability of the modification and the possibility to go back to a previous version.
- **Change log.** The correct use of CVS allows you to automate the change log writing by means of the commit log that each developer has to write. The collection of these logs, when well written (and they must be well written), generates the documented history of the code.

Speaking according to Agile manifesto, if there is value in the code, we have more in a CVS repository.

Test Practices

This section describes the test methodology that must be adopted during the development of the code. Two main test categories that exist in ADPD are the same with respect to XP: unit test and functional test. It is important to understand what each test category represents and where it has to be applied. In the following, an introduction to both categories of testing will be performed.

Unit Test

A unit test is the basis for implementing regression testing defined in the deployment section, which allows you to verify the impact of a modification on the previously developed code. The main recipe for implementing a correct unit test practice is to follow the strategy, *code a little, test a little, code a little, test a little*. This does not mean that a unit test is a short test but that you have to test each function that you code. Unit tests are written by the programmer, but this practice also deeply impacts management, allowing better control of the project. Let me give you an example of unit tests related to object oriented. I suggest that you write at least a unit test for each class. The class unit test can be created incrementally as you add functionalities to the class. Suppose that you have to create a class that has a constructor and a couple of functional methods; once you have coded the constructor, you can create the first part of the unit test that, for example, performs the following tasks:

- Create an instance of the class with the constructor and verify that the initialization parameters have been collected and stored correctly;
- Create two instances of the class with the same initialization parameters, and verify that the resulting objects are equal; and
- Create two instances of the class with different initialization parameters, and verify that the resulting objects are different.

You have simulated the possible error condition of the constructor. Now, you can add a method (code a little) and add to the unit test one or more lines of code to verify the behavior of the method (test a little). Each programmer should spend about 25% of his or her time writing tests.

Let me show you a sample written in an object-oriented meta-language related to a class that implements a complex number:

```
Class ComplexNumber {
real : float
img : float
Constructor(float real, float img) : void
Getreal() : float -- returns real part
Getimg(): float -- returns img part
}
```

The unit test can be a class (as usually done in Java or when a test suite is present) or a method that can be conditionally not compiled for release (as often happens in SmallTalk or C++). In any case, the UnitTest is something like the following code (where Assert is a function that exists with error when the condition is not satisfied).

```
Unit Test {
      a: ComplexNumber(10,5);
      Assert(a.Getreal()==10 AND a.Getimg()==5);
      b: ComplexNumber(10,5)
      c: ComplexNumber(11,6)
      Assert(a==b)
      Assert(a<>c)
}
```

In the class of complex number, you would like to add the sum functionality by means of the method sum that performs the addition between the current instance and the object it receives as argument.

```
Sum(ComplexNumber b) {
-- code here --
}
```

The unit test can be integrated by a line that tests if the sum is executed correctly.

```
Unit Test {
-- previous code here --
d: ComplexNumber(1,1)
Assert(c==b.sum(d))
}
```

This example shows how to incrementally update a class unit test. For large classes, sometimes it is necessary to implement more than one unit test.

Test Suite

The perfect complement for unit testing is a suite for automating the execution of unit tests and automatically collecting the results in a standard format. If you are not able to use a suite that already exists (for an example, refer to http://www.xprogramming.com/software.htm), you should arrange something for your team. A simplification of a suite test that can be applied profitably consists in a directory in the CVS repository where you put all the files that execute a unit test. Before committing, you can manually or automatically execute all tests with a script that collects results, and if all tests successfully pass, it authorizes the commit.

Of course, the integration of the test suite in the development environment, if you use one, is preferable. One of the most used for Java is the JUnit suite, which is integrated in some editors and also can be used with commercial editors and suites.

Functional Test

While unit tests are created, implemented, and executed by developers for code verification with the aim of creating an environment suitable for regression testing and low maintenance costs, functional tests are created and sometimes implemented by the customer with the aid of the team for the parts that involve code writing. The concept of a functional test is very important, since it supports the concept of small releases. When a functionality is selected for implementation in release, it is necessary to define the functional test that has to be satisfied by the correctly implemented functionality.

It is also important to note that when the functional test works (as well as the unit tests), it means that the functionality can be considered stable. It does not mean that the functionality will not be modified in the future, since continuous improvement is one of the main results that can be obtained with Agile programming, but only that the written code is working correctly and according to user specification. It also means that if there is no change in the requirement, this function is completed, while if changes in the requirement will be necessary, the code can be considered a stable point, to change how the function operates.

The functional tests can be integrated or not as the test suite mentioned previously. In general, they are separate, since if the requirements change, functional tests can be deeply modified, and at a general level, they can be considered as a higher abstraction layer, even if they are strictly bound with code.

Deployment and Release Practices

Regression Testing

All the practices that have been discussed previously are focused on obtaining a robust code that implements the functionality selected by the customer without changing the behavior of the previously working functionalities. This is possible by a correct implementation of unit tests, which allows the application of the regression testing methodology.

According to webopedia.com (www.webopedia.com), the definition of regression testing is the following:

The selective retesting of a software system that has been modified to ensure that any bugs have been fixed and that no other previously working functions have failed as a result of the reparations and that newly added features have not created problems with previous versions of the software. Also referred to as verification testing, regression testing is initiated after a programmer has attempted to fix a recognized problem or has added source code to a program that may have inadvertently introduced errors. It is a quality control measure to ensure that the newly modified code still complies with its specified requirements and that unmodified code has not been affected by the maintenance activity. (http://www.webopedia.com/TERM/r/regression_testing.html)

As evidenced in this definition, regression testing and, therefore, unit tests increase the quality of the code by identifying hidden or newly introduced bugs.

ADPD development strategy ensures regression testing, which is enforced by the fact that maintenance is the status in which code is at each point of the project, regardless of the phase of the life cycle. Therefore, an always-on maintenance code must be controlled according to defined procedure for quality control. Regression testing is one of the most suitable.

General and Management Practices

Project Documentation

As evidenced in Chapter IX on Agile development, it is better to have a working code with respect to comprehensive documentation. However, having no documentation at all is not a good practice. There are two different types of documentation in the project: the automatically generated documentation and the so-called ADPD project document, referred as PD in the following. While the first documentation type has been described in the section related to the development, the latter must be detailed in this section, since it is one of the main duties of the project manager. There are two different approaches for realizing a PD: (1) to realize a classical document as reported in the following that can fit better the needs for large organizations with quality standards to be respected; and (2) a more Agile way of compiling documentation with the use of tools for automatic code generation starting from UML diagrams. This second approach will be detailed in Chapter XIII, which discusses relationships among UML and ADPD, while in the following paragraphs, a short description of the classical way to document the project is presented together with a possible table of contents of PD.

The skeleton of PD is defined in the WS phase. In general, this document is written following the guidelines of the company quality plan developed by the Quality Assurance Department, but in any case, it must contain a short description of the project scope and target and a general description of the architecture to be used and deployed in the WS phase. After this introductory section, a section in which all the task cards are collected is needed in order to collect the history of each task, the statistics, and the changes performed. The last section of the document must contain a list of all the releases of the product with a short description of all the implemented functionalities. It is also necessary to report the measurement performed and the relevant corrective actions that have been approved during the daily meetings.

A basis for building the summary of the PD, together with the suggested maximum length of each section, can be extracted for the following list, taking in account that PD must be functional to the scope of the project, but that it also must be compliant with the specifications of the Quality Department.

1. Project Background and Introduction. 2 pages.
2. Scope and Target of the Project. 2 pages.
3. Architecture Description. 4 pages.
4. Project History
    - 4.1. Task 1
        - 4.1.1. Task Card and Story Card. Depends on number of stories and complexity of tasks.
        - 4.1.2. Task-Relevant Decision 1. 1 page.
        - 4.1.3. ....
        - 4.1.4. Task-Relevant Decision *n*. 1 page.
    - 4.2. ....
    - 4.3. Task *m*
        - 4.3.1. ....
5. Project Measurement. 2 pages with adopted metrics description.
    - 5.1. Effort Tracking. Depends on project size.
    - 5.2. Project Metrics. 3 pages.
    - 5.3. Other Metrics. Depends on metrics adopted.

Agile Intergroup Improvement Team

The Agile Intergroup Improvement Team (AIIT) is an engineering task force in which it is mandatory to include all team managers of the different teams of the company and company senior management, with particular reference to technical management.

AIIT is important and necessary where the company is large enough to have more than one team working on different projects. AIIT is an engineering group that works at a company level in order to comply with organizational needs that are not considered in XP and in other Agile methodologies.

The main activities of AIIT are related to decisions that can influence the strategy of the whole company in terms of standard tools and methodologies to be employed and in terms of training to be scheduled.

The need for AIIT is born from the fact that, during the development of projects in a company, it is commonly assumed that an engineering group meets periodically for establishing strategies, dealing with quality control problems, defining company approaches to methodologies, and carrying out other activities. This team is required both from the classical approach to software quality, such as Software Capability Maturity Model, and also by quality control procedures, such as ISO 9000.

To this end, AIIT has to do the following:

- Revise methodology improvements in order to verify if they can be applied to all teams in the company. Adopt pair programming or not, decide duration of daily meetings, train on-the-job approaches, and so forth.
- Revise and approve the tools that one of the teams has adopted with success, obtaining improvements in productivity, better quality code, or better usability in practice. If some of these advantages are demonstrated, AIIT can extend the adoption of the tool to other teams that need such improvements,
- Plan training at the company level in order to reduce skill shortages of developers. Training can be on-the-job, performed by company people, or performed in outsourcing by external companies.
- Plan training activities for management (e.g., team managers) in order to better focus the activities to be performed, to guide a team, and to focus team managers on how to obtain better results in the case of poor results, deadlines not met, bad quality code, or bad feedback from a customer. This training usually is performed by an external company, even if it can be done by internal skilled team managers.

Track and Measure

It is important to track the project evolution in terms of assignment of tasks and roles in order to identify responsibility. Agile methodologies, in general, do not care much about management; the major drawback, if people are not responsible for their actions, is the total loss of control over the project. It is necessary to establish tracking mechanisms that are useful, not only to identify who has done something wrong, but also to know who among the developers has modified and, therefore, knows details of a specific part of the code. This tracking activity also is useful when one person decides to leave the team or the company, since you can identify in a short time who has shared the knowledge of a particular functionality and identify how many functionalities have been developed only by that person. You also can easily identify the amount of training time you will need in order to transfer the knowledge to other people.

The tracking activity can be achieved by applying the task and story card in which it is evidenced for each task/story developed and who the manager was for each functionality.

Other important data to the tracked, measured, and analyzed are the efforts planned before project start by marketing/sales or senior management, a priori estimated by developers during the planning game, and a posteriori evaluated when the task/story has been completed.

This approach for effort measurement has three main advantages:

- Gives feedback to senior management and marketing/sales about effort estimation during negotiation with a customer related to team capability in the project domain.
- Learn from estimation and subsequent evaluation how to evaluate correctly the effort for each microphase of the project. This increases the capability of developers to estimate their productivity on the basis of the task to be realized.
- Evaluate productivity of the team and have a clear picture of the tasks that will delay the scheduling. If the effort collection and/or task card writing is automated, you also can utilize a tool that automatically gives scheduling feedback. This is a way for senior management to evaluate the capability of team managers with respect to planned deadlines.

Effort measurement is not the only way to perform measurement of the project. Several other aspects of the project can be measured and evaluated to have feedback about project evolution and quality. In Chapter XIV, which relates to software metrics, several examples of parameters to be kept under control are presented and commented on. Apart from metrics for effort estimation that can be applied or not, several other project metrics to evaluate management, productivity, and suitability of the adopted methodology are presented, together with metrics for object-oriented systems and cognitive metrics in order to measure the understandability of the code and, therefore, the project.

Fifteen-Minute Daily Standing Meeting

The 15-minute daily standing meeting can be a good replacement for pair programming in all situations in which it cannot be applied. It is necessary to specify the two main aspects of this practice: why daily and why 15 minutes standing.

- **Daily meeting.** It is important to share knowledge each day, because the daily activities, task-related choices, problems, and solutions have to be communicated to the other members. This allows you to present to the other team members what has been done during the previous day. The frequency of the meeting is important in order to be sure to transfer everything and to transfer it in a short period of time.
- **Fifteen-minutes standing.** BA meeting with a duration of 15 minutes seems to be too short to communicate anything to anyone, but if the previous hypothesis (daily meeting) is complete, then 15 minutes can be enough to review a standard day of development. Considering the total time of the meetings in a standard month (21 days), it is more than five hours of meeting, and therefore, it can be considered equivalent to at least a half-day meeting each month. The advantage of having 15 minutes each day is that the focus of the meeting is on a small number of problems that are addressed quickly. The concept of a standing meeting is also important, since if you are compelled to stand up in front of a blackboard, you are not inclined to waste time, and therefore, there is a higher probability that the daily scheduled time will be enough.

If, during the meeting, some problems arise, it might be necessary to have a restricted meeting with the developers involved with the problem in order to find a suitable solution. The identified solution also will be communicated to the other members in the next daily meeting. With this approach, only a limited number of persons has to deal with a meeting longer than 15 minutes, while the others can immediately start to code or to perform the other daily activities.

Training

Training is a very important activity to perform and must be focused both on developers (for reducing skill shortage or for introducing a new technology or language) and on team managers in order to focus the effort of management in obtaining the best results from the methodology and the best integration in the company environment and quality system.

Training is planned at a company level and not at a team level during AIIT meetings in order to solve problems that can arise at the team level.

References

Beck, K. (1999). Embracing change with extreme programming. *IEEE Computer, 32*(10), 70-77.

Beck, K. (2000). *Extreme programming explained: Embrace change.* Boston, MA: Addison-Wesley Professional.

Fioravanti, F. (2003). The impact of eXtreme programming on maintenance. In M. Polo, M. Piattini, & F. Ruiz (Eds.), *Advances in software maintenance management: Technologies and solutions* (pp. 75-92). Hershey, PA: Idea Group Publishing.

Paulk, M. C., Curtis, B. Chrissis, M. B., & Weber, C. (1993, February). *Capability maturity model for software, Version 1.1* (Publication CMU/SEI-93-TR-24, DTIC No. ADA263403). Pittsburgh, PA: Software Engineering Institute.

Paulk, M. C., Weber, C. V., Garcia, S. M., Chrissis, M. B., & Bush, M. W. (1993, February). *Key practices of the capability maturity model, Version 1.1* (Publication CMU/SEI-93-TR-25, DTIC No. ADA263432). Pittsburg, PA: Software Engineering Institute.

Lessons Learned

Target

Agile and Defined Project Development (ADPD)

Practices

ADPD basis on the following practices:

Small releases (mandatory)

On-site customer (strongly recommended)

Planning game (mandatory)

Management of requirements (mandatory)

Pair programming (optional, but recommended)

Coding standards (mandatory)

CVS (mandatory)

Tests (mandatory)

Project documentation (strongly recommended)

AIIT (strongly recommended)

Track and measure (optional, but recommended)

Fifteen-minute daily meeting (can be a replacment for pair programming)

Chapter XII

ADPD and SW-CMM

ADPD has been discussed in the previous chapter and introduced as an Agile methodology, but focused on reaching the Level 3 of SW-CMM (Paulk, Curtis, Chrissis, & Weber, 1993; Paulk, Weber, Garcia, Chrissis, & Bush, 1993).

In this chapter, all the relationships between ADPD and SW-CMM at Level 3 will be discussed in order to verify how it is possible to adopt an Agile methodology and at the same time be compliant with standard methods such as the SW-CMM.

In the chapter not related to Agile methodologies, a short introduction to SW-CMM has been reported, but in order to have clear detail of the matching between SW-CMM Level 3 and ADPD, it is necessary to describe in more detail the CMM Key Process Areas (KPAs) related to Levels 2 and 3.

In Table 1, the KPAs for the target maturity levels are reported.

KPA 2.4 will not be addressed in this discussion, since the target environment discussed in Chapter VII does not include the case in which subcontracting exists and since subcontracting requires a development method that is more structured; therefore, it is difficult to achieve by the ADPD or Agile methodologies, in general. Subcontracting can be considered for the sake of simplicity as COTS (*components off the shelf*); all the other KPAs must be addressed and satisfied. Paulk (2001) examines the relationships between XP and SW-CMM, evidencing if the KPAs are addressed totally, partially, or not at all.

Table 1. Key process areas for maturity Levels 2 and 3

Maturity Level	Key Process Area
2: Repeatable	KPA 2.1 Requirement management
2: Repeatable	KPA 2.2 Software project planning
2: Repeatable	KPA 2.3 Software project tracking and oversight
2: Repeatable	KPA 2.4 Software subcontract management
2: Repeatable	KPA 2.5 Software quality assurance
2: Repeatable	KPA 2.6 Software configuration management
3: Defined	KPA 3.1 Organization process focus
3: Defined	KPA 3.2 Organization process definition
3: Defined	KPA 3.3 Training program
3: Defined	KPA 3.4 Integrated software management
3: Defined	KPA 3.5 Software product engineering
3: Defined	KPA 3.6 Intergroup coordination
3: Defined	KPA 3.7 Peer reviews

Table 2. XP addressing of CMM Levels 2 and 3 according to Paulk (2001)

Maturity Level	Key Process Area	XP Addressing Level
2: Repeatable	KPA 2.1 Requirement management	Addressed
2: Repeatable	KPA 2.2 Software project planning	Addressed
2: Repeatable	KPA 2.3 Software project tracking and oversight	Addressed
2: Repeatable	KPA 2.4 Software subcontract management	Not addressed but not necessary
2: Repeatable	KPA 2.5 Software quality assurance	Partially addressed
2: Repeatable	KPA 2.6 Software configuration management	Partially addressed
3: Defined	KPA 3.1 Organization process focus	Partially addressed
3: Defined	KPA 3.2 Organization process definition	Partially addressed
3: Defined	KPA 3.3 Training program	Not addressed
3: Defined	KPA 3.4 Integrated software management	Not addressed
3: Defined	KPA 3.5 Software product engineering	Addressed
3: Defined	KPA 3.6 Intergroup coordination	Addressed
3: Defined	KPA 3.7 Peer reviews	Addressed

According to his analysis, the activities to be enforced in order to comply with Level 3 are reported in Table 2.

In the rest of the chapter, each KPA with the related goals will be discussed in order to verify if the improvement to XP inserted in ADPD has successfully exploited the target of obtaining Level 3 compliance to SW-CMM.

More focus will be dedicated to the activities partially or not addressed, while for the others, it will be verified that the changes with respect to XP have not changed the addressing level of the KPAs.

The detailed description of the goals of each KPA and of KPAs can be found in Paulk, Curtis, et al. (1993) and Paulk, Weber, et al. (1993).

KPA 2.1 Requirement Management

KPA 2.1 is related mainly to the establishment of a common understanding between the customer and the team about the customer's requirements. The following are the main goals to be achieved:

- **Goal 1.** System requirements allocated to software are controlled to establish a baseline for software engineering and management use.
- **Goal 2.** Software plans, products, and activities remain consistent with the system requirements allocated to software.

The management of requirements is one of the main activities performed in XP and ADPD, since the customer is an active part of the team and the XP Planning game is the formalization of the process of continuous refinement of the requirements to be implemented. During this process, the main activities to be performed and the priority among the requirements are established.

ADPD methodology requires that, for each activity, one or more task cards have to be created and ordered by priority (between one and 100, where one is the highest) in order to satisfy Goal 1 and have a clear view of what has to be implemented and to get control over the satisfaction of user priorities.

ADPD encourages the continuous refinement of requirements and customer involvement in that process, since the priority is related not only to the fact that the functionality has to be implemented, but also to the fact that after the single story is identified by the customer, the development team refines it by dividing it into prioritized activities and submits it again to the customer for validation. A user requirement that states that there must be a Web interface based on the look and feel of the customer's Web site for managing the company DHCP server is decomposed in several phases such as: (1) creating the library function to implement the functionality; (2) creating a raw interface that works and operates correctly with the library function; and (3) refining the Web site in order to satisfy the customer's requirements regarding look and feel. To this end, if the customer's initial priority for the whole task was 10, then the development team can define a priority of 10 for subtasks (1) and (2), while task (3) can be delayed in time, assuming for it a priority of 20.

The decomposition of stories in tasks defined by the development team and agreed to by the customer allows you to implement functionalities in a smaller time frame, allowing the customer to review the functionalities and delaying activities that are not strategic. This process allows you to satisfy Goal 2 in the sense that the continuous review of well-formalized requirements allows you to synchronize what has been planned as requirements with what is developed by the team.

KPA 2.2 Software Project Planning

KPA 2.2 is focused on establishing in the project the concept of planning, allowing management to have overall control. The goals to be achieved to comply with this activity are the following:

- **Goal 1.** Software estimates are documented for use in planning and tracking the software projects.
- **Goal 2.** Software project activities and commitments are planned and documented.
- **Goal 3.** Affected groups and individuals agree to their commitments related to the software project.

In XP, KPA 2.2 is addresses by the presence of the planning game and small releases. In projects where requirements can change often and then the projects rapidly evolve in unexpected directions, it is necessary to plan often, since it is impossible to plan well.

ADPD adopts and refines the mechanism of the planning game and enforces the use of small releases, being compliant to the general requirement of the KPA under analysis.

ADPD also tracks and monitors software estimates and a posteriori verification in each task card in order to comply with Goal 1.

Goal 2 seems to be in contrast with the Agile manifesto, since the working code has to be preferred to comprehensive documentation, but it is also true that the production of no documentation generates only bad results. The ADPD development team has to track in the task card the evolution, completion, and problems that arise form the task, documenting the evolution of the related activities. The commitment is also documented, since the developer who takes a task card must put on his or her name.

The commitments of the group to the software project and then the satisfaction of Goal 3 are evidenced by the fact that each part of the system is improved as soon as the possibility of a simplification exists.

KPA 2.3 Software Project Tracking and Oversight

KPA 2.3 is focused on the traceability of the software process in order to allow management to verify that the project is not deviating from the plans. The goals to be achieved to comply with this activity are as follows:

- **Goal 1.** Actual results and performances are tracked against the software plans.
- **Goal 2.** Corrective actions are taken and managed to closure, when actual results and performance deviate significantly from the software plans.
- **Goal 3.** Changes to software commitments are agreed to by the affected groups and individuals.

XP is compliant to this KPA in a general sense, since the small stories, the agreement with the user on the functionalities to be implemented, and the project velocity due to the small releases mechanism help to identify as soon as possible if the software project deviates from the plan defined with the user.

The process of effort estimation that each developer does when a story is chosen among the set of the stories to be implemented can be verified when the story has been finished, and then a tracking of the project is performed continuously.

ADPD adopts all these techniques, and the measurement process is stressed in order to verify if the project deviates from the plan both from the time scheduling point of view and from the software quality point of view. One of the main activities of ADPD is the 15-minute daily standing meeting in order to know from each team member, from the customer, and from management if any problems arose in the previous day in order to have a clear view of the divergences from the planned activities. If all is okay, no change is made; otherwise, management, customer, and team members who have found the problem have a short meeting in order to plan corrective actions. This practice alone allows you to match Goal 1 and Goal 2. Goal 3 is well-matched due to the on-site customer that agrees that each functionality will be implemented and chooses the functionalities and the stories to be implemented at each release in the release meeting, where all the components of the team must participate.

KPA 2.4 Software Subcontract Management

As previously evidenced, this KPA is not considered in this dissertation, since the company that can be a target for the ADPD adoption usually does not require external subcontracting.

KPA 2.5 Software Quality Assurance

KPA 2.5 is strictly bounded to the 2.3, since it is present to give management a clear view of the product and software process and of its adherence to standard methodologies agreed to by the team. The goals to be achieved in order to comply with this activity are the following:

- **Goal 1.** Software quality assurance activities are planned.
- **Goal 2.** Adherence of software products and activities to the applicable standards, procedures, and requirements is verified objectively.
- **Goal 3.** Affected groups and individuals are informed of software quality assurance activities and results.

- **Goal 4.** Noncompliance issues that cannot be resolved within the software project are addressed by senior management.

In Agile methodologies, the figure of software quality assurance group is not present as a separate identity with respect to the development team, since quality assurance is performed by the team under management supervision. The team leader, the manager of the team, is the person responsible for the application of the software quality assurance policies and standards. Software quality assurance is enforced in XP mainly by pair programming and by unit and functional tests. In ADPD, pair programming can be replaced easily by the daily meeting. Although I consider it a great value, I found many problems applying pair programming on the field, as discussed in Chapter XI. Daily meeting with problem discussion allows team members to share knowledge and to transfer to management a clear picture of what is going wrong and why in order to verify nonconformities from what has been planned for the quality assurance process. The practice of writing unit tests and functional tests enforces quality control, since each team member writes a test to verify if his or her functionality conforms to what has been planned. The execution of all the tests after each modification and before each software commit in the software repository allows team members to enforce quality control in the software, not allowing software that does not conform to all the previous tests. Software quality is tested at a higher level by the adoption of specific software metrics, as introduced in Chapter XI and as it will be discussed in Chapter XIV.

ADPD practices and measurement processes enforce software quality and allow you to establish a set of planned activities to verify nonconformities. To this end, Goal 1 is satisfied. Regarding Goal 2, the test execution and the software quality measurement are objective ways to track the software quality process. At the same time, since all team members are informed about tests and about measurements on software, complying with Goal 3 is automatically achieved.

When a problem arises during the daily meeting, management, the customer, and involved team members have a meeting in which management gives the guidelines to solve the nonconformities, complying with Goal 4.

KPA 2.6 Software Configuration Management

KPA 2.6 is focused on guaranteeing over the software product life cycle the completeness and congruency of the product. The goals to be achieved in order to comply with this activity are as follows:

- **Goal 1.** Software configuration management activities are planned.
- **Goal 2.** Selected software work products are identified, controlled, and available.
- **Goal 3.** Changes to identified software work products are controlled.
- **Goal 4.** Affected groups and individuals are informed of the status and content of software baselines.

As a general concept, software configuration management is an activity that is inserted by default in XP methodology due to the collective ownership of code. Collective ownership implies that RCS or CVS is implemented in the software project.

ADPD maintains this practice and enforces it in the mandatory adoption of CVS similar systems in order to deal with the problem of concurrent modifications for large projects, satisfying the requirement of Goal 1. XP and ADPD, with their small releases and the cooperation among all team members in selecting the functionalities, allow you to identify and control all the single software products to be realized, complying with Goal 2. The adoption of CVS allows you to track and control all modifications, allowing each individual in the development team to be advised of the status revision and changes performed in each single software work, satisfying the requirements of Goal 3 and Goal 4.

KPA 3.1 Organization Process Focus

The organization process focus purpose is related to the establishment of a set of responsible persons and of the associated responsibility related to the process of software development with the aim of improving the capability of the organization's software processes.

The main activity of organization process focus is devoted to the maintenance of the knowledge of the software process standard and to the melioration of the coordination activities. The company must plan to use stable resources to monitor these activities in order to have clear commitments for current and future software projects. The goals to be achieved to comply with this activity are the following:

- **Goal 1.** Software process development and improvement activities are coordinated throughout the organization.
- **Goal 2.** The strengths and weakness of the software processes used are identified relative to a process standard.
- **Goal 3.** Organization-level process development and improvement activities are planned.

This KPA is addressed only partially by XP, since it is not considered at company level but only at team level. The main problem of XP regarding this KPA and, more generally, CMM Level 3 is related to the fact that XP as it is does not address organizational problems. In my opinion, there are several situations in which the XP approach is sufficient; for example, in small software houses, where the team *is* the company, and therefore, if KPA is addressed at the team level, then it is addressed at the company or organization level. In addition, very small companies are not the only target organizations for agile methodologies, and then, a method for addressing the KPA-related goals must be defined. In ADPD, the organizational level is addressed only when necessary; for example, where several Agile teams operate in the same company, and at the same time, the Agile methodology is adopted across several projects. In this case, ADPD highly suggests that the company create a software engineering team called AIIT (Agile Intergroup Improvement Team) composed of all the Agile team managers and by senior management, who contribute to identify software process strengths and to improve the development process when weaknesses are identified. ADPD, therefore, is compliant with Goals 1 and 2 of this KPA, at least when organizational problems must be addressed. Goal 3 is addressed by the same team, with sharing among all the team managers of the knowledge and process improvements to be applied. For example, if a team finds that the currently adopted revision system of the company is no longer suitable for addressing all the needs of a specified team, then the team manager can propose a new tool that can be employed successfully. It is a requirement of AIIT to evaluate if this feature can be extended to all the team in order to globally improve the software process.

KPA 3.2 Organization Process Definition

The main purpose of KPA 3.2 is related to the development and continuous improvement of the software process in order to provide the basis for long-term advantages resulting in a global benefit to the whole organization. For example, the maintenance of a database of the projects developed by the company with the problems that arose and the solution adopted to solve them can help in the continuous improvement of software process organization; the maintenance of the company-adopted software life cycle and methodologies for development and management is another key point. The goals to be achieved to comply with this activity are as follows:

- **Goal 1.** A standard software process for the organization is developed and maintained.
- **Goal 2.** Information related to the use of the organization's standard software process by the software projects is collected, reviewed, and made available.

As discussed for KPA 3.1, KPA 3.2 is partially addressed by XP because of the lack of commitments with organizational issues at a company level. On the other hand, if an Agile methodology is adopted in all the development teams of the company, at least Goal 1 is satisfied, since the software life cycle is well-defined and adopted in the company. ADPD by itself also addresses Goal 2, since one of the requirements of the already cited AIIT is to share among the teams the knowledge and improvements related to the software process life cycle and to the tools to be adopted.

KPA 3.3 Training Program

It is very important that KPA 3.3 be implemented in a company, since its main purpose is to increase and improve the skills and capacities of individuals with the scope of allowing them to perform their role adequately. To this end, training program KPA considers training at all levels — from the organization level to the individual level — considering also the team and project level.

Several different approaches can be identified for training, and all of them contribute to guide individuals toward a successful training, improving their skills with (1) on-the-job training, (2) classroom training, and (3) guided self study. The goals to be achieved to comply with this activity are the following:

- **Goal 1.** Training activities are planned.
- **Goal 2.** Training for developing the skills and knowledge needed to perform software management and technical roles is provided.
- **Goal 3.** Individuals in the software engineering group and software-related groups receive the training necessary to perform their roles.

XP practically does not address this KPA apart from the adoption of pair programming, which provides on-the-job training with the aim of reducing skill shortage. This kind of training is not managed or planned and is not focused on the development of management skills. In order to address this very important KPA — ADPD — that does not stress the concept of pair programming as a mandatory practice because of the difficulties in its adoption in real environments, several mechanism are provided that allow it to be compliant with training process areas. The reduction of skill shortage must be a key point to be addressed by each Agile methodology, since the main basis for the success of such practices relies on the individual's capacities and skills. The daily meeting of ADPD is a way to identify weaknesses in individuals or in the group, not only regarding the project's problem but also regarding the missing skills or knowledge of the individuals or the group. As a consequence of such identification, in the AIIT meetings, the team managers identify if a technical training program is needed, and in that case, they plan when and how to train people. During the same meeting, it also is evaluated if some of the managers need some special focus or training in order to reach a result that is similar to the mean result of the company's teams. Feedback about project results, user satisfaction, and developer's satisfaction and commitment with the team manager are evaluated in order to verify if some sort of training can be identified. The adoption of simple feedback mechanisms at the company level and not just at the team level and the creation of AIIT allows you to address all the goals of this KPA.

KPA 3.4 Integrated Software Management

The purpose of KPA 3.4 is related to the coherent integration of software engineering and management activities in order to fit the organization's standards and assets. The goals to be achieved to comply with this activity are the following:

- **Goal 1.** The project's defined software process is a tailored version of the organization's standard software process.
- **Goal 2.** The project is planned and managed according to the project's defined software process.

XP, as it is and as evidenced in the previous sections, does not address this KPA, since it basically does not address organizational problem on the large and then at company level.

ADPD's main aim is to cover all the KPAs of SW-CMM Level 3 and then to address problems at the company level regarding the organizational processes.

ADPD has a small set of documents that have to be produced by management and by each development team. These documents have to be inserted in the organization's standard software process in order to satisfy the requirement of this KPA. The review process of the project at both team (daily meetings) and company (AIIT meetings) levels is defined by ADPD allowing you to define a software process that can be planned and managed.

It is necessary to remember that ADPD is an Agile methodology, and then, the focus on the documentation can be lower with respect to other software development and management methodologies. Since it is impossible to assure that all the team members and the manager will be with the company forever, some documentation is useful for reducing skill shortages when some persons leave the company. The ADPD project document that must be created and maintained during the project life is the main example of the applicability of documented processes to an Agile methodology. ADPD is agile enough to allow the user to define the project document and the other related documentation in the form that best agrees with the company's standards.

KPA 3.5 Software Product Engineering

The purpose of KPA 3.5 is related mainly to the need to adopt an engineering process that allows you to produce software products effectively and efficiently. The main focus of this KPA is the definition of the activities to be performed during the project life cycle, such as requirement definition and selection, software development and implementation, test, and documentation review. The goals to be achieved to comply with this activity are as follows:

- **Goal 1.** The software engineering tasks are defined, integrated, and consistently performed to produce the software.
- **Goal 2.** Software work products are kept consistent with each other.

Both XP and ADPD define guidelines and processes that fully address the goals of software process engineering, since the main scope of a development and management methodology is to define how to operate on the software product during the project lifetime.

It is not possible to evidence how XP and ADPD comply, since the adoption of a methodology that allow you to guide a product during its lifetime according to a predefined life cycle guarantees the compliance to this KPA. ADPD, if possible, is more compliant with respect to XP, because it addresses the problems related to the documentation and to the coordination at a higher level with respect to the team allowing a better consistency among products developed by different teams or by the same team in different periods of time.

KPA 3.6 Intergroup Coordination

The purpose of KPA 3.6 is to establish mechanisms for team members and team managers to interact actively with the customer in order to address the customer's needs. With this aim, technical review must be planned and conducted on a regular basis in order to ensure that all team members and the customer are aware of the status and the plan or modification to the plans. The goals to be achieved to comply with this activity are the following:

- **Goal 1.** The customer's requirements are agreed to by all affected groups.
- **Goal 2.** The commitments among the engineering groups are agreed to by the affected groups.
- **Goal 3.** The engineering groups identify, track, and resolve intergroup issues.

XP's focus on communication is the better guarantee of successfully applying the practices contained in these KPA goals, since the on-site customer, the peer review mechanism, and the collective ownership of the code allow you to address them. The agreement on the requirements (Goal 1) is one of the main activities to be performed in Agile methodologies, such as XP and ADPD, and the commitments and agreement among all members and the customer (Goal 2) also is satisfied in the largest sense.

ADPD, apart from the maintenance of the already evidenced practices, guarantee the full satisfaction of Goal 3 by the adoption of the AIIT engineering group.

KPA 3.7 Peer Reviews

The purpose of KPA 3.7 is the removal of defects from the software work products early and efficiently. Peer review also requires that the software be examined in order to identify defects and project parts where modifications are needed. The goals to be achieved to comply with this activity are as follows:

- **Goal 1.** Peer review activities are planned.
- **Goal 2.** Defects in the software work products are identified and removed.

In order to comply with peer review, it is necessary to define a set of instruments that can be used to perform the software product review. This activity can be performed by direct code inspection (i.e., XP pair programming) or by indirect code evaluation (i.e., software metrics and regression testing techniques). While XP uses and encourages both practices by the adoption of pair programming and unit and functional tests, ADPD does not put so much emphasis on pair programming, since if encouraging results are coming from its adoption from the defect removal point of view, it is not fully compliant with the concept of peer review in this KPA, where it is assumed that peer reviewers are external to the team and particularly skilled people are requested to deal with such activities.

The adoption of functional and unit tests is without any doubt a powerful way to inspect code by examining its working functionalities on the field, since examining the union of unit tests is very useful, if some part of the code has changed the global system behavior by inspecting the single functionalities, while functional testing does not stress single functionalities but give a clear picture of the compliance of the software works with user specifications and requirements.

APDP does not stress the team with the adoption of metrics for fault prediction, since the models are often difficult to find and are dependent on the language adopted and on the project type. In the chapter related to software measurement, some experience from the field is reported and can be used as a guideline for adopting a measurement framework that can aid in the prediction of faults.

Conclusion

The conclusion that can be drawn from the considerations performed in this chapter is that it is possible to have an Agile methodology that completely complies with SW-CMM Level 3 without adding exceptional overhead to the agility.

Let me evidence the main differences that bring ADPD to be compliant with the KPAs that XP does not addresses in order to understand the amount of overhead needed.

- **Fifteen-minute daily meeting.** ADPD uses this practice as a replacement or improvement of XP pair programming, since pair programming is difficult to apply in real environments that have worked in the past without Agile methodologies.
- **Software metric adoption.** The team manager is requested to check software product against a set of software quality metrics in order to verify the compliance of the project with respect to the expected goals.
- **AIIT establishment.** The AIIT creation allows you to export the knowledge developed in each team to all the other teams, improving the global quality of the projects developed in the company and allowing you to have a better control at the organizational level for training activities that are not demanded only for self study or for pair programming.
- **Project document.** The creation of a master document for the project in which the team manager includes the most important knowledge and nonconformities allows you to reduce skill shortage and to address organizational problem according to predefined policies.

Table 3. Summary of SW-CMM Levels 2 and 3 with XP and ADPD compliance level

Key Process Area	XP	ADPD
KPA 2.1 Requirement management	Addressed	Addressed
KPA 2.2 Software project planning	Addressed	Addressed
KPA 2.3 Software project tracking and oversight	Addressed	Addressed
KPA 2.4 Software subcontract management	Not addressed but not necessary	Not addressed but not necessary
KPA 2.5 Software quality assurance	Partially addressed	Addressed
KPA 2.6 Software configuration management	Partially addressed	Addressed
KPA 3.1 Organization process focus	Partially addressed	Addressed
KPA 3.2 Organization process definition	Partially addressed	Addressed
KPA 3.3 Training program	Not addressed	Addressed
KPA 3.4 Integrated software management	Not addressed	Addressed
KPA 3.5 Software product engineering	Addressed	Addressed
KPA 3.6 Intergroup coordination	Addressed	Addressed
KPA 3.7 Peer reviews	Addressed	Addressed

All the practices added to ADPD with respect to XP do not have a strong influence on the daily team working, since the manager is the person that must perform these tasks in order to obtain a high level view at the company level.

Team members and the developer can operate with the traditional agility that the methodology promises in order to steer the project toward a success story and to have at the same time a coordination at management level that in the long term only can improve the benefit of the Agile methodology in general.

References

Paulk, M. C. (2001). Extreme programming from a CMM perspective. *IEEE Software,* 18(6), 19-26.

Paulk, M. C. Curtis, B. Chrissis, M. B., & Weber, C. (1993, February). *Capability maturity model for software, Version 1.1* (Publication CMU/SEI-93-TR-24, DTIC No. ADA263403). Pittsburgh, PA: Software Engineering Institute.

Paulk, M. C., Weber, C. V., Garcia, S. M., Chrissis, M. B., & Bush, M. W. (1993). *Key practices of the capability maturity model, Version 1.1* (CMU/SEI-93-TR-25, DTIC No. ADA263432). Pittsburgh, PA: Software Engineering Institute.

Lessons Learned

Target

ADPD and SW-CMM

Practices

Adopting an Agile methodology, it also is possible to be compliant with SW-CMM Level 3.

The key practices for ADPD compliance are:

Fifteen-minute daily standing meeting

Software metrics

AIIT

Project document

Chapter XIII

ADPD and UML Adoption

In this book, the world of management and Agile development always suggested that we adopt the simplest technology and methodologies that can fit the project you are dealing with.

These are the questions that can arise: How can UML fit these requirements? Can UML be employed with Agile methodologies and particularly with ADPD? How many types of diagrams should be used profitably with ADPD?

This chapter will try to answer these and other questions that are asked considering UML as a tool for aiding development and management of Agile projects. Agile developers usually draw UML diagrams on a board in order to have a topic to discuss about formalized well-know common language. On the other hand, when these diagrams are transferred to a tool capable of managing UML notation, you obtain the advantage of having a documentation automatically generated that can be updated to your needs.

As introduced in Chapter XI, UML and the automated documentation that some tools can generate, starting from a set of UML diagrams, can substitute the ADPD project document. This approach to documentation compels the project manager to make some choices and decide if some parts of the project have to be documented or not. In any case, it is better that this choice be performed by the project manager, who can select the most important features to be documented among the whole project instead of compelling the reader of the documentation to cut according to his judgment.

UML in Short

This section is not an exhaustive essay on UML diagrams and their usage nor is it an introduction focused on the general concepts of UML. The main purpose of this section is to propose the author's view of UML and UML adoption, to suggest further reading for interested readers, and to give a brief introduction to tools that can be usefully employed to approach UML for the first time.

UML is the acronym for Unified Modeling Language, and, as the name suggests, it can be usefully employed to model with a (visual) language all the processes. UML tries to unify by the adoption of a set of diagrams all the possible options for modeling business processes, interaction among software models, and human description of class hierarchy or module dependencies together with fast descriptions of modules or class functionality and responsibilities.

When this section was written, UML was at its 2.0 specification, and therefore, it can be considered mature enough to be used.

In order to give the reader a clearer view of the diagrams and to introduce some free tools (or free downloadable versions of commercial tools) for UML adoption and Java development, I have decided to adopt two free tools that can be downloaded from the Internet: NetBeans 3.6 IDE for Java (www.netbeans.org) and Smart Development Environment Version 1.1 of Visual Paradigm in its community version for NetBeans and SunOne (www.visual-paradigm.com). The snapshots of this section have been obtained during the usage of such tools. The tool used in this chapter has implemented Version 1.4, and the standard UML diagrams that it offers are described in the following:

- **Use case diagram.** Use case diagram describes what a system does from the point of view of an observer that is external to the system. The focus of a use case diagram is to describe what the system has to do without specifying how the system does such functions. Use case diagrams are closely connected to XP metaphors or to agile stories, since use case describes what happens when an actor (i.e., a person or another system) interacts with the system under description.
- **Class diagram.** A class diagram's aim is to show the classes belonging to the system and their relationships. This overview of the system is not a dynamic view, since no description of what happens when two classes interact is given with the interaction link.

- **Sequence diagram.** A sequence diagram is a dynamic diagram that shows what happens during time. In this diagram, all the details of the operations are specified, and the messages that each object involved in the operation sends to the others is detailed together with the time instant at which it happens. The diagram is built with time that progresses from up to down, and the objects are ordered from left to right according to the time instant in which they appear in the sequence of messages.
- **Collaboration diagram.** Collaboration diagrams contain and express the same information with respect to sequence diagrams, but their focus is not on timing but on objects roles. A collaboration diagram is a graph in which edges are object roles, and arcs are the messages.
- **State diagram.** State diagrams are the classical diagrams for representing state-machines. They are useful when it is necessary to define the state changing of an object, while they are not suggested when cooperating objects have to be represented.
- **Activity diagram.** An activity diagram can be described as a flowchart with the support of parallel elaboration. It can represent business processes and workflows as simple flowcharts. Originally, it was considered a special case of state diagram, but especially with UML Version 2.0, it has obtained a personal identity and role in the UML world.
- **Component diagram.** Component diagrams are adopted to divide the system into parts described by their interface. The interaction among the interfaces also can be documented with these diagrams.
- **Deployment diagram.** Deployment diagrams document the physical configurations of software and hardware, with particular care to assign software parts to the correct hardware parts.

Visual Paradigm also supports the following diagrams in its Smart Development Environment (SDE):

- **Textual analysis.** "Textual analysis is one of the way of analysis requirements. You can find out and highlight the candidate actors, use cases and classes from the problem statements. The candidate elements can be used to create UML models and diagram elements" (Manual of SDE).
- **Business workflow.** Business workflow diagrams are useful for representing business processes and workflow of documents in business processes.

- **CRC cards.** "CRC cards are another method of analysis requirements. You can walk through the required system to identify classes and use CRC cards to record their names, responsibilities and collaborations." (Manual of SDE).

The reader interested in having more details on UML can refer to Fowler (2004), Rumbaugh (1999), Booch (1998), Larman (2001), Mellor (2002), and Favre (2003).

UML is a visual language that can be used with pen and paper or on a dashboard and that also can be usefully integrated with RAD and IDE for development.

UML and ADPD Life Cycle

During the ADPD life cycle, UML can be adopted usefully in different phases with the aim of simplifying and unifying the notation used on the team and for automating the generation of the project documentation.

Walking Skeleton Phase

UML is adopted mainly for the analysis of the project, especially for the part related to the business analysis of the use cases. A business use case is very similar to the formalization of the XP metaphor, since it collects what the system has to do without considering any architectural details.

Suppose that you have to create the simple system for an e-business shop in which the user can select the items, confirm the basket, select the desired payment method, and finally buy the items in the basket, paying by credit card, paying when the items arrive at home, and so forth. The bank is present to authorize the payment with credit card.

Use Case Adoption

Use cases can be divided in two main groups: business level and system level. Business level use cases are high-level descriptions of the system, adopted

Figure 1. Business use case diagram for the Web system

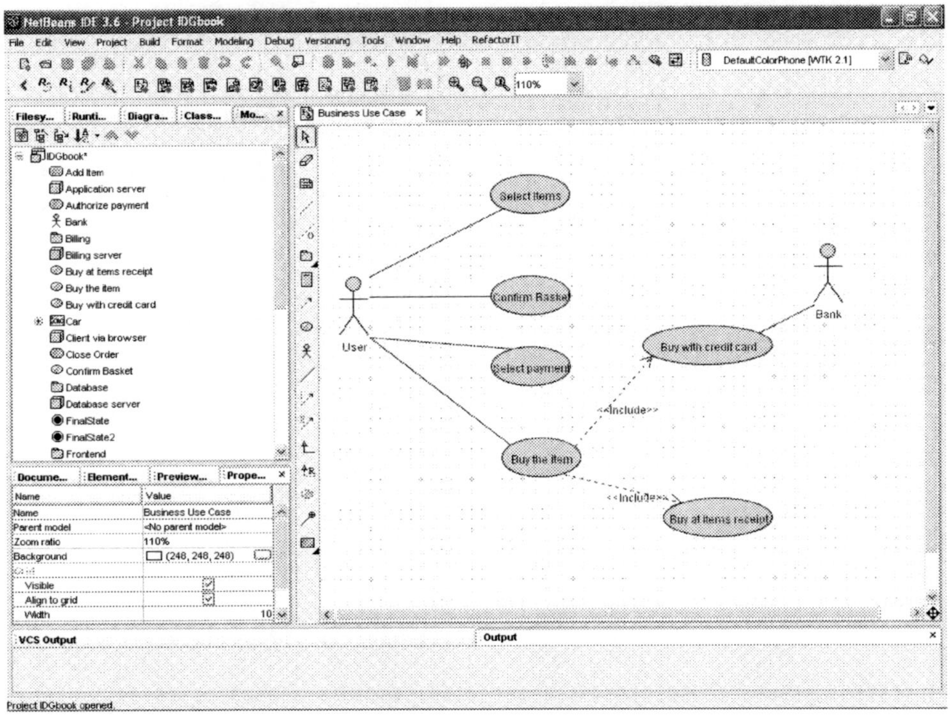

mainly during the Walking Skeleton phase to give the customer a global idea of the system at "kite level," according to the notation of Cockburn (2001a), which is detailed in the following. System level use cases are adopted mainly in development phases, when it is necessary to have an in-depth detail of the operation to be performed.

The system supposed in the previous section can be described by the business level use case reported in Figure 1. A description can be attached to each diagram element in order to automatically generate system documentation in both PDF and HTML formats. The work of drawing and specifying some details in the description has the positive payload of having an automated documentation of the project.

The example reported previously is a very high-level diagram, where the bank actor is so undefined that we do not know at this level what kind of entity it is —human, Web service, library of the project, and so forth.

I think that use case diagrams can be very useful in presenting information to customers who are not technically skilled, since they can understand what you likely want to do at first glance. The use cases also are useful in order for

Table 1. Text use case for buying items

User buys products
Use case level: Sea Level
1. User browses the Web site, selecting items to buy 2. User verifies the basket and checks out 3. Use selects payment method 4. User pays by credit card 5. Bank authorizes payment
Extensions 4a: User pays when he or she receives the items .1 System prepares the shipment with delayed payment and surcharge

developers and software architects to identify which operations have to be completed on a system in order to have a desired result. Several experts such as Fowler (2004) suggest that you use text use case instead of graphical diagrams. I introduce these kinds of use cases (not formalized in UML) in order to give the reader the possibility to choose the notation he or she prefers.

The text use case for the business use case diagram is summarized in Table 1.

Table 1 collects more information with respect to the graphic diagram, and therefore, it is more suitable for people who are closer to the code and to the implementation of the system. The table is divided in four parts, detailed from up to down:

1. **Use case title.**
2. **Use case level.** According to the classification in Cockburn (2001a), use cases can be classified among (1) sea level, when the described action involves mainly the principal actor and the system in a restricted area; (2) fish level for all the use cases that exist only because they are included by a sea level use case; and (3) kite level, which is general use cases that can show the adoption of sea level use cases in a more general context, generally at the business level.
3. **Use case description.** The sequence of activities performed by an actor to reach the desired result (in the example, the result is to successfully buy something online).
4. **Extension description.** When it is possible to have more than one action for a single item inside a use case, this section is filled with possible alternatives that can bring to the target results or completion with an error state.

Component Diagram

Once you have defined what the system has to do, it is time to describe how the system is organized at a high level in terms of macro components. UML 2.0 has adopted the package diagram that can be more suitably employed, but the components diagram present in the 1.4 specification is a superset and, therefore, also can be adopted. The component diagram that I will show has the same semantic and appearance of a package diagram.

The architecture of the simple system described previously can be expressed by the component diagram depicted in Figure 2.

You have to remember that in the case of a toy system, the specification can be complete, but when you deal with a complex system, only the main parts of the system can be described, leaving to the code and to the code documentation the description of the details.

Figure 2. Component diagram (UML 1.4) or package diagram (UML 2.0) for the Web system

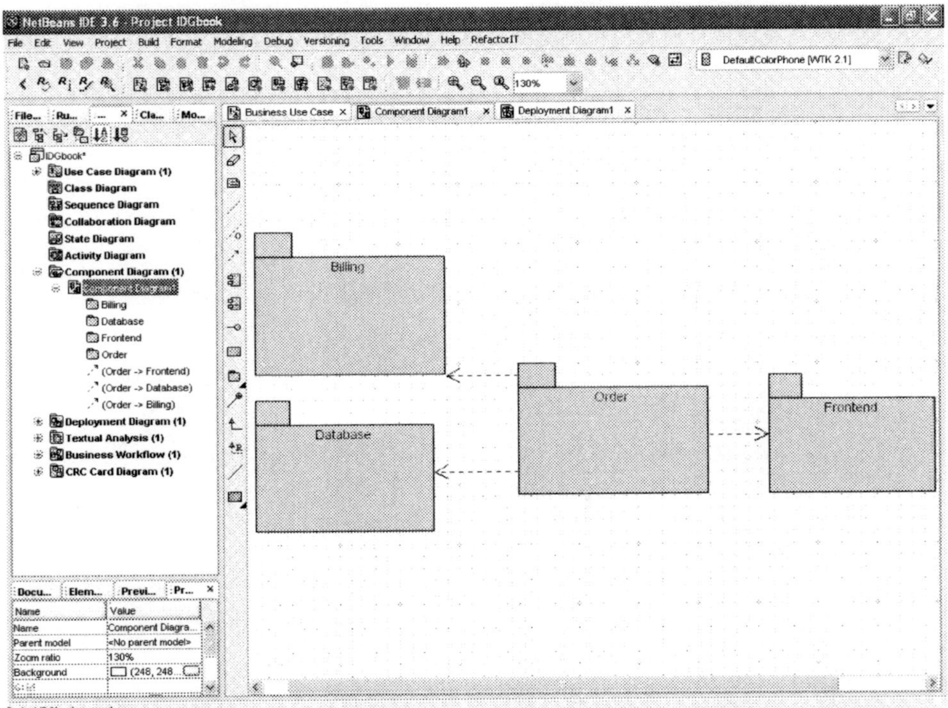

Deployment Diagram Adoption

In order to have a test plant at the customer site or in the development environment, it is necessary to have a clear idea of how to implement system deployment. UML helps you with a diagram that can identify the matching between the hardware you have adopted and the software modules you have to deploy.

Figure 3 reports the deployment diagram for the simple Web system described in the first part of the chapter.

As already evidenced, in this case, the same toy system is deployed. Some notes have been attached to some deployment units in order to show the bounds (if any), such as operating system, DB type, and so forth.

CRC Cards Adoption

CRC cards are not a UML standard but usually are employed in a project session by project managers and are often integrated in UML case tools. CRC

Figure 3. Deployment diagram for the Web system

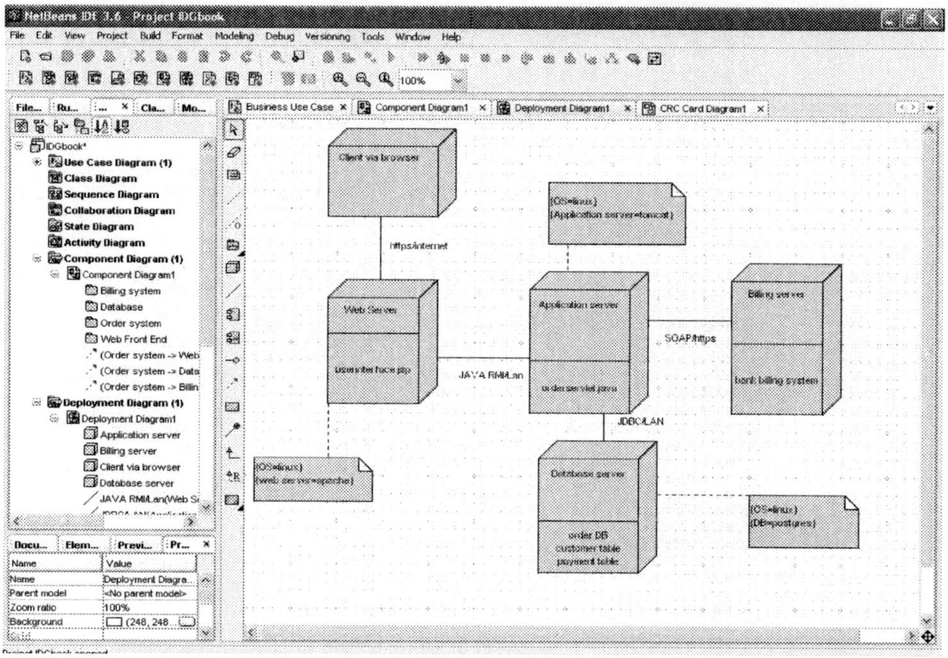

cards are very useful to describe the responsibility of each class of the system you are implementing and can be a sound basis for building more complex class diagrams.

There are several different types of CRC cards that can be adopted in Agile methodologies.

The most complex and complete I have found is in the SDE tool presented in this chapter, where all inheritance relationships and class components can be described fully.

This first example is very similar to a class of a UML class diagram but with a low formality, and can be adopted as an advanced description of classes, leaving to class diagrams the details of the most important sections of the system. An example of such a CRC card is in Figure 4.

The simplest is that reported in Fowler (2004), which is based on the original work in Cunningham (1989), and reports only the responsibility and collaborators of the class without any details about the position in the class hierarchy, the attributes, or methods, and so forth.

This second CRC card type can be described by the SDE tool, as reported in Figure 5.

Figure 4. Complex CRC cards as considered by Visual Paradigm SDE

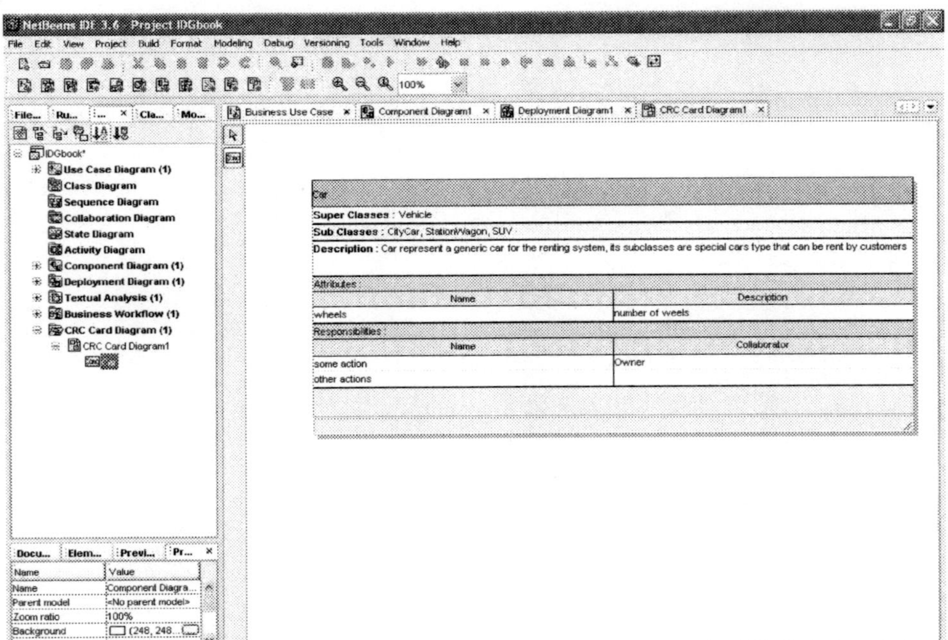

You can adopt all the notations that are in the middle between these extremes in order to use the most suitable one for your team. You can remove all the details you classify as marginal or not useful and keep only the parts you consider important, remembering that the second notation is the commonly adopted one in software project management. CRC cards often are written on a piece of paper in order to simulate message passing by moving them on the table or raising them when the related object has been activated. You can formalize CRC cards with the adoption of a case tool, for simplifying their maintenance, in terms of modification of the documentation that CRC card represent, or only for comparing them with the class diagrams they are related to.

Class Diagram Adoption

Once you have completed this operation, you are close to the development activity of the walking skeleton phase, and it is time to start considering classes and their interactions. UML class diagrams allow the developer and project manager to detail the project description at the desired level. When you adopt an Agile methodology, I suggest to avoid a very detailed description. Some class diagrams that evidence the critical dependencies must be present when you have to communicate to other people the internal implementation details.

Figure 5. The classical CRC card as reported in the literature

I also suggest that you adopt class diagrams in all situations in which CRC cards in their simpler form cannot solve your problems. Class diagrams also can be represented inside the package they belong to in a package diagram, but putting too much information together can be confusing and can tailor the specification according to the reader's needs and point of view instead of focusing on the main message that the project manager would like to transfer.

I do not want to introduce class diagrams in detail, since every person that has seen a UML has a 95% probability of having encountered a class diagram; what I want to specify is only a set of suggestions to usefully employ class diagrams in an Agile methodology. The main suggestion is to adopt them, but with care. Other suggestions are listed in the following:

- Class diagrams model static behavior and, therefore, cannot capture the dynamic mechanisms of message passing and dynamic interactions.
- Do not model all the possible interactions (especially association, which can produce frequent misunderstanding).
- Adopt the programming language standards when implementing characteristics such as packages (or namespaces), attributes, and method visibility (especially for protected and package visibility).

Draw diagrams for evidencing complexity or for delegating the development for critical parts only, and update them as often as possible; obsolete diagrams are not only useless but can be dangerous, since they can provide false input to developers and software architects.

Class diagrams complete the list of the diagrams usually adopted in the walking skeleton phase. It is now time to give some hints related to the possibility of adopting UML diagrams and notations during the release phases.

Release Phase

During the release phase, some UML notations and diagrams can be employed usefully with the same objectives reported in the walking skeleton phase.

Use Case Adoption

During the release phases, it can be useful to describe particular activities with a text use case for clarification with the customer, who at this point of the project is involved deeply in the decision process and is also more skilled with respect to the technical language and the operations that have to be implemented in the story selected for the release.

Activity Diagrams Adoption

Whenever you have an object whose behavior is particularly complex or shows parallel information flow (i.e., multi-threaded applications), you can adopt an activity diagram that allows you to model the information flow of the object under inspection.

Activity diagrams are a very powerful information source for all the people that can understand the symbol meanings. It is important to adopt them only when

Figure 6. Example of activity diagrams with fork and join to show parallel execution of flows

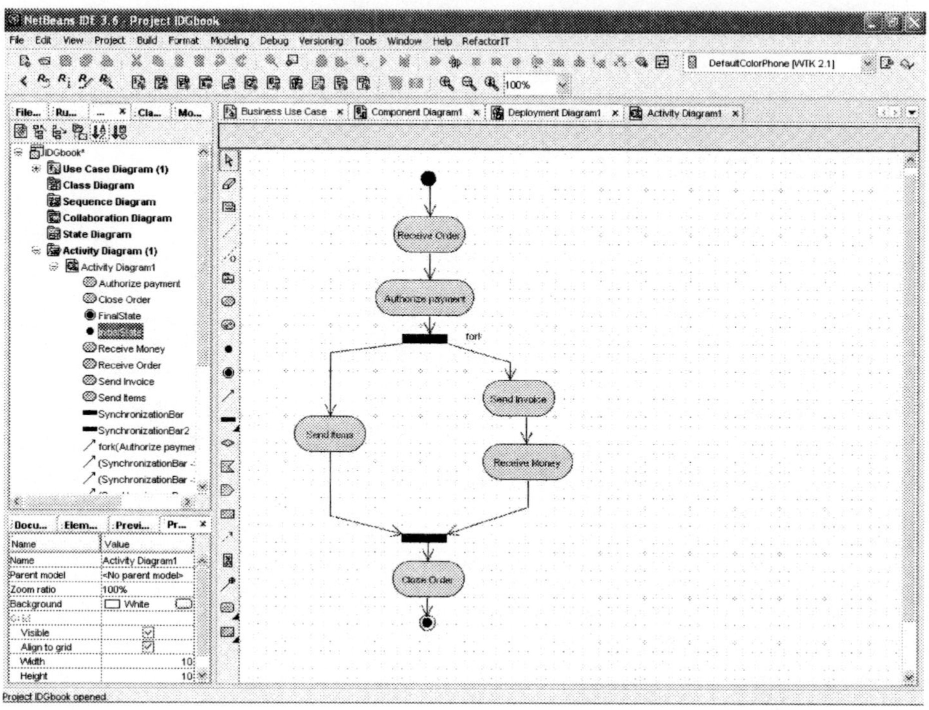

Figure 7. Example of a state diagram for updating the basket of the customer

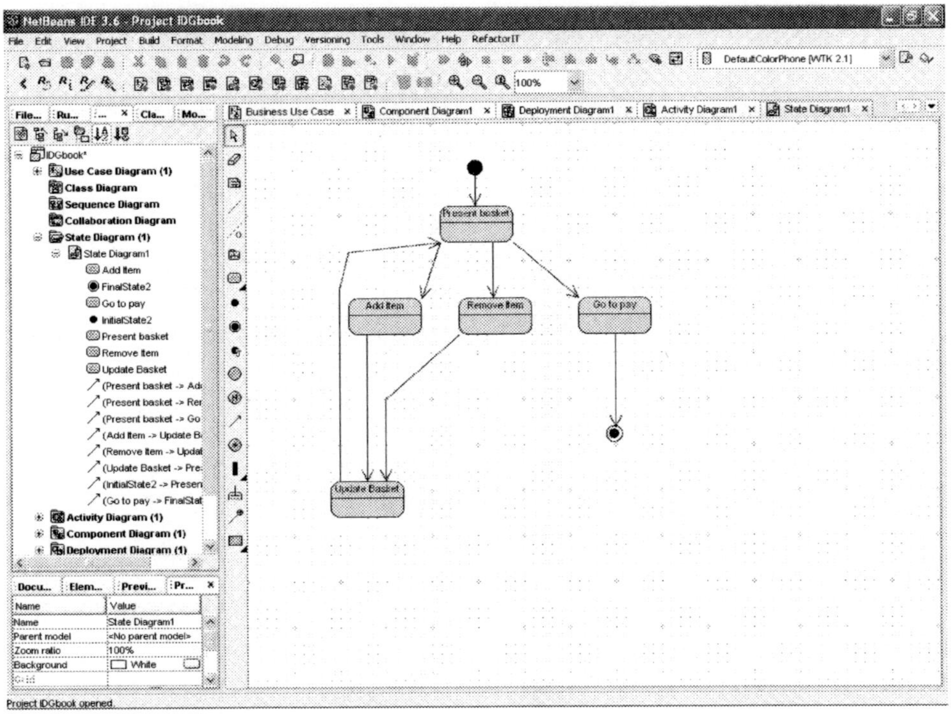

people are skilled in the usage of such diagrams and, as always, to use them only when it is strictly necessary.

State Diagrams Adoption

State diagrams can be employed usefully to detail the behavior of a class that is particularly complex and difficult to understand or which knowledge has to be shared among different persons on the team. A state diagram starts with the different states that the class can assume during its life and continues defining the transition among the states and the conditions under which it is possible to pass from one state to another.

The states that have to be considered are high-level states that are visible from the external of the class. Internal implementation details usually are not shown in state diagrams, even if nobody denies you the ability to describe the class at a more detailed level.

As always, you have to remember that you are developing according to the principles of Agile development, and therefore, you have to document the system inside the code and use other documenting methodologies when the code itself or automated documentation are not enough to describe the process with the desired and necessary clarity.

References

Booch, G., Rumbaugh, J., & Jacobson, I. (1999). *The unified modeling language user guide*. Boston, MA: Addison-Wesley Professional.

Cockburn, A. (2001a). *Writing effective use case*. New York, NY: ACM Press.

Cunningham, W., & Beck, K. (1989). *A laboratory for teaching object-oriented thinking*. Paper presented at OOPSLA'89, New Orleans, Louisiana.

Favre, L. (Ed.). (2003). *UML and the unified process*. Hershey, PA: IRM Press.

Fowler, M. (2004). *UML distilled : A brief guide to the standard object modeling language* (3rd ed.). Boston, MA: Addison-Wesley.

Larman, C. (2001). *Applying UML and patterns: An introduction to object-oriented analysis and design and the unified process*. Upper Saddle River, NJ: Prentice Hall.

Mellor, S., Balcer, M., & Balcer, M. J. (2002). *Executable UML: A foundation for model driven architecture*. Indianapolis, IN: Addison-Wesley.

Rumbaugh, J., Jacobson, I., & Booch, G. (1999). *The unified modelling language reference manual*. Boston, MA: Addison-Wesley.

Lessons Learned

Target

ADPD and UML

Practices

UML can be used profitably in all methodologies since it introduces a common notation, well understood by all persons involved in the development. UML tools aid in the automatic generation of documentation.

UML diagrams that are more useful in Agile methodologies and in ADPD also are:

- Use case diagrams
- Deployment programs
- CRC cards (also adopted widely if they are not standard in UML)
- State diagrams
- Activity diagrams

Chapter XIV

Software Measurement

The problem of measurement in software engineering has been addressed by many authors, and one of the most common questions is, "Can we learn from measurement in physics and can we transform this to software engineering measurement?" (Zuse, 1997, 1998).

An engineering measure, from the physical point of view, is relevant if it can quantify the object under measurement, since qualitative measures usually are considered too coarse. The problem arises when we shift this concept in software engineering, where nearly all the possible measurements are qualitative ones. All of the characteristics defined by ISO9126 (1991) are qualitative and not directly related to precise *physical* or tangible phenomena.

On the other hand, a wide skepticism of using numerical values is diffused, because it can be hard to give the requested semantic to the number.

Metrics, that are the measures performed on code, can be split into two categories: metrics for software complexity/size measurement and effort estimation, and metrics for qualitative characteristics evaluation. In the first part of the chapter, the former type of metrics is discussed, while in the second part, a general overview of quality in use by metrics will be performed. Apart from this general distinction, a more accurate taxonomy of the software metrics is reported in order to classify them on the basis of the applicability field in which they can be adopted.

Metric Taxonomy

Metrics can be classified according to different criteria. A first classification can be performed on the basis of its capability to predict and/or to evaluate a posteriori system characteristics.

The main difference between these two classes of metrics is in the use or not of the functional code. In general, predictive metrics are evaluated only on the basis of the class interface (e.g., C or C++ Header files, Java class definition, without inline code, etc.), while a posteriori metrics also need class code (method implementation).

In general, a posteriori metrics consider all class aspects — attributes, methods interface, and method implementation (both locally defined and inherited). Predictive metrics also can be evaluated, if the implementation phase has not been performed yet, such as in the early phase of system development. These metrics also can be used to predict the adaptive maintenance effort by knowing only the interface that classes will have at the end of the system adaptation. This can be very useful for evaluating the adaptive maintenance effort needed during its planning phase.

A metric is either able to measure directly a software characteristic or not; thus, it can be classified as direct or indirect. Direct metrics should produce a direct measure of parameters under consideration; for example, the number of Lines of Code (LOC) for estimating the program length in terms of code written. Indirect metrics usually are related to high-level features; for example, the number of system classes can be supposed to be related to the system complexity by means of a mathematical relationship, while LOC (as an indirect metric) is related typically to development effort. Thus, the same measure can be considered as a direct and/or an indirect metric, depending on its adoption. Indirect metrics have to be validated for demonstrating their relationships with the corresponding high-level features. This process consists of (1) evaluating parameters of metrics (e.g., weights and coefficients) and (2) verifying the robustness of the identified model against real cases. The model can be linear or not, and it must be identified by using both mathematical and statistical techniques (Briand, 2000a, 2000b; Nesi, 1998; Rousseeuw, 1987; Schneidewind, 1992, 1994).

Metrics are frequently reclassified on the basis of the phase in or for which they can produce significant estimations; therefore, a distinction can be made among analysis, design, and code metrics. An exact classification of metrics, according to this model, is quite difficult, since the boundaries among phases depend on the methodology and the development life cycle used.

Another classification is based on technical, cognitive, and process-oriented views of the system. The technical view refers to software engineering aspects of system specification (size, complexity, etc.); the cognitive view takes into account the external understandability and verifiability of the system; and the process-oriented view refers to system aspects that are influenced by or can influence the process of system development (i.e., productivity, reuse, cost of development, cost of maintenance, etc.). Metrics of each view can be used in different phases of system evolution: cognitive metrics during system development and/or in system maintenance; technical metrics for the evaluation or certification of some specific characteristics of the system; and process-oriented metrics for evaluating the impact of technology on the whole development process.

Metrics also can be divided on the basis of the aspect they caught, and therefore, they can be functional, behavioral or structural. Functional metrics are those such as LOC that deal with the pure evaluation of code line/statements, while structural ones are those that consider several system aspects like the number of key classes or the system complexity. Behavioral metrics are those related to system comprehension, understandability, or reusability.

Several classifications can be applied only to object-oriented metrics. One of the most used deals with the level of applicability; thus, method-, class-, and system-level metrics can be identified. Class-level metrics are the most important, since, according to OOP, all components (structural aspects) should be defined in terms of classes. In this case, functional, behavioral and structural aspects are considered.

During the classification of metric frameworks, the distinction between metrics that can cope with quality or that can exploit in a correct way OOP have been introduced. The reference to quality has been specifically introduced, taking into account ISO9126.

For the functional part, metrics for effort estimation can be divided in volume (also called size) and complexity metrics. Volume and size metrics, in general, are related to a simple token counting of class members and program components, while complexity metrics take into account code structure (i.e., loop, nesting level of code structure).

Another type of metrics that will be discussed in this chapter is the so-called quality in use metrics that are useful for tracking project behavior and are only indirectly related to code. Code or classes are used only to normalize the metric in order to a have a measure that does not depend on the project size. For example, a fault measure can be the simple fault counting, but it is different, if you have 10 faults in a 1,000 LOC system or if you have the same 10 faults in a 100,000 LOC system. A better measure can be the number of faults normalized with respect to the LOC — faults/KLOC.

A short introduction to code duplication measurement is reported at the end of the chapter.

Functional Metrics

Functional metrics can be adopted for both procedural and object-oriented software products, since they are independent of the software paradigm chosen for the development. On the other hand, functional metrics usually are adopted in non-object-oriented environments, even if some object-oriented metrics use functional metrics at their basis. The more commonly adopted metrics in this category are the line of code (LOC) and the McCabe cyclomatic complexity (*Vg* or *Vg'*) (McCabe, 1976).

These metrics are very simple in their definition but are discussed not only for dealing with the concept of bad or good measures but because they are still under evaluation whether they can measure effectively some aspects of software engineering.

In this chapter, COCOMO (COnstructive COst MOdel) is considered. COCOMO is the model for estimating effort with functional metrics historically considered and also widely adopted. It is considered at the end of the functional metric section.

Line of Code

LOC measure is probably one of the first raw measures used to evaluate the complexity and size of program, since it was used to count the lines of old-style fixed format assembler programs. The first problem arose when free format assemblers were introduced, because several statements could be written on the same line. The advent of high-level languages complicated the LOC life, because a higher level of abstraction was introduced in the programming concept — a line of code no more corresponds to an instruction executed by the CPU.

In the literature, a lot of LOC counting methods have been presented and commented on, though one of the more widely-accepted definitions is that given in Conte (1986, p. 35):

A line of code is any line of program text that is not a comment or blank line, regardless of the number of statements or fragments of statements on the line. This specifically includes all lines containing program headers, declarations, and executable and non-executable statements.

Some of the LOC definitions are language-dependent in the sense that they are strictly related to the grammatical structure of the language under evaluation. This can bring about a more precise measure, even if it compels you to redefine LOC for different languages or different dialects.

In order to avoid the usage of a language-dependent LOC definition, the definition provided in Conte (1986) can be adopted widely because it is not possible to know in advance the language used in the reader's team. This approach is not the perfect LOC, but it is a good compromise between language independence and accuracy in the estimation. On the other hand, it has some drawbacks due to the lack of a formal fixed structure of the language used for coding.

In Figure 1, two ways of writing the same *C* program that simply prints out five times a statement are reported. Figure 1(a) has three LOCs, while Figure 1(b) has only one. The two programs perform exactly the same task, but from a cognitive point of view, the second one can be more difficult to understand because of its non-linear style of programming. In this example, the use of ";" for counting the lines (since ";" is the statement terminator for *C* language) (Li,

Figure 1. Example of C code with different LOC but having the same functionalities

```
int i;
for(i=0; i<5; i++)
    printf("Iteration %d", i)
```

(a)

```
for(int j=0;j<5 ;printf("Iteration %d",j), j++);
```

(b)

1993) can resolve the problem, and therefore, this kind of approximation should be accepted. It is possible to propose other examples in which a greater complexity is coded in the same or lower number of LOCs.

Cyclomatic Complexity

Any program can be represented by a graph in which each node represents a control structure (e.g., *if*, *while*, etc.), and each edge represents a sequence of lines of code. In Figure 2, an example is reported.

The cyclomatic number derives by the graph theory and was used by McCabe (1976) as the basis for his complexity metrics. It is related to the maximum number of linear-independent paths that can be found in a program graph. The simplification of the concept is: How many different paths can be followed inside a program from its start to its end? As this number increases, the program became more difficult to understand.

In the following, the most commonly adopted formulation of the *Vg* metric is reported:

$$Vg = e - n + p + 1$$

This definition can be found in Henderson-Sellers (1992), where *e* is the number of edges, *n* is the number of nodes, and *p* is the number of connected components of the graph. The *p* is essential to compose some graphs into an equivalent monolithic one.

It can be assumed that the total complexity of a program is related to the sum of the complexity of the *p* functions that compose the program. Each function is a graph whose complexity can be estimated by *Vg*. Note that *Vg* metric is not additive in the sense that we cannot simply add the *Vg* of the subgraphs to obtain the *Vg* of the composed one. The sum of the complexities of the functions of a program is greater or equal to the complexity of the equivalent monolithic program, and therefore, this measure should be normalized, as reported in Figure 3.

In the left part of Figure 3, a flow graph containing two calls to subroutine is depicted, while in the right one, the composed flow graph is presented. It is evident that it is not possible to simply add up the *Vg* of the three graphs on the left part to obtain the *Vg* or the monolithic graph.

Figure 2. Mapping of a C program in an equivalent graph

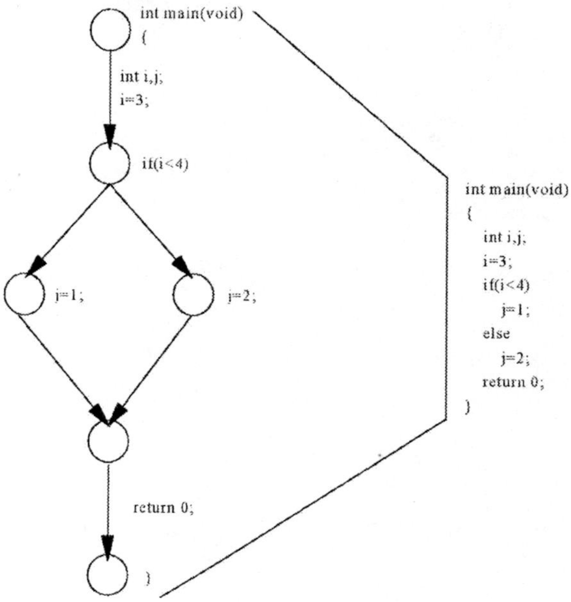

Figure 3. Example of Vg composition rules

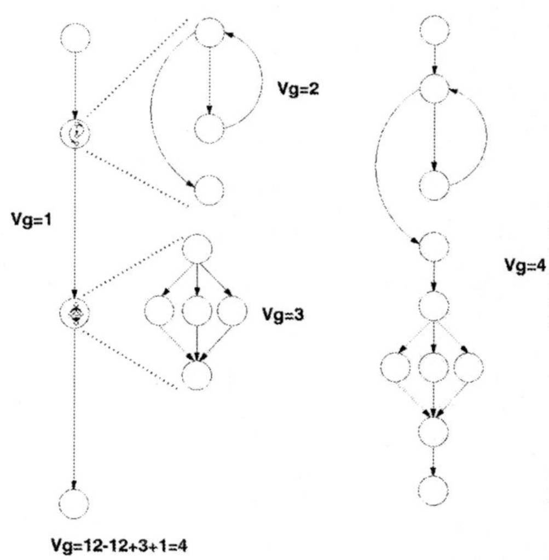

On the other hand, this can be a limitation when additive property is needed, for example, by a complex metric that adopts *Vg* as its basis. In order to avoid this drawback, a different version of the classical and more commonly adopted McCabe metric is introduced to the reader. This metric will be called *Vg'* and has the following structure:

$$Vg' = e - n + 1$$

It is evident that this metric is independent of the number of flow-graphs (the p term has been eliminated, and, as shown in Figure 4, it is fully additive). The Vg' measure is also equivalent to the number of decision nodes with an out-degree greater than or equal to 2. The following relationship also states:

$$Vg' = Vg - p$$

In Figure 5, some of the most common constructs of structured programming languages are reported along with their corresponding Vg and Vg' cyclomatic complexity.

The COCOMO Model

The first version of COCOMO has been presented with details in Boehm (1981). This model allows the estimation for the effort of a project on the basis the KLOC, which we plan to have. The main drawback for the applicability of

Figure 4. Example of Vg' composition rules

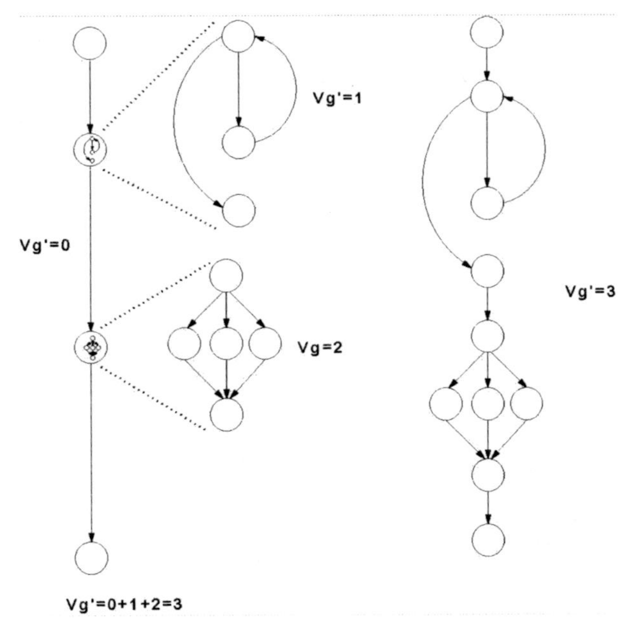

the model can be the fact that it was developed having in mind waterfall life cycle and validated with projects developed according to that methodology.

Boehm, speaking about COCOMO validation, affirms that this model has an accuracy of +/– 20% in 70% of the project, against which has been validated in the same project domain. It can be not so satisfactory but can be a good starting point for a raw estimation of the software engineering economist. I also add the following note: Boehm affirmation is true if you are able to correctly estimate the KLOC. This is why the COCOMO model has been refined over time by adopting more complex models in order to compensate the error in the KLOC estimation and by inserting more general quality parameters.

There are at least two models of COCOMO (Basic and Intermediate) that can be used to estimate and/or predict the effort of a project, and they will be presented in this section.

The basic model is comprised of two equations for estimating the effort in people/months (E) and the time in months (T) requested for the project.

$$E = a \cdot KLOC^b$$
$$T = c \cdot E^d$$

Figure 5. Example of common programming construct with Vg and Vg' values

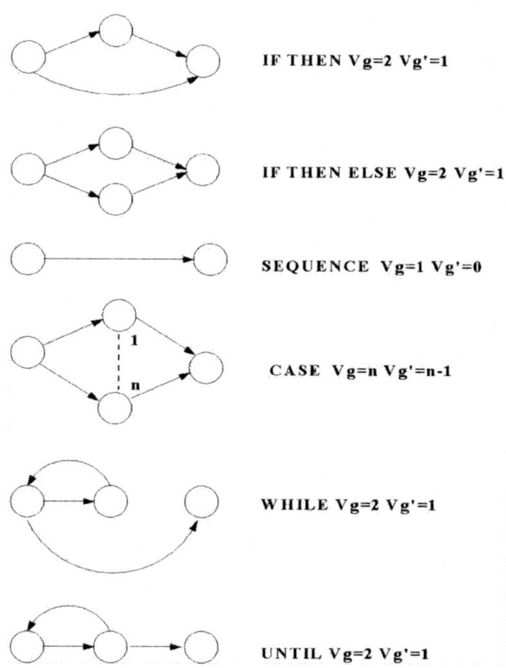

The coefficients proposed by Boehm (1981) have been estimated on the basis of project typologies. Boehm defines three project sets:

- **Organic.** Simple or small projects in which requirements can change. A sample of this kind of project is classical Web services in two- or three-tired applications.
- **Semi-detached.** This project type contains all complex projects that are not real-time or safety-critical systems.
- **Embedded.** This group contains real-time and safety-critical systems, which in general are very complex systems in which requirement are established and never changed.

On the basis of the preceding taxonomy, a table of coefficients can be drawn, as shown in Table 1.

In order to have a view of the values of *E* and *T* that COCOMO produces, a sample for different projects sizes is presented in Table 2.

The ratio between *E* and *T* is very different among the different project. Simpler (organic) projects require a small group of programmers, because the group must be agile enough to react to requirement changes.

Table 1. Coefficients for basis of COCOMO model

	a	b	c	d
Organic	2,4	1,05	2,5	0,38
Semi-detached	3	1,12	2,5	0,35
Embedded	3,6	1,2	2,5	0,32

Table 2. E and T evaluated by COCOMO for different project sizes

KLOC	Organic	Semi-detached	Embedded
10	$E = 26.93$ $T = 8.74$	$E = 39.55$ $T = 9.06$	$E = 57.06$ $T = 9.12$
30	$E = 85.35$ $T = 13.55$	$E = 135.36$ $T = 13.93$	$E = 213.23$ $T = 13.91$
50	$E = 145.93$ $T = 16.61$	$E = 239.87$ $T = 17.02$	$E = 393.61$ $T = 16.92$
100	$E = 302.14$ $T = 21.9$	$E = 521.34$ $T = 22.33$	$E = 904.28$ $T = 22.08$

A more complex and also accurate model is the intermediate COCOMO model that has a correction coefficient named *effort adjustment factor* (EAF). The following equation is then obtained:

$$E = a \cdot KLOC^b \cdot EAF$$
$$T = c \cdot E^d$$

EAF is the product of 15 factors that can be obtained by a table in which several aspects, such as reliability, database, and team experience are considered at different levels (e.g., poor, normal, good, very good, etc.). EAF normally lies between 0.94 and 1.40.

The coefficients of the model change (at least *a* and *b*) because of this adjustment. The complete table for intermediate COCOMO model is reported in Table 3.

Toward Object-Oriented Metrics

The presented metrics are not very suitable for evaluating complexity or size of object-oriented systems, since they are not capable of considering all of the object-oriented aspects (Fioravanti, 1999, 2001b; Henderson-Sellers, 1991; Nesi, 1998; Thomas, 1989). The lack of precision and the coarseness with respect to object-oriented systems of the presented measures have not been considered a severe limitation for their adoption in more complex measurement environments. These metrics are considered as basic metrics to build more complex structures that do not depend only on the code structure but also on several high-level features that easily can discriminate among different levels of complexity.

Table 3. Coefficients for intermediate COCOMO model

	a	b	c	d
Organic	3,2	1,05	2,5	0,38
Semi-detached	3,0	1,12	2,5	0,35
Embedded	2,8	1,2	2,5	0,32

Object-Oriented Metrics Overview

Several object-oriented metric suites for effort estimation and/or prediction are present in the literature (Briand, 1999, 2000; BritoeAbreu, 1994; Bucci, 1998; Chidamber, 1991, 1998; Fioravanti, 1998a, 1998c, 2001a, 2001b; Halstead, 1977; Henderson-Sellers, 1994; Kim, 1997; Li, 1993; Thomas, 1989).

In this section, an overview of some of the metrics contained in the frameworks of the cited literature will be analyzed in order to give the reader a clear picture of the different approaches that can be adopted in the complex field of software measurement and assessment.

The main characteristic of object-oriented metrics is related to the fact that the measure is no longer performed at the level of raw code, but different evaluations are performed to try to extract measures that are more focused on object-oriented concepts, such as methods, attributes, and classes. Some of the object-oriented metrics can be evaluated at the system level (giving a measure of the complexity of the whole system), which is equivalent to the functional measure for the total number of LOC of the system. The main characteristics that can be measured for each class are related to the class components that can be summarized as follows:

- **Local methods.** All the methods that are defined in the class and are not inherited by the class.
- **Inherited methods.** All the methods that the class inherits from its super-classes.
- **Local attributes.** The properties defined locally in the class and not inherited by the super-classes.
- **Inherited attributes.** The properties inherited from the super-classes.

Of course, the relationship among classes is also important and must be carefully considered, such as the number of super-classes and subclasses and the relationships in terms of methods of a class that call methods of other classes.

Chidamber and Kemerer Suite

Chidamber and Kemerer's suite (CK) is related strictly to the measurement theory (Chidamber, 1991, 1998), and it has been defined with the aim to assess the software development process as seen by expert object-oriented developers.

The CK suite is mainly comprised of the following six metrics:

- **WMC (weighted methods per class).** Supposing that a class contains *n* methods, WMC is the weighted sum of the methods where the weights can be (1) one, and the result is the count of the local methods; (2) LOC of each method, and the result is the size of the local methods; and (3) *Vg* of each method, and the result is the total complexity of the methods locally defined in the class.
- **DIT (deep inheritance tree).** The length of the maximal path to the root of the class hierarchy.
- **NOC (number of child).** Equals the count of immediate subclasses.
- **CBO (coupling between objects).** The number of non-inheritance-related couples between a class *C* and any other class. CBO is approximately equal to the number of couples with other classes, where a method call or instance of other classes constitutes couples.
- **RFC (response for a class).** The cardinality of the set of all methods that can execute in response to the arrival of a message to an object of a class. More simply, it can be considered as the sum between the number of methods of a class and the number of methods of other classes called by the class methods.
- **LCOM (*l*ack of *co*hesion in *m*ethods).** Approximately equal to the number of method pairs that do not have common instance variables minus the number of method pairs that do.

Apart from the formal definition of the metrics, some hints on the applicability of the metrics can be suggested. WMC can be considered a measure of the complexity and size of the class. DIT is related to the number of parent classes that the class under evaluation has and then to the impact that a modification in the upper level of the hierarchy can have in the class. NOC is related to the number of direct subclasses, and then to the impact that a modification performed on the class under examination can have on its derived classes. CBO is related to the coupling between classes and then to the interrelation of classes and to the difficult level of maintaining severely coupled classes. RFC is another measure of the cohesion of the class, related to the concept of methods called by the class methods. LCOM is related to the class variables or attributes that can be shared among class methods and then to the impact that a change performed on a class variable can have on the whole class; a larger value indicates less cohesion.

Li and Henry Metrics

In Li and Henry's framework (LH) (Li, 1993), three sets of metrics have been defined. The first set contains all the metrics of Chidamber and Kemerer, except for CBO; the second group contains message-passing coupling (MPC), data abstraction coupling (DAC), and number of methods (NOM); while the third group includes Size 1 and Size 2. In the following, a short description of the metrics not already covered during the discussion of the CK suite is reported:

- **MPC.** The number of send statements defined in a class that equals the number of procedure calls originating from a method in the class and going to other classes. Every call is counted as many times as it exists in the code.
- **DAC.** The number of abstract data types defined in a class. An object-oriented paradigm offers the opportunity of using abstract data types as instance variables, along with the use of the inherent data types, such as integer and boolean. All the relationships usually known as aggregation relationships are counted by this metric.
- **NOM.** The number of local methods of a class.
- **Size 1.** The number of semicolons (";") in a class. This is a sort of LOC for *C*-style programming languages.
- **Size 2.** The number of locally defined attributes and methods for a class.

For this new set of metrics, it also is necessary to clarify their impact on practical aspects. MPC deals with cohesion aspects measuring indirectly the amount of classes needed by the class under examination for its correct functionality, and therefore, it is related to maintenance aspects, since a change in one of the target classes can influence its behavior. DAC is a measure of the aggregation and encapsulation of data in the class. NOM is self explanatory and is related to the complexity of a class by counting its functionalities. Size 1 is a modified version of LOC, while Size 2 adds the local attributes to the NOM measure, taking into account the class state by its attributes.

Thomas and Jacobson Class Complexity

Class complexity defined by Thomas and Jacobson (1989) deals with aspects related to local attributes and methods and is a weighted sum of all local and inherited methods and attributes, or more formally:

$$TJ = \sum_{i=1}^{NAL} w_i' A_i + \sum_{i=1}^{NML} w_i'' M_i$$

where NAL is the number of locally defined attributes, A_i is the generic class attribute, NML is the number of locally defined methods, and M_i is the generic class method.

On the basis of the weight, we can create different metrics for measuring size or complexity of the class. Again, these metrics can be based on the functional metrics we have discussed in the first part of this chapter.

- **TJ_{NAM}.** When weights are imposed to 1, that is the counting of locally defined attributes and methods. Note that TJ_{NAM} is equivalent to Size 2 metrics of the LH framework.
- **$TJCC_{LOC}$.** When weights are proportional to the equivalent size of the attributes and methods. Size of an attribute is 1 for basic types such as integer, Boolean, pointers or reference (if defined in the language), and so forth, while in the case of an abstract data type, it is equal to the $TJCC_{LOC}$ of the class of the attribute. Size of methods is generally considered equal to the LOCs of the method.
- **$TJCC_{Vg'}$.** When weights are proportional to the equivalent complexity measured by the Vg' cyclomatic complexity of class attributes and methods, with rules for attribute complexity similar to that of $TJCC_{LOC}$.

Henderson-Sellers Class Complexity

Class complexity defined by Henderson-Sellers (1991) is an extension of the class complexity defined by Thomas and Jacobson (1989) and adds a component related to inherited methods. It can be formalized as follows:

$$TJ = \sum_{i=1}^{NAL} w_i^{'} A_i + \sum_{i=1}^{NML} w_i^{''} M_i + \sum_{j=1}^{NMI} w_i^{'''} M_j$$

where NAL is the number of locally defined attributes, A_i is the generic class attribute, NML is the number of locally defined methods, NMI is the number of inherited methods, M_i is the generic local class method, and M_j is the generic inherited class method.

Also for HS class complexity, several metrics can be obtained on the basis of HS formulation, in particular:

- **HS_{NAM}.** When weights are imposed to 1.
- **$HSCC_{LOC}$.** When weights are proportional to the equivalent size of attributes and methods.
- **$HSCC_{Vg'}$.** When weights are proportional to the equivalent complexity measured by the means of *Vg'* cyclomatic complexity of attributes and methods.

TAC++ Framework

TAC++ (Tool for Analysis of C++ code) framework born at the University of Florence and formalized with my PhD dissertation. In this section, only a short introduction to some of its components is reported, and references to a full and comprehensive description are present in the text.

Class Complexity Metric for Effort Estimation

Class Complexity (CC) is the most famous metric defined in the TAC++ that has been validated both from a theoretical point of view in Fioravanti (2001b) and also empirically as the publications of the author in the reference section demonstrate. CC is an evolution of the metrics proposed in HS and TJ frameworks and is mainly related to the evaluation of effort needed to produce a software program. Its adoption has been extended to evaluate maintenance effort and estimate in predictive ways the future development effort.

The cost of development (i.e., the effort) is one of the main issues that must be kept under control. To this end, a linear or non-linear relationship between software complexity or size and effort (i.e., people per months or people per days needed for system development), from requirements analysis to testing, or in some cases, only for coding, is commonly assumed. To this end, the problem of effort evaluation is shifted into the problem of complexity or size evaluation. When software complexity evaluation is performed on code, this can be useful for controlling costs and development process efficiency as well as for evaluating the cost of maintenance, reuse, and so forth. When software evaluation is performed before system building, metrics are used for predicting costs of development, testing, and so forth.

As pointed out by many authors, traditional metrics for complexity and size estimation often used for procedural languages can be difficult to apply for evaluating object-oriented systems (Henderson-Sellers, 1994; Li, 1993; Nesi, 1998).

On the basis of the previous assumptions and taking in account the experience of the metrics proposed by HS and TJ, a more complex metric has been defined. CC is defined as the weighted sum of the complexity of local attribute (CACL), local methods (CL), inherited attribute (CACI), inherited methods (CI), local methods interface (CMICL), and inherited method interface (CMICI).

$$CC_m = w_{CACL} CACL_m + w_{CACI} CACI_m + w_{CMICL} CMICL_m + w_{CMICI} CMICI_m + w_{CL} CL_m + w_{CI} CI_m$$

In this way, CC_m takes into account both structural aspects (attributes, relationships of containment) and functional/behavioral (methods, method cohesion by means of $CMICL_m$ and $CMICI_m$) aspects of class. In CC_m, the internal reuse is considered by means of the evaluation of inherited members. Weights in the equations can be evaluated by a regression analysis performed on real projects. As for TJ and HS, CC_m can be regarded as the definition of several fully object-oriented metrics based on functional metrics: McCabe and LOC, $CC_{Vg'}$ and CC_{LOC}, respectively.

Let me give some more explanation on how to evaluate CC metric in a practical context. Each term will be discussed in order to have a clear understanding on how to measure it.

CACL

CACL is the complexity of the local attributes. Each local attribute of the class has the following measure:

- Basic types (e.g., integer, bool, float, etc.), pointers, and references have a complexity equal to one; and
- Abstract data types have a complexity equal to the CC of the related class.

In case a recursive definition exists (i.e., a class that has an attribute of the same class type or is defined in terms of the same class type), the calculation of CC for that attribute stops.

CACI

CACI is calculated as CACL but for each inherited attribute. In the case of multiple inheritance, all the upper branches have to be considered.

CMICL

CMICL is the complexity of local interface of methods. It is evaluated calculating the complexity of each parameter of each local method of the class by adopting the same procedure described for CACL.

CMICI

CMICI is the same as CMICL but evaluated for each parameter of each inherited method.

CL

CL is the complexity of the code of local methods evaluated in terms of *Vg'* or LOC, depending on the feature (complexity or size) we would like to evaluate. *Vg'* has been chosen with respect to *Vg* for two reasons: it is additive and it is evaluated always for a single code tree, which is the method.

CI

CI is evaluated as CL but calculated for all the methods that are inherited by the class.

A Posteriori Effort Estimation Metric

As a sample of a posteriori effort estimation metric, CC_{LOC} will be considered, and some consideration for suggested values of the coefficients will be presented on the basis of the project type. For obtaining such coefficients, a regression analysis on the basis of the previous project has been performed, and the values of the coefficients have been obtained for different types of projects. A possible range of values to be applied to the metric (if the company that would like to adopt CC has no archive of previous projects to perform a regression analysis based on its data and on its project types) are suggested. General conclusions about coefficients also are drawn.

For simple projects or projects with a low level of structure in terms of inheritance complexity or for the first phases of complex projects, when the class definition is not yet standardized and documentation and design are not stable, the ranges of values shown in Table 4 can be adopted. The left number is for simpler projects, while the right one is for more complex projects.

The coefficients in Table 4 also can be applied to projects developed with Agile methodology, since several of the hypotheses for the application of Agile methodologies are satisfied.

For more complex projects where inheritance is a beneficial feature and for final phases of complex projects where interfaces are stable and documentation has been approved, different values can be assumed (see Table 5).

Examining the coefficients intervals, some conclusions about the coefficient meaning can be drawn.

Table 4. CC coefficients applicable to simple projects or to first phases of complex projects

w_{CACL}	0.001	0.003
w_{CACI}	-0.030	0.100
w_{CMICL}	0.200	0.550
w_{CMICI}	0.100	-0.030
w_{CL}	0.020	0.010
w_{CI}	0.003	0.001

Table 5. CC coefficients applicable to complex projects

w_{CACL}	0.002	0.001
w_{CACI}	0.100	0.080
w_{CMICL}	0.100	-0.100
w_{CMICI}	0.200	0.350
w_{CL}	0.050	0.150
w_{CI}	-0.010	-0.040

- **w_{CACL}.** The coefficient related to the complexity of local attribute. It is quite independent by the project type, and its value is quite constant, demonstrating that the addition of local attributes is always a cost, even if it is lowered by the coefficient absolute value.
- **w_{CACI}.** The behavior of this coefficient and, therefore, its value is very different with respect to CACL. For very simple projects or for the first phases of a complex project, the inheritance of attributes can be considered a saving in effort (negative coefficient) (see Table 4), since the local attributes are always a cost, and therefore, avoiding defining them locally and inheriting them is a saving. When the architecture becomes more complex, the inheritance of attributes becomes a cost that is greater in absolute value (even if normalized with respect to value or the respective metric) with respect to that of local attributes (see Table 5). It can be deduced that when inheritance is well exploited, it is better to have attributes in leaf classes than in the classes close to the root. It is also a good object-oriented practice to put the status on objects that have to be instantiated, which are usually those on the leaves of a hierarchy tree.
- **w_{CMICL}.** The complexity of method interface is a cost in a simple project when the specifications are not well defined, since method interface can

change often. For stable projects, when design and documentation are stable, it also can be a saving in effort, since it is a well-known interface guarantee to write code in a faster way, when the number of classes is high.

- $\mathbf{w}_{CMICI}$. The behavior of the CMICI coefficient is opposed with respect to CMICL, denoting that in the first phase of a project, the method inheritance saves time, and a change in its interface has a low impact on total effort, while when the hierarchy is large and the project is complex, a modification in the interface of inherited methods can provoke a disaster, since several other classes usually have to be modified, which is the reason it is considered a cost.
- $\mathbf{w}_{CL}$. CL coefficient is stable and always positive. The same considerations performed for CACL are valid.
- $\mathbf{w}_{CI}$. CI coefficient is low in absolute value, since the related metric CL is quite large. For simple projects, it shows that the reuse of code is a cost (even if it can be lower with respect to define all methods locally), while it can bring savings to an effort when the hierarchy is stable. The general conclusion is that code inheritance is always an advantage, since it reduces the code duplication in the project. The discussed advantage becomes a benefit for large projects, allowing saved effort.

The empirical correlation found between real effort and effort estimated by CC has been calculated between 0.75 and 0.9. It is interesting to note that the highest correlation values have been obtained for simple projects, and therefore, the coefficient that can be used for agile methodologies is very relevant.

A Priori Effort Estimation Metric

Some readers may not find the previous section useful, since it is focused on how to evaluate the effort of a project after the project has been completed and, therefore, gives no information on future efforts needed. Apart from the fact that the trend of a project in time can give suggestions for the next step of the project effort, it is possible to adopt CC metric in a predictive manner, so that the effort can be estimated in advance. In order to perform such an analysis, it is necessary to base our assumptions only on class interface, since the code of methods (locally defined and inherited) may be unknown, because it has not been written yet. The metric that can be used then is CC, with the removal of CL and CI terms.

Table 6. Coefficients that can be applied to simple projects or to first phases of complex projects for predicting effort on the basis of the predictive form of CC

w_{CACL}	0.002	0.003
w_{CACI}	-0.050	0.100
w_{CMICL}	0.150	0.200
w_{CMICI}	0.040	-0.020

Table 7. Coefficients that can be applied to complex projects for predicting effort on the basis of the predictive form of CC

w_{CACL}	0.005	0.015
w_{CACI}	0.130	0.350
w_{CMICL}	0.250	0.500
w_{CMICI}	-0.020	-0.015

The importance of coefficient validation and estimation is greater for a priori metrics with respect to a posteriori ones, since effort estimation cannot be based on raw code, and therefore, it is influenced by the programming style and by the project typology.

For this predictive metric, it also is possible to suggest values; for the already identified simple projects, Table 6 can be adopted.

Moreover, for the mentioned complex projects, Table 7 can be considered valid.

Regarding coefficient trends, as a project evolves, the same consideration performed before are valid, considering that the effects of the CMICL and CL coefficients are merged as the effects of CMICI and CI. Attributes-related coefficients are quite independent of the metric adoption in a predictive manner or not.

From several experiments performed, the metric seems to have the same accuracy in terms of the correlation between estimated and predicted effort that is between 0.9 (for simple projects) and 0.7 (for complex ones).

Structural Metrics Overview

Among the structural metrics defined in the framework, in this chapter, only the NAM, NSUP, and NSUB metrics will be discussed.

Table 8. Mean and maximum reference values for NAM, NAI, NAL, NMI, and NML metrics (NAM is evaluated with all weights imposed to one)

	Mean values	Maximum values
NAM	80	160
NAI	12	30
NAL	6	15
NMI	40	90
NML	20	40

NAM is an extension of Size 2 metrics and takes in account not only aspects related to local methods and attributes but also considers the inheritance by adding to Size 2 two terms related to inherited attributes and methods. All the terms are weighted for allowing a tuning of the metric on the basis of an empirical validation such as in Rousseeuw (1987) and Fioravanti (2001b).

The NAM metric has the following formulation:

$$NAM = w_{NAL}NAL + w_{NAI}NAI + w_{NML}NML + w_{NMI}NMI$$

When all weights are equal to one, NAM is the simple attributes and method counting (both locally defined and inherited).

Regarding the values that the single components can assume, we can consider as a reference Table 8, in which are reported the values suggested by the author.

The other metrics (NSUP and NSUB) are a more complex reformulation of DIT and NOC of CK suite, as a complex inheritance tree suggests.

The structure of the inheritance hierarchy impacts on system maintainability, reusability, and so forth, since a high number of super-classes can get classes hard to be understood and tested. DIT metric estimates the number of direct super-classes until the root is reached. It ranges from *0* to *N* (*0* in the case of root classes). On the other hand, DIT is an over-simplification of the real condition, since the depth of class three is not fully evaluated. No explicit rules were given for solving multiple inheritance cases, even if in literature it can be found that for the case of multiple inheritance, DIT metric evaluates the maximum value among the possible paths toward the several roots (e.g., five for class M in Figure 6) or the mean value among the possible values three, four, and five; thus, four. Class *M* presents seven super-classes, and thus, its

Figure 6. A specialization hierarchy with multiple inheritance

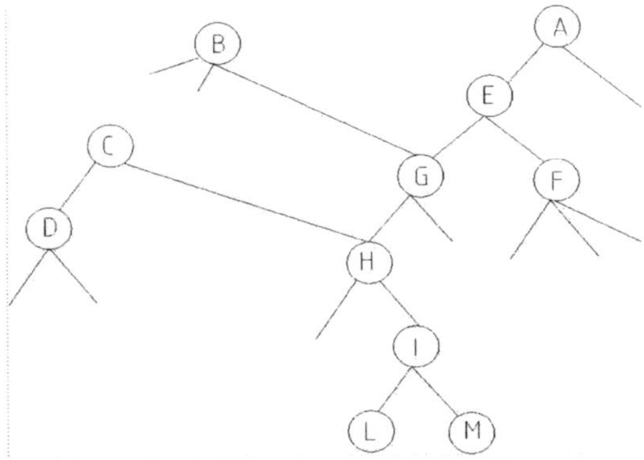

complexity obviously depends on all these classes. For this reason, metric NSUP, Number of SUPer-classes, has been defined, and it counts the number of super-classes till the roots are reached. Please note that the difference between DIT and NSUP can be relevant, even if the height of the inheritance tree is limited to three.

In order to better analyze the position and the relevance of a class in the hierarchy, it is very important to evaluate the number of its direct subclasses. NOC metric estimates the number Of children, considering only the direct subclasses, and it ranges from 0 to N (0 in the case of a leaf). Classes with a high number of children must be designed carefully and tested, since their code is used by several entities. On the other hand, a high number of children can be due to a lack of specialization. Thus, this metric can be useful for identifying critical classes. Comments similar to that expressed for DIT also can be made for NOC. According to the example of Figure 6, class E has two children without considering that it presents at least six subclasses (considering only those reported in the figure). For this reason, NSUB, *n*umber of *sub*-classes, has been defined. NSUB counts the subclasses until leaves are reached. Thus, NSUB can be regarded as a more precise measure of class relevance in the system.

The experience of the author in the evaluation of object-oriented systems and the literature on the topic allow us to define with a certain degree of accuracy some parameters for measuring if an object-oriented design can be considered bad or good on the basis of these metrics. Table 9 contains the reference values that can be used.

Table 9. Mean and maximum values that can be considered for DIT, NSUP, NOC, and NSUB metrics

	Mean values	Maximum values
DIT	2	5
NSUP	2	6
NOC	2	20
NSUB	5	60

Quality in Use Metrics

Several quality in use metrics can be defined and adopted during project development. These metrics can be a strong aid in verifying the productivity of the team, the fault proneness of the system, and also if the methodology adopted for the development is suitable or not. Quality in use metrics measure all the aspects that are not directly related to code but that are related to people, to management, and to usability of the system.

Fault Proneness Metrics

Before defining metrics for measuring a system faulty, it is necessary to define what a fault is. The usually adopted definition for a fault is an incorrect behavior or the result of the software system as the response to correct input data.

My experience on real systems and especially in *n*-tiered projects suggests that this definition should be modified and adapted to the layer in which the fault occurs. There are at least two different kind of faults: engine faults and presentational faults. The previous definition can be applied only to the so-called *engine faults*, which are the incorrect results produced by the business logic middleware or in the database layer code. The business logic (e.g., Enterprise Java Beans, middleware system that interfaces with databases, or legacy systems) is expected to operate on correct input data, and therefore, the previous definition applies.

Presentational faults are a larger family, since the presentation layer that interacts with the user also has to deal with random data in input and, therefore, must be robust to the so-called *monkey test*, in which incorrect data are presented to the system. The presentation layer must filter the input data in order to pass only the correct data to the business logic. This is the reason for which a fault in the presentation layer has a different definition: a presentational fault is an incorrect behavior or result of the software system when correct data are presented in input or when incorrect data flow from the presentation layer to the business logic layer.

A sample of engine fault is a function that, with valid data in input, produces a wrong result, while a presentational fault also occurs when the presentation layer does not block the user input when numerical data are required and a string is inserted.

Taking into account the previous definition, the system fault (SF) metric can be defined as follows:

$$SF = \frac{faults}{KLOC}$$

Another metric for measuring the fault proneness of a system can be the system test fault (STF), which is measured during the test phase of a traditional methodology such as spiral, waterfall, and so forth. It is similar to SF, but the counted faults are only the faults identified in the system test phase.

Note that this metric cannot apply to Agile methodology, since regression testing is usually adopted, and therefore, no release can be produced if some faults are detected.

In the metric literature, several metrics for fault prediction in software systems have been defined, even if a detailed dissertation about these kinds of metrics is out of the scope of this book, since a strong mathematical and statistical introduction is needed. An introduction to these models and metric is reported in Chapter XV, as related to maintenance. Readers interested in these results and in the related mathematical tools for validation can refer to Fioravanti (1999, 2001a, 2001b), Briand (1997), Duntenam (1989), and Hosmer (1989).

Project Metrics

It is necessary to control the several different aspects of project management: team productivity (TP), customer change requests (CCR), and schedule adherence (SA) (Moller, 1993). These metrics can be used profitably to verify how teams work (TP), how profitably the management drives the project (SA), and how the methodology employed is suitable for the domain of the project (CCR).

The metrics have the following definitions:

$$TP = \frac{KLOC}{ManDays}$$

$$CRR = \frac{NumberOfChangesRequested}{KLOC}$$

$$SA = \frac{PlannedWork - ActualWork}{PlannedWork}$$

TP metric can be applied at team level, but also can be employed for measuring the productivity of individuals. It is not usually recommended for measuring the performances of individuals, since the LOCs have no intrinsic quality, and therefore, a difficult task that requires a lower number of LOCs seems to be less productive with respect to another simpler task that requires large LOCs.

The TP value considered at project level operates as a mean operator, giving a global value to the team productivity quite independently of the productivity of individuals. Individual productivity shall be considered when the global productivity is lower than the mean of the projects of the same type previously developed in the company in order to identify if a lower productivity shall be due to some individuals of the team who are not working at their best.

It is not possible to give reference values for TP, since the TP value depends on several different parameters, such as project type (Web project, embedded system, real-time system, safety-critical system, etc.); development language (object-oriented or not, C++, Java, PHP, etc.); team cohesion (newly created team or a team that previously has developed different projects); and development and management methodology (waterfall, spiral, fountain, Agile such as XP, etc.). Therefore, the company has to create an archive of projects during time in order to identify a suitable range for TP.

Once the team activity has been measured in terms of productivity, it is also necessary to measure the quality of management by means of an SA metric. The project manager usually has a time window in which the final release must be on the market. At the same time, the project manager at the start of the project is asked to declare the planned resource and time necessary to develop the project. The actual effort spent with respect to the plan can be performed not only when the project is in the deployment phase but also for intermediate releases or at predefined milestones, depending on the methodology chosen.

Sometimes, the methodology used can be the weak point or the silver bullet for driving a project on the road toward success. It is necessary to track if the chosen methodology is suitable.

To this end, CCR metric is defined and used. Suppose that you are using an evolutionary methodology and that CCR assumes large values; this means that (1) the requirement collection and/or design phases have not been performed correctly and perhaps the project is compromised in its results; or (2) the evolutionary methodology is not the right choice, since the requirements cannot be defined in advance, and then it is time to move toward an agile methodology such those described in this book. On the contrary, if CCR is very low and an agile methodology has been selected, perhaps it is time to plan something more or to move quickly toward a more classical methodology, such as an evolutionary one.

Cognitive Metrics

Cognitive metrics are related to the quality in the sense of understandability and, therefore, related to the quality in use of the classes instead of considering the quality of the whole project.

One of these metrics is the *c*lass *c*ognitive *i*ndex (CCGI), which measures how much the class is understandable by considering the ratio between the complexity of its interface (external class description [ECD]) and the total complexity of the class (defined in terms of ECD and internal class implementation [ICI]). The formal definition of CCGI is:

$$CCGI = \frac{ECD}{ECD + ICI} = \frac{CACL + CACI + CMICL + CMICI}{CACL + CACI + CMICL + CMICI + CL + CI}$$

and the typical values that this metric should assume is about 0.6. If the value of CCGI is below 0.35, it means that the ICI part is too large with respect to

ECD and, therefore, that there is too much code for the implemented interface. Classes with a CCGI larger that 0.85 can be considered as skeleton or template classes with little implementation.

The general conclusion about CCGI metric is that having the same number of LOC, the classes with more attributes and/or methods are more understandable; CCGI metric is then able to measure a qualitative feature as understandability.

Duplication Analysis Metrics

Software developers often operate with the cut-and-paste method instead of reusing the already written code or without refactoring an already present code in order to adapt it to the new needs. This process results in producing duplicated parts (also known as clones) in the source code.

Clone detection in medium and large software systems has been investigated by several authors (Baker, 1995; Ducasse, 1999; Johnson, 1993; Kontogiannis, 1997; Mayrand, 1996), and clone elimination has been presented in Baxter (1998) and Johnson (1993). Several techniques have been reported in the literature to approach the clone identification problems (Baxter, 1998; Ducasse, 1999; Johnson, 1993), and several results also have been presented (Baker, 1995; Baxter, 1998; Ducasse, 1999; Mayrand, 1996). In particular, several approaches give only information on the amount and location of clones (Baker, 1995; Ducasse, 1999), while other works also present results on the aspects of clone similarities (Baxter, 1998; Kontogiannis, 1997; Mayrand, 1996).

The real problems in code duplication analysis are mainly the code preprocessing and the extraction of high-level features and duplication-related metrics (Fioravanti, 2001c).

In order to make more effective the code duplication analysis, a preprocessing phase is recommended. This phase tries to eliminate all the noise factors that can be summarized as follows:

- **Comments.** A developer has copied a piece of code and has added only some comments.
- **Blank lines.** In the same case, one or more blank lines can be added to improve readability without changing anything in the code.

- **Different formatting styles.** After the cut and paste, the braces can be put according to a different style without changing the functionality of the code.
- **Variable names.** Sometimes, we find duplicated sections in different files that differ only for the name assigned to the variables. In order to eliminate such a problem, all variable names should be replaced with the related type.

These noise factors are typically present in the source code. After the preprocessing phase, the code is independent of the formatting and of variable names. This allows performing a more precise code duplication detection and analysis. This phase prepares the code to be correctly processed in order to extract code duplication information.

Metrics for code duplication analysis can be extracted from the reference reported in the bibliography, since a detailed description of a framework for duplication analysis is perhaps an argument sufficient for another book.

References

Abreu, F. B., & Carapuca, R. (1994). *Object-oriented software engineering: Measuring and controlling the development process.* Paper presented at the Fourth International Conference on Software Quality, McLean, VA, USA, October 3-5.

Boehm, B. (1981). *Software engineering economics.* Upper Saddle River, NJ: Prentice Hall.

Briand, L., Daly, J. W., Porter, V., & Wüst, J. (1998). *A comprehensive empirical validation of product measures for OO systems* (Tech. Rep. No. ISERN-98-07). Kaiserslautern, Germany: Fraunhofer Institute for Experimental Software Engineering.

Briand, L., Devanbu, P., & Melo, W. (1997). An investigation into coupling measures for C++. In *Proceedings of the International Conference on Software Engineering.* Boston.

Briand, L., Wüst, J., Ikonomovski, S., & Lounis, H. (1998). *A comprehensive investigation of quality factors in object oriented design: An indus-*

trial case study (Tech. Rep. No. ISERN-98-29). Kaiserslautern, Germany: Fraunhofer Institute for Experimental Software Engineering.

Briand, L., Wüst, J., Daly, J., & Porter, V. (2000). Exploring the relationships between design measures and software quality in object-oriented systems. *Journal of Systems and Software, 51*, 245-273.

Briand, L., Daly, J., & Wüst, J. (1999). A unified framework for coupling measurement in object oriented systems. *IEEE Transactions on Software Engineering, 25*(1), 91-121.

Bucci, G., Fioravanti, F., Nesi, P., & Perlini, S. (1998). *Metrics and tool for system assessment*. Paper presented at the International Conference on Engineering of Complex Computer Systems, Monterey, California.

Chidamber, S. R., Darcy, D. P., & Kemerer, C. F. (1998). Managerial use of metrics for object oriented software: An exploration analysis. *IEEE Transactins on Software Engineering, 24*(8), 629-639.

Chidamber, S. R., & Kemerer, C. F. (1991). *Towards a metrics suite for object-oriented design*. Paper presented at the OOPSLA'91.

Conte, S. D., Dunsmore, H. E., & Shen, V. Y. (1986). *Software engineering metrics and models*. Menlo Park, CA: Benjamin/Cummings.

Duntenam, G. (1989). *Principal component analysis*. Thousand Oaks, CA: Sage University.

Fioravanti, F. (1999b). A metric framework for the assessment of object oriented system. Doctoral dissertation, University of Florence, 1999.

Fioravanti, F., Migliarese, G., & Nesi, P. (2001c). Reengineering analysis of object-oriented systems via duplication analysis. In *Proceedings of the 23rd International Conference on Software Engineering*. Toronto, Canada.

Fioravanti, F., & Nesi, P. (2001a). *A study on fault-proneness detection of object-oriented systems*. Paper presented at the Fifth European Conference on Software maintenance and Reengineering, Lisbon, Portugal.

Fioravanti, F., & Nesi, P. (2001b). Estimation and prediction metrics for adaptive maintenance effort of object-oriented systems. *IEEE Transactions on Software Engineering, 27*(12), 1062-1084.

Fioravanti, F., Nesi, P., & Perlini, S. (1998a). *Assessment of system evolution through characterization*. Paper presented at the International Conference on Software Engineering, Kyoto, Japan.

Fioravanti, F., Nesi, P., & Perlini, S. (1998b). *A tool for process and product assessment of C++ applications*. Paper presented at the Conference of Software Maintenance and Reengineering, Florence, Italy.

Fioravanti, F., Nesi, P., & Stortoni, F. (1999). Metrics for controlling effort during adaptive maintenance of object oriented systems. In *Proceedings of the IEEE International Conference on Software Maintenance*. Oxford, England.

Halstead, H. M. (1977). *Elements of software science*. New York: Elsevier.

Henderson-Sellers, B. (1991). Some metrics for object-oriented software engineering. In *Proceedings of the International Conference on Technology of Object Oriented Languages and Systems*.

Henderson-Sellers, B. (1992). Modularization and McCabe's cyclomatic complexity. *Communications of the ACM, 35*(12), 17-19.

Henderson-Sellers, B., Tegarden, D., & Monarchi, D. (1994). *Metrics and project management support for an object-oriented software development*. Paper presented at the TOOLS 13, Versailles, France.

Hosmer, D., & Lemeshow, S. (1989). *Applied logistic regression* (1st ed.). Indianapolis, IN: Wiley.

ISO9126. (1991). *ISO/IEC, ISO 9126*. Retrieved from http://www.iso.org/iso/en/CatalogueDetailPage.CatalogueDetail?CSNUMBER=39752&scopelist=

Kim, E. M. (1997). *Program complexity metric and safety verification method for object oriented system design.* Doctoral dissertation. Department of Information and Computer Sciences, Graduate School of Engineering Sciences, Osaka University, Osaka, Japan.

Li, W., & Henry, S. (1993). Object-oriented metrics that predict maintainability. *Journal of Systems and Software*, *23*(2), 111-122.

McCabe, T. J. (1976). A complexity measure. *IEEE Transactions of Software Engineering, 2*(4), 308-320.

Moller, K. H., & Paulish, D. J. (1993). *Software metrics*. Los Alamitos, CA: IEEE Computer Society Press.

Nesi, P., & Querci, T. (1998). Effort estimation and prediction of object-oriented systems. *Journal of Systems and Software, 42*(1), 89-102.

Rousseeuw, P. J., & Leroy, A. M. (1987). *Robust regression and outlier detection*. Indianapolis, IN: Wiley.

Schneidewind, N. F. (1992). Methodology for validating software metrics. *IEEE Transactions on Software Engineering, 18*(5), 410-422.

Schneidewind, N. F. (1994). Validating metrics for ensuring space shuttle flight software quality. *IEEE Computer, 27*(8), 50-57.

Thomas, D., & Jacobson, I. (1989). Managing object-oriented software engineering. In *Proceedings of the TOOLS '89*, Paris, France.

Zuse, H. (1997). Measurement in physics and software engineering: Part I. *Metric News, 2*(2).

Zuse, H. (1998). *A framework of software measurement.* Magdeburg, Germany: Otto-von-Guericke-Universitat.

Lessons Learned

Target

Software measurement

Practices

Software measurement is a very complex activity.

Some of the most important parameters in software measurement are qualitative and not quantitative.

Software measurement can be a practical way of controlling project and quality.

Metrics also can be profitably applied in the identification of code duplication.

Software metrics can be applied to the estimation of:

- Effort
- Project structure
- Fault proneness
- Cognitive aspects

Chapter XV

Project Maintenance

Maintenance is a phase that is usually placed after project completion when problems start to arise. Agile development changes this approach in depth, since maintenance is always the current status of the project. In this section, after a short introduction about maintenance model, the application of these models in classical and Agile methodologies will be discussed in order to highlight differences and focus the reader on the different approaches to this activity that can cost a lot if not well realized.

The last part of this section is dedicated to metrics for the estimation of maintenance effort and on metrics for the prediction of faults in order to guide the reader in this very complex environment. All of you can select the metrics that seem to be well suited for approaching the problem of effort measurement or fault proneness detection.

Maintenance Models

The three main maintenance models and activities usually are referred to as corrective maintenance, adaptive maintenance, and preventive maintenance. In the following, a brief description of all of them will be reported. In the next sections, the suitability of each model with respect to the methodological approaches that have been presented will be discussed.

Corrective Maintenance

Corrective maintenance usually is referred to as maintenance, since it is the universally recognized reason for which a program is maintained. As we will discuss, it is actually not the sole maintenance activity that can be carried on.

Corrective maintenance is applied each time the customer finds an error in your program and you change the code in order to solve the problem. The error detection is often present during the internal testing phase or during the first deployment of the system, at least in a spiral-oriented life cycle. To this end, this phase is considered an extra project activity to be performed after the deployment of the product on the customer site. On the other hand, it is possible to apply corrective maintenance in the daily activities of the team, if you find the error before the customer does.

Corrective maintenance usually is performed on code, and therefore, it is a low-level activity and rarely implies strong modifications in the architectural aspects of the project or in the requirements. The impact of the single maintenance activity is usually small and limited to a bugged class or part of the code that, once fixed, will allow the disappearance of the error.

Adaptive Maintenance

Adaptive maintenance is a very different maintenance phase, since it impacts the code, but it originates not by an error but by a change in the requirements or in the adopted technologies.

If not correctly managed or supported by a methodology that allows changes in the requirements, it can have a large impact on the code and on the time to deliver the maintained product. This is caused by the fact that the changes in the requirements usually impact the architecture of the system, and the changes in technologies impact a large part of code or even an entire subsystem.

An example of adaptive maintenance can be the change of the input file of the system that from a raw ASCII format becomes a structured XML. This can happen when your system interfaces other systems you do not control. For this example, you have two choices:

- The new XML format contains the same data of the ASCII file, and the change has been performed for embedding a semantic in the configuration file and for future expansion. In this case, you can decide to write a translator from the new format to the old to leave your system as is. In this case, you have to spend some time writing the module, but the system will remain constant, and you have the time to migrate your system toward the new input format without generating too many problems. If this is the case, you are a lucky person.

- The new XML format contains data that are compatible but not exactly the same or also contains new data you have to consider in your system. In that case, you are not so lucky, since you are compelled to modify the system in any case, and the translator is no more a feasible solution. You have to modify the code that uses the new data and rewrite the input module that loads data for your system, adopting new tools that support the technological innovation—the XML format.

Adaptive maintenance activities are common in systems that require you to cooperate with another system, often a legacy system, when deep changes can be made in the interfaces. This can be one of the main reasons for the interest in the standardization at least at the level of Web services of the format for data exchanging.

Preventive Maintenance

Preventive maintenance is not so common in software activities, since it is usually present in a hardware system that also may not be related to information technology. A typical preventive maintenance that you have experienced in your life and that is related to the car you have is the scheduled change of some parts during periodic maintenance. These changes usually are bounded to the MTBF (*mean time between failures*) and the MTTF (*mean time to failure*) of mechanical or electronic parts. The justification for that approach can be summarized as follows: Spend something today to avoid spending a lot tomorrow. This is true if you are quite sure of what you will spend tomorrow, but it is not really clear if this approach also can be applied profitably to software. Preventive maintenance in software systems is focused mainly on introducing features that can be used in the future, because a change in technology or in the requirement is facing the project. It is a maintenance activity performed in order to avoid dealing with adaptive maintenance activities.

Another situation of preventive maintenance application can be the generalization of a software product in order to cover a wider range of possible customers. For example, if you have realized a system for a customer, and you want to transform it into a product that some other customers can use profitably and, therefore, buy, you add functionalities not really needed by your customer but that can aid in the generalization of the project. I prefer to consider this activity as a new project instead of a maintenance activity on the old, since this allows an easier scheduling not bounded by the original customer's needs.

Maintenance in Classical Methodology

Classical methodologies such as waterfall or spiral-oriented methodologies do not consider maintenance inside the life cycle of the project as a specific phase or activity to be performed during the project development apart from some corrective maintenance that is performed only when an error occurs. The corrective maintenance costs are quite high, and, as shown in Chapter XI, the costs of a single corrective activity increase in a linear way, at least during each iteration of the project. Moreover, the total corrective maintenance cost influences the total cost of the project in a strong manner.

Corrective maintenance is also an activity that usually is performed after the project test and deployment, since it is during this phases that the larger number of errors appears.

Corrective maintenance can be considered a post-project phase, not inserted in the life cycle, but subsequent to the system deployment on the customer's site. If it is evident in these methodologies how corrective maintenance is approached, it is not so clear how adaptive and corrective maintenance is considered during the project. Classical methodologies are not very flexible in changing user requirements, and therefore, each time a change in technology or a modification of a requirement compels you to revise the system from the adaptive maintenance point of view, it takes a large effort to deal with such modifications. Preventive maintenance is usually not considered, since the requirement and design of the system often offer more functionalities with respect to those that are strictly needed. This approach can prevent preventive maintenance actions, but the drawback is that several times, a lot of not useful functionalities are inserted in the system in an early phase of development.

Maintenance in Agile Methodologies

Agile methodologies offer a better approach to corrective maintenance costs, since the main hypothesis and the main promise of all Agile methodologies are the guarantee of a constant maintenance cost for a single modification.

In Agile methodologies such as ADPD, maintenance in the sense of corrective and adaptive models is the normal condition of the project. The global approach to error identification by regression testing is a way to continuously act with corrective maintenance activities in order to avoid the failure of a single unit test. The costs of corrective maintenance are considered during the development, since the failure of a unit test or of a functional test compels you to revise the code before its integration into the system. Corrective maintenance is a real project phase and can be performed every time an integration is performed, and since the concept of small releases applies, the corrective maintenance activities are performed so often that this kind of maintenance can be considered the stable situation for the project.

Adaptive maintenance is usually applied often during an agile project development, considering that requirements can change often.

Regarding preventive maintenance, there are two different approaches. The first approach (preventive maintenance in the large) affirms that it is never applied in Agile methodologies, since you never do today something that possibly will be useful tomorrow. It is better to apply tomorrow an adaptive maintenance process in order to satisfy the new needs instead of adding a functionality that may not be useful tomorrow. The second approach consists of considering preventative maintenance (considered in the small sense) as a daily activity that is performed each time a developer modifies for improving the code of another developer, as often happens in XP. My personal point of view is that the second approach is not considered valid, since it is true that you modify the code of other developers, although it is for performing a simplification for adding a new functionality that is planned in the current release and not for the sake of simplification or generalization.

Metric and Models for Estimation of Maintenance Effort

Several metrics and models have been proposed for the estimation of development effort. Some of these metrics, if revised in the model, can be applied successfully to the estimation and prediction of the maintenance effort.

It is important to focus on the concepts of maintenance and, therefore, on the model that can be applicable for the estimation of this particular effort. To this end, in Fioravanti (1999b), a general model has been developed and validated. It allows you to use several metrics for the estimation, and then it generalizes the concept of maintenance effort estimation. From the model point of view, there is no distinction on the basis of the maintenance type that has to be performed.

The system/class effort for the maintenance activity typically is spent to perform several operations: the comprehension/understanding, the addition and/or deletion of parts, and the modifications/changes of other portions:

$$Eff_m = Eff_{add} + Eff_{und} + Eff_{del} + Eff_{chang}$$

where Eff_m is the maintenance effort, Eff_{add} is the effort for adding new code, Eff_{und} is the effort for understanding the system, Eff_{del} is the effort for deleting no more used code, Eff_{chang} is the effort for changing existing code.

The term Eff_{chang} can be eliminated, since the changes can be regarded as decomposed in the phases of deleting and rewriting (adding) specific parts. In this way, the model is reduced to three terms:

$$Eff_m = Eff_{add} + Eff_{und} + Eff_{del}$$

The previous listed terms for the maintenance effort have to be estimated by using specific metrics.

For the sake of clarity, in Figure 1, a typical maintenance activity is depicted with a system before and after maintenance, reused code, added code, and deleted code.

Figure 1. Model for maintenance effort estimation

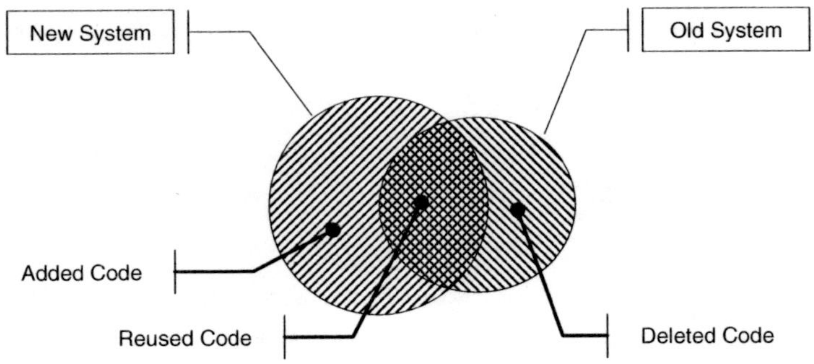

An estimation of the effort related to the added parts, Eff_{add}, can be performed by using:

$$Eff_{add} \approx M_a - M_r$$

where M_a is a system/class measure of effort on the system after the activity of maintenance; and M_r, is a measure obtained on the reused code of the system/class before the maintenance.

The cost of understanding the system before maintenance is spent deciding which actions to implement during the process. In a first approximation, it is reasonable to suppose that Eff_{und} is related to the class/system measure before the maintenance with a certain percentage. For this reason, the effort of understanding can be estimated approximately by using:

$$Eff_{und} \approx k_{und} \cdot M_b$$

where effort is directly related to the effort for developing the size/complexity of system/class before the maintenance process and k_{und} specifies the relationship (as a scale factor) between effort of understanding and the effort used for producing the code before the maintenance process. This scale factor should be determined during a validation process. If the team that performs the maintenance activity is the same that has generated the application, then the effort for comprehending the system can be neglected with respect to other factors. Thus, under this condition, which is usually the most common, the effort is due mainly to the addition and deletion of code pieces and, thus, Eff_{und} can be considered null.

In most cases, Eff_{del} may be very difficult to estimate directly on the code. If an LOC-based metric is used, the counting of the number of removed lines of code can be an approximated solution to perform its estimation. Unfortunately, this approach cannot be used when more complete and complex metrics are used, since structural and functional aspects and the class definitions and relationships have to be considered.

Typically, programmers are quite reluctant to the deletion of methods, since, in many cases, it may be difficult and time-consuming to be sure that they are not used by other classes or by other team members, unless you have implemented unit tests and regression testing for verifying the impact of deletion. Thus, the code deletion in classes typically is limited to parts of methods and only in some cases to entire methods or attributes. This produces a well-known maintenance problem for object-oriented systems: the presence of non-used methods and attributes. In general, Eff_{del} can be estimated approximately by using:

$$Eff_{del} \approx k_{del} \cdot M_{del} = k_{del}(M_b - M_r)$$

where M_{del} is a system/class measure of code deleted from the before version of the system during the activity of maintenance, k_{del} specifies the relationship (as a scale factor) between deleting effort and the measure of the deleted code, and M_b is a system/class measure of code before the maintenance activity. The effort for deleting is considered proportional to size/complexity that is deleted from the system/class before the adapting maintenance process. The scale factor is needed, since the activity of deletion has a different effort cost with respect to the addition or understanding. The scale factor should be estimated during the validation process.

Typically, the deleted parts are only a limited percentage of the system/class before the maintenance process.

For these reasons, the model assumes the following form:

$$Eff_m \approx M_a - M_r + k_{und} \cdot M_b + k_{del}(M_b - M_r)$$

In this equation, the values of metrics can be obtained on the basis of the code, if the reused portion of the before system is known. The estimation of the unknown parameters k_{und}, k_{del} could be performed by a validation process based on a multi-linear regression technique.

This model can be simplified by considering that the reused parts can be represented as a percentage of the system/class before the adapting maintenance process:

$$M_r = k_b \cdot M_b$$

then:

$$Eff_m \approx M_a - k_b \cdot M_b + k_{und} \cdot M_b + k_{del} \cdot M_b - k_{del} \cdot k_b \cdot M_r$$

This can be rewritten obtaining the model:

$$Eff_m \approx M_m = M_a - w_M M_b$$

where M_m is a metric for effort estimation during maintenance, typically related to effort, while the weight w_M is defined as:

$$w_M = k_b - k_{und} - k_{del} + k_{del} \cdot k_b$$

The scale factors included in w_M are hidden in a unique weight, and their estimation is impossible by using this last model. Weight w_M can be estimated by means of a validation process with a linear regression.

This model can be used directly at system level. If the model is used at class level, the basic costs of addition, deletion, and understanding are referred to each class. This means that the model can be used, assuming a unique value for weight w_M, and therefore, that changes to perform maintenance that can be considered uniform on all system classes.

On the other hand, during maintenance, several distinct actions may be performed, which may be non-uniformly operated on all classes. This model takes into account (1) the addition of new classes or parts of them for addressing new functionalities, (2) the deletion of classes or parts of them in the before version, (3) the performing of changes in the before version, and (4) the reuse of classes or portions of them from the before version.

In any case, the structure of the empirical relationships between effort and the measure holds the structure of the proposed equation.

CC-Based Metrics for Maintenance

Considering that M equals the CC metric defined in Chapter XIV, the complexity/size enforced in the system during maintenance, CC_{am}, can be expressed as follows:

$$CC_m = CC_a - w_{CC_b} CC_b = CC_a - CC_b$$

Imposing $w_{CC_b} = 1$ means that w_{CC_b} is included in the weights of CC_b that change their meanings. Since CC is defined as the weighted sum of six terms, the whole metric CC_m can be regarded as a metric with 12 terms and their corresponding 12 weights, six for CC_a, and six for CC_b, as in the second part of the equation just given. A complete validation of CC_m metrics has to be performed by considering the whole structure of CC. This validation also allows you to identify terms of metric CC_m that are relevant for maintenance effort estimation. Metric CC_b also takes into account some cognitive aspects of the system and can partially model the effort for comprehending the system before adaptation.

NAM-Based Metric for Maintenance

Considering M equal to NAM in the equation related to the model, the size enforced in the system during maintenance, NAM_m, can be expressed as:

$$NAM_m = NAM_a - w_{NAM} \cdot NAM_b = NAM_a - NAM_b$$

A complete validation has to be performed by considering the whole structure of NAM for both NAM_a and NAM_b for estimating the weights.

Therefore, once a draft analysis of the maintenance phase is performed, the number of members that the classes will present at the end of the maintenance process is known. Exploiting this early knowledge, it could be possible to use NAM_m metric for predicting the effort for the maintenance activity.

Other Metrics for Maintenance

The previous approach can be used for defining metrics for the adaptive maintenance on the basis of the previously-mentioned metrics for effort estimation.

For Size 2 metric, for example, a different approach has to be used, since it does not include weights in its definition. For this reason, in order to estimate the model applying techniques reported in Rousseeuw (1987) for Size 2 metric, it is necessary to adjust the model according the following equation:

$$Effort = Size2_a - w_{Size2} \cdot Size2_b$$

and then,

$$Size2_a - Effort = w_{Size2} \cdot Size2_b$$

In this last form, weight w_{Size2b} can be estimated with a linear regression.

Metrics and Model for Fault Detection

The problems related to software quality aimed at reducing the number of faults by identifying the classes that can contain bugged code and, therefore, program faults is a complex topic.

In the literature, several models have been presented, and nearly all models are very complex and empirically validated on a small project set. The mathematical instruments adopted in all these studies for identifying the metrics that are correlated with an high probability to program faults are very complex to describe (principal components analysis [Duntenam, 1989], logistic regression [Hosmer, 1989], etc.) and, therefore, are also beyond the scope of the book. In the text, the reader can extract the reference to the research paper and to the basic mathematical instruments adopted. In this section, only four models will be presented, and some results of the application of these models on a small dataset of small projects developed by students participating in an upper division undergraduate or graduate level course offered by the Department of Computer Science at the University of Maryland.

The models presented in this book have been extracted from Fioravanti (2001a) and Briand (2000). These models can be compared, since they have been validated against the same cited dataset. These models are presented according to the criterion of increasing complexity and accuracy.

Model I

The first model discussed in this book has been presented in Briand (2000), and it is based mainly on three metrics related to size aspects of the project. The adopted metrics are:

- **NM (number of methods).** The number of all methods (inherited, overriding, and non-inherited) of a class.
- **NMpub (number of public methods of a class).** The number of public methods implemented in a class.
- **NumPara (number of parameters).** The sum of the number of parameters of the methods implemented in a class.

The model assumes the following complex mathematical expression:

$$prob = \frac{e^{(c_0 + C_1 \cdot NM + C_2 \cdot NMpub + C_3 \cdot NumPara)}}{\left(1 + e^{(c_0 + C_1 \cdot NM + C_2 \cdot NMpub + C_3 \cdot NumPara)}\right)}$$

The coefficients estimated with this model are reported in Table 1.

A class to which this model is applied is considered faulty, if probability is greater than 0.75. The model correctly classifies 62.83% of the classes.

Table 1. Coefficients used in model I

Metric	Coefficient	Value
Intercept	C_0	-0,338
NM	C_1	0,449
NMpub	C_2	-0,314
NumPara	C_3	-0,060

Model II

Model II also has been presented in Briand (2000), and it is based on seven metrics related to coupling and cohesion aspects of the classes and then of project. The adopted metrics are:

- **RFC_{inf} (response set for class).** The response set of a class consists in set *M* of methods of the class and the set of methods directly or indirectly invoked by methods in *M*. In other words, the response set is the set of methods that potentially can be executed in response to a message received by an object of that class. RFC is the number of methods in the response set of the class (Chidamber, 1991).
- **NOP (number of parents).** The number of classes from which a given class inherits (Lorenz, 1994).
- **RFC_1.** Same as RFC_{inf}, except that methods indirectly invoked by methods are not included in the response set this time (Chidamber, 1991).
- **NMI (number of methods inherited).** The number of methods in a class that the class inherits from its ancestors and does not override (Lorenz, 1994).
- **FMMEC (counts of interaction between classes).** Counts the number of times a method of a friends classes is used (Briand, 1997).
- **NIHICP (information flow based non-inheritance coupling).** Number of methods weighted by method parameters number in classes not bounded by inheritance (Lee, 1995).
- **CLD (class to leaf depth).** CLD of a class is the maximum number of levels in the hierarchy that is below the class (Tegarden, 1992).

The mathematical model is the same with respect to Model I, but it is comprised of eight terms and coefficients. The coefficients are reported in Table 2.

Table 2. Coefficients used in model II

Metric	Coefficient	Value
Intercept	C_0	-3,332
RFC_{inf}	C_1	0,175
NOP	C_2	3,152
RFC_1	C_3	0,221
NMI	C_4	-0,297
FMMEC	C_5	0,550
NIHICP	C_6	-0,055
CLD	C_7	-2,572

This second model correctly classifies about 82.30% of classes, meliorating very much the previous result. The cut-off probability is now 0.65.

Model III

This model also is defined in Briand (2000), and the approach consists of mixing coupling and cohesion metrics with size metrics in order to verify if considering both aspects can bring about a better result.

This model is comprised of nine metrics that have been discussed in the previous models—apart from the following:

1. **OCAEC (counts of interaction between classes).** This metric counts the number of time an attribute of a class is used in other classes not coupled by inheritance or friendship (Briand, 1997).
2. **OMMIC (counts of interaction between classes).** This metric counts the number of time a method of coupled classes but not coupled by inheritance or friendship is used in the target class (Briand, 1997).
3. **NMA (number of methods added).** That is the counting of method that are not inherited and not overridden (Lorenz, 1994).

It is possible to draw the same table for this model in order to give the reader a starting point and some reference values in the case of a real application of the suggested model.

Table 3. Coefficients used in model III

Metric	Coefficient	Value
Intercept	C_0	-2,836
CLD	C_1	-3,518
NOP	C_2	4,171
OCAEC	C_3	-1,048
RFC_{inf}	C_4	0,464
FMMEC	C_5	0,351
NM	C_6	-0,726
NMA	C_7	0,526
NumPara	C_8	-0,119
OMMIC	C_9	-0,269

This model correctly classifies 80.53% of the classes with a threshold probability of 0.7. The accuracy of this model is lower with respect to the model that has only coupling/cohesion metrics, denoting that size metrics are not so suitable for faulty classes identification.

Model IV

The last model presented in this section has been presented in Fioravanti (2001a) and is comprised of 12 metrics.

The large number of metrics used suggests not to deeply inspect this model. The reader that is interested can find all the details in Fioravanti (2001a), where a more complex model has been identified.

Model IV correctly classifies about 85% of the classes. The other model reaches an accuracy in the identification of more than 97%.

The main problem in these last models is the high number of metrics employed to reach a good accuracy in the estimation and/or prediction of classes with faults.

Model IV is a hybrid model and contains coupling/cohesion metrics, structural aspects that sometimes in the literature have been strongly related to cohesion and a couple of metrics related to functional aspects. The large part of the metrics adopted is cohesion/coupling related confirming the results obtained also for the first three models presented.

Conclusion

The models developed in the literature and in this section for detecting faults proneness classes are very complex and require a strong background from both the mathematical and metrics knowledge points of view and, therefore, can be difficult to apply for projecting maintenance phases without building or having an automated tool that collects metrics. On the other hand, these models evidence that some characteristics of software systems are strictly related to faulty classes. One of these aspects is the cohesion and coupling inside the system, which cannot be avoided but must be carefully considered when projecting and developing a software project. The main suggestion that models in the literature can give to a project manager that is leading a team is to take more care to the correct implementation of coupling and cohesion with respect to system size (i.e., increase size), if this can reduce coupling/cohesion in order to limit the risks of having faulty classes.

References

Briand, L., Devanbu, P., & Melo, W. (1997). *An investigation into coupling measures for C++*. Paper presented at the International Conference on Software Engineering, Boston, Massachusetts.

Briand, L., Wüst, J., Daly, J., & Porter, V. (2000). Exploring the relationships between design measures and software quality in object-oriented systems. *Journal of Systems and Software, 51*, 245-273.

Chidamber, S. R., & Kemerer, C. F. (1991). *Towards a metrics suite for object-oriented design*. Paper presented at the OOPSLA'91, Phoenix, AZ.

Duntenam, G. (1989). *Principal component analysis*. Thousand Oaks, CA: Sage University.

Fioravanti, F. (1999). A metric framework for the assessment of object oriented system (Doctoral dissertation, University of Florence, 1999).

Fioravanti, F., & Nesi, P. (2001). *A study on fault-proneness detection of object-oriented systems*. Paper presented at the Fifth European Conference on Software Maintenance and Reengineering, Lisbon, Portugal.

Hosmer, D., & Lemeshow, S. (1989). *Applied logistic regression.* Indianapolis, IN: Wiley.

Lee, Y., Liang, B., Wu, S., & Wang, F. (1995). *Measuring the coupling and cohesion of an object oriented program based on information flow.* Paper presented at the International Conference on Software Quality, Maribor, Slovenia (pp. 81-90).

Lorenz, M., & Kidd, J. (1994). *Object-oriented software metrics.* Englewood Cliffs, NJ: Pearson Education POD.

Rousseeuw, P. J., & Leroy, A. M. (1987). *Robust regression and outlier detection.* Indianapolis, IN: Wiley.

Tegarden, D., Sheetz, S., & Monarchi, D. (1992). *A software complexity model of object-oriented systems.* Paper presented at the OOPSLA '92, Vancouver, Canada.

Lessons Learned

Target

Project maintenance

Practices

Three main types of management exist:

- Corrective
- Adaptive
- Preventive

Maintenance effort can be estimated by evaluating system size/complexity before and after maintenance.

Automated fault detection is a difficult task; the main suggestions for handling it are:

- Limit cohesion
- Limit coupling
- Increase size (this can limit cohesion and coupling)

About the Author

Fabrizio Fioravanti obtained his MS and PhD from the University of Florence in 1996 and 2000, respectively. Since 1992, he had been a consultant for several companies covering different roles in several IT related topics. During 2000, he was assigned professor of computer architecture for the BS in electronic engineering at the University of Florence. He was also co-chair and on the program committee for IEEE International Conferences. Fabrizio Fioravanti wrote several papers and book chapters on software engineering related fields. In 2001, he was R&D chief officer for an Italian IT company. Since 2004, he has been project manager for Exitech, Italy, an IT company involved in software product development. He has been a member of IEEE since 1992, and his main research and applicative interests are related to Agile methodologies for developing and managing IT project, software engineering, and object-oriented and software metrics.

Index

Symbols

10-20-30 minutes organization 17
15-minute daily standing meeting 13

A

a priori effort estimation metric 211
activity diagram 178
adaptive maintenance 225
ADPD (Agile and Defined Project Development) 95, 108, 134, 158, 176, 228
ADPD life cycle 135, 179
ADPD planning game 142
Agile development 4, 176, 224
Agile Intergroup Improvement Team (AIIT) 152, 171
Agile life cycle 137
Agile Manifesto 96, 134
Agile methodology 3, 65, 72, 95, 104, 143, 158, 184, 228
Agile methods 65
Agile teams 67, 101
AIIT establishment 173
alpha test 76
appearance 34
automatic or metric-driven cost estimation 92

B

bank and security systems 67
behavior 47
beta test 76
body 34
brainstorming 12
business logic 215
business workflow 178

C

CBO (coupling between objects) 203
CC coefficients 210
CC-based metrics 233
certification 41
change log 146
Chidamber and Kemerer's suite (CK) 203
class cognitive index (CCGI) 218
class complexity 205
class complexity metric 206
class diagram 177
class-level metrics 193
CLD (class to leaf depth) 236
COCOMO (constructive cost model) 51, 194, 198
code 13, 99, 119, 120, 147, 229
code description document (CDD) 76

code revision 100
coding 3, 80
coding standards 120, 145
cohesion 236, 239
collaboration diagram 178
collective ownership 120
color usage 27
commercial partner 42
communication 2, 21, 37, 45, 109
component diagram 178, 182
component reuse 68
concurrent versions systems (CVS) 99, 165
conference 24
conference presentation 32
constructive criticism 47
consultant 1
continuous feedback 110
continuous integration 117
controller 5
corrective maintenance 225
cost evaluation 74
cost-driven project 101
COTS (components off the shelf) 158
coupling 236, 239
courage 11, 57, 111
CRC cards 139, 179
critical activities 15
customer 41, 115, 171
customer change requests (CCR) 216
CVS repository 146
cyclomatic complexity 196

D

daily meeting 164
data abstraction coupling (DAC) 204
database layer code 215
deadlines 17
decision tree analysis 89
decision-making process 59
delegation 56
deployment diagram 178, 183
developer 1, 5, 115, 142
development life cycle 138
development phase 75, 84
development time 52
direct feedback 3, 38
DIT (deep inheritance tree) 203
documentation 100, 109
duplication analysis metrics 219
duplication-related metrics 219
duration 22

E

economic loss (EL) 86
effort adjustment factor (EAF) 201
effort estimation 206
embedded project 200
engine faults 215
engineered product 80
engineering measure 191
estimated effort 52, 66
estimated project duration 52
estimation of development effort 229
extra resources 17
eXtreme Programming (XP) 78, 108

F

failure 60
fan-in and fan-out of the modules 89
fault proneness metrics 215
faulty event (FE) 86
feasibility document (FD) 74
feasibility study 73
feedback 3, 38, 46, 57, 73, 110, 154, 168
fifteen-minute daily standing meeting 155, 173
fixed contract 101
FMMEC (counts of interaction between classes) 236
forty-hour weeks 122, 125
functional metrics 194
functional test 149

G

Gantt diagram 15, 50, 75
glue person 5
graphic appeal 22

H

hands-on training 41

I

IKIWISI (I'll know it when I see it) 65, 80, 113
indirect feedback 3, 38
information flow 187
information technology 65
inherited attributes 202
inherited methods 202
innovator 5
integrated software management 169
integration 76
integration and test 131
intergroup coordination 171
internal class implementation (ICI) 218
IT project group 6

K

Key Process Areas (KPAs) 158
knowledge 105

L

language 22
LCOM (lack of cohesion in methods) 203
Li and Henry's framework (LH) 204
life cycle 73
line of code (LOC) 194
LOC measure 194
LOC-based metric 231
local attributes 202
local methods 202
long-term motivation 48
long-term prospects 18
look 34

M

management meeting 24
management of requirements 143
management presentation 30
marketing presentations 31
McCabe metric 197
meeting 13
message-passing coupling (MPC) 204
meta-models 72
metaphor 112, 120
metric taxonomy 192
metric-driven cost estimation 92
metrics 192, 229
monkey test 215
monthly strategy 14
MTBF (mean time between failures) 226
MTTF (mean time to failure) 226

N

NIHICP (information flow based non-inheritance cou 236
NM (number of methods) 235
NMI (number of methods inherited) 236
NMpub (number of public methods of a class) 235
NOC (number of child) 203
NOP (number of parents) 236
number of methods (NOM) 204
NumPara (number of parameters) 235

O

object-oriented metrics 201
object-oriented systems 231
on-site customer 112, 141, 171
on-the-job training 42
online presentations 21
organic project 200
organization process definition 167
organization process focus 165
overtime 17

P

pair programming 118, 144, 164
paper presentation 27
Pareto law (80-20 law) 88
peer reviews 171
people management 44
PERT diagrams 15
planning game 114, 117, 142
planning of risk control 85
positive feedback 47
presentation 20
presentations with slides 23
preventive maintenance 226
problem solving 44, 47

problem-oriented format 26
Program Evaluation and Review Technology (PERT) 15
programming 143
project development 98, 143
project document 173, 176
project documentation 151
project leader 4
project lifetime 66
project maintenance 224
project manager 4, 39, 183
project measurement document (PMD) 76
project metrics 216
project specification document (PSD) 75
project technology 68
prototype 77
prototyping life cycle 78

R

Raleigh-Norden equation 52
rapid application development (RAD) environment 77
RCS 165
real-time systems 68
reduction risk coefficient (RRC) 86
refactor 112
refactoring 120
regression testing 150
release phase 140, 186
requirement management 160
requirement specification document (RSD) 74
requirements and analysis 130
resources 53
responding to change 103
reviewer 5
revision control system (RCS) 99
RFC (response for a class) 203
risk 118
risk analysis 85
risk classification 85
risk exposure (RE) 86
risk identification 85
risk management 84
risk monitoring 85
risk solving 85
risk/cost factor 89

S

safety critical systems 68
sandwiched presentations 24
schedule adherence (SA) 216
scheduling 143
scheduling activities 16
SDE tool 184
semi-detached project 200
sequence diagram 178
short-term motivation 48
short-term objectives 18
simple design 117
simplicity 3, 10, 37, 56, 110
Size 1 metric 204
Size 2 metric 204
slide presentation 23
small releases 116, 141
Smart Development Environment (SDE) 178
software subcontract management 163
software configuration management 165
software capability maturity model (CMM-SW) 134
software development 72, 114
software engineering 65
software management 72
software measurement 191
software metric adoption 173
software metrics 154
software product engineering 170
software product life cycle 165
software project oversight 162
software project planning 161
software project tracking 162
software quality assurance 163
speech 28
spiral life cycle 81, 137, 225
state diagram 178
structured presentation 25
SW-CMM 158
system fault (SF) metric 216
system test fault (STF) 216
system test plan (STP) 74
system-level metrics 193

T

TAC++ Framework 206
task cards 142
tasks relationships 16
team 4
team behavior 11
team leader 4, 39
team manager 10, 20, 142, 153
team meeting 24
team members 164
team motivation 44, 48
team presentation 30
team productivity (TP) 216
team working 1
technical partner 42
technical presentations 31
technical skills 104
technology 2, 40, 64
test integration 131
test plan 92
test practices 147
tests 117
textual analysis 178
throw-away prototype 77
time management 10
TJ framework 207
traceability 146
training 36, 156
training program 168
turnover 105

U

UML 176
UML case tools 183
unit test 147
use case diagram 177

V

value 2
vice presidents 13
voice 33

W

walking skeleton (WS) 138
walking skeleton phase 179
waterfall life cycle 73, 136, 199
waterfall methodology 227
weekly planning 14
WH (what and how) 56
WMC (weighted methods per class) 203

X

XML 225
XML schema 113
XP 95, 135, 158
XP life cycle 117, 130
XP planning game 110
XP rules 112, 142